INDEBTED MOBILITIES

Indebted Mobilities

INDIAN YOUTH, MIGRATION, AND THE
INTERNATIONALIZING UNIVERSITY

Susan Thomas

The University of Chicago Press   CHICAGO AND LONDON

University of Chicago Press, Chicago 60637
The University of Chicago Press, Ltd., London
© 2024 by The University of Chicago
For more information, contact the University of Chicago Press,
1427 E. 60th St., Chicago, IL 60637.
Published 2024

33 32 31 30 29 28 27 26 25 24   1 2 3 4 5

ISBN-13: 978-0-226-83068-1 (cloth)
ISBN-13: 978-0-226-83070-4 (paper)
ISBN-13: 978-0-226-83069-8 (e-book)
DOI: https://doi.org/10.7208/chicago/9780226830698.001.0001

Library of Congress Cataloging-in-Publication Data

Names: Thomas, Susan (Professor of education), author.
Title: Indebted mobilities : Indian youth, migration, and the
internationalizing university / Susan Thomas.
Description: Chicago : The University of Chicago, 2024. |
Includes bibliographical references and index.
Identifiers: LCCN 2023023180 | ISBN 9780226830681 (cloth) |
ISBN 9780226830704 (paperback) | ISBN 9780226830698 (ebook)
Subjects: LCSH: Students, Foreign—United States. | Immigrant
students—India. | Immigrant students—United States.
Classification: LCC LB2376.5.I5 T56 2024 | DDC 378.1/982691—
dc23/eng/20230602
LC record available at https://lccn.loc.gov/2023023180

DEDICATED TO MY FATHER AND MOTHER:
THOMAS ZACHARIAH
SARA THOMAS

Contents

Introduction · Going Global

In the early days of my fieldwork at Riverside,[1] I spent much of my time hanging around awkwardly in the administrative office managing the overseas students on campus. It was here that I met Ani, a young graduate student from the southern Indian state of Tamil Nadu who worked part time at the office. In between running errands and providing the students who streamed in through the doors the paperwork they needed, Ani would sneak in time to chat with me. Despite my various attempts at explaining to him the methodological nature of what Clifford Geertz had called "deep hanging out," he found this ethnographic practice entirely strange and took every opportunity to tell me so.[2] Many of our early exchanges involved him teasing me, questioning, "What exactly do you think you are doing?" I quickly learned that being subjected to relentless teasing and playful confrontation was a ritual among Ani and his friends, and I had to learn how to surrender to it quickly to be a part of their social group.

One afternoon early on, Ani offered to give me a break from the office and show me the university campus after his shift was over. I eagerly accepted, happy to spend time with my new friend and escape the tedium of the office's routines. We wandered along the paved paths through the campus grounds, only half-heartedly paying attention to our surroundings and the students scurrying by us. The New York suburban campus, Riverside University, was notorious for its unappealing aesthetic. On more than one occasion, it had made national lists of poorly designed campuses, specifically being noted for its prisonlike architectural style. One could see the more recent self-conscious attempts to distance itself from this reputation, like the beautifying of the campus with pockets of ornamental greenery and landscaping. In the midst of ongoing state withdrawal of funding, the public university had also managed to secure some large private donations from wealthy alumni, allowing the administration to make additions to the campus's assortment of academic buildings. Set against a backdrop of drab, monolithic block architecture reflecting the campus's origins in the Cold War era, there were now the occasional brightly colored, high-tech buildings with a futuristic aesthetic. Ani did not comment on the odd contrast; his only gestures to the campus buildings were to the places where he and his friends commonly held part-time jobs. This was an early reference to how their roles as workers were essential to these young people's relationship to the campus.

Ani and I eventually reached the university's boundaries, where he pointed over to a bar called Andies. It was the only nearby semblance of the famous American nightlife that many of the migrant youth I met would claim they heard so much of long before they arrived. Ani sighed and clasped his hands behind him, "Anyway, it's boring. This is it." I gave him a sympathetic smile, sensing his resignation to unmet expectations. I took it as a chance to ask the simple question, "So, tell me, why did you decide to come here?" Ani paused. Glancing over at Andies, he shrugged, asking rhetorically, "I don't know. Say you could go to the moon. Wouldn't you?" He must have not noticed the look of bewilderment that flashed briefly across my face. Punctuating his allusion to both the fantasy of "America" and the sense of the impossibility of reaching it, Ani continued, "I think coming here was more important than even coming to graduate school."

Conjuring up images of travel to the United States as akin to arriving on the moon was a striking sentiment. When the contemporary figure of the student-migrant is often conceived of as a highly calculating subject easily and strategically pursuing the educational choices afforded by neoliberal forces, how do we interpret Ani's metaphorical musing? This question becomes particularly compelling as the world continues to reel from the profoundly damaging effects of the COVID-19 global pandemic. As the virus began to spread across borders and all manner of life, institutions of higher education scrambled to manage its impact on their own campuses. In the midst of sending students home, transitioning to remote teaching, and dealing with massive financial losses, these institutions found that the presence of student-migrants and their education in the United States had become an urgent concern. This was transpiring while student-migrants were already coping with the challenges posed by the international travel restrictions that were implemented to reduce the spread of the virus. To make matters worse, the Trump administration's incendiary, xenophobic, and ethnonationalist rhetoric contributed to the very real threat of racial violence against Asian populations, including overseas students, who overwhelmingly arrive from the Asian region. However, when the alarming July 6, 2020, US Immigration and Customs Enforcement (ICE) directive mandated that any student-migrants taking a fully online course load would be required to transfer or leave the United States, there was immediate and widespread panic. As most campuses were operating entirely remotely at the time, this move would mean the loss of large numbers of enrollments, which would be economically catastrophic for universities across the nation that were already grappling with the financial strain of pandemic lockdowns.

Revealing how dependent US institutions of higher education have become on overseas-student enrollments, educational institutions led by Harvard College and MIT rushed to file a lawsuit against the Trump administration. The overwhelming pressure resulted in ICE rescinding the directive within days, rendering the dilemma of student-migrants' presence a seemingly fleeting incident within the public discourse around the pandemic crisis. Yet, the directive highlighted the familiar tension between restrictive immigration policies and the economic importance of migrant populations. More specifically, the situation was an instantiation of how, in key historical conjunctures, student migration is implicated in broader sociopolitical and economic turmoil concerning the United States' place as a global power.

At the same time, the incident also exposed the inadequate attention paid to the everyday lives of young people who move across US borders to study on American campuses. It is a neglect that has been exacerbated by the portrayal of student-migrants as merely economic subjects critical to the revenue-generation schemes of educational institutions, which was the impetus for the immediate national reaction to the ICE directive. Such portrayals have become especially prevalent over the course of the last few decades as campuses across the country, and the world, declare they are "going global." This market-driven trend, now commonly referred to as "internationalization," involves a number of different strategies intended to reap the benefits of the neoliberal globalization of higher education, but enrolling students from overseas continues to be the most coveted of these efforts. Recognizing it as a highly lucrative enterprise, educational institutions across the world seek out global markets for student-consumers, competing to bring them to study on their campuses. Over the last twenty years, the largest markets have been located in the Asian region, with India consistently serving as one of the key sources of student-migrants, alongside China.[3] Beyond their importance to the revenue schemes of institutions, Indian student-migrants are typically fluent in English and overwhelmingly enroll in professional fields considered to be critical to the global knowledge economy. A function of the growing gulf between the kind of moral education provided by the humanities and the technical education meant to produce knowledge workers,[4] US institutions are increasingly promoting and investing in the latter; however, inadequate enrollments by American students mean that Indian student-migrants are also contributing much-needed intellectual and technical labor on campuses. As educating other nations' students has become a multi-billion-dollar industry for the United States, which continues to be the most sought out destination for students from India, the presence of Indian student-migrants on American campuses is crucial to the globally competitive edge the United States boasts.

Assumed to be a rationally calculating, ambitious, and globally minded consumer of higher education pursuing the choices afforded by internationalization, the Indian student-migrant figure embodies *Homo economicus*, an idealized migrant subject in the contemporary period, a fetishized example of neoliberal globalization's success story. In this book, I take as my point of departure that such idealizing masks crucial stories of longings and struggle that are formative to the educational circuits of neoliberal empire. I offer an ethnographic rendering of the migratory lives of middle-class youth from India studying at a public university in New York, which I call Riverside University; the chapters of this book uncover such stories situated in the nexus of the historical, material, political, and affective forces through which they are forged. I contend that the transnational circulations of these student-migrants are marked by important considerations of surveillance, labor, and exclusion that come to bear on the racial and class locations of these young people. Further, the gendered contours of these migrations illustrate that the professional fields important to the global knowledge economy continue to be dominated by men and are often read as implicitly culturally masculine. For this reason, this book attends particularly to Indian student-migrant men's encounters with the internationalizing university. An examination of these encounters reveals how educational migratory routes are sites of Indian middle-class men's desires to become modern figures in an age of neoliberal globalization, but these desires are entangled in particular webs of obligation attached to the imagined future returns of an American education. Such obligations translate into a cultural logic of indebtedness—materially, affectively, and morally. This logic of indebtedness, the notion of owing and being owed, shapes the racial, class, and gender sensibilities of Indian middle-class youth whose migratory lives are simultaneously marked as indispensable and disposable to the internationalizing university.

EDUCATIONAL IMAGINARIES
OF NEOLIBERAL EMPIRE

With the election of the Biden administration, the US government rushed to undo any damage to the United States' role in international education the reactionary policies and rhetoric of the Trump administration may have caused. This was evidenced by the joint statement released in July 2021 by the State Department and Department of Education, with the support of the Departments of Commerce and of Homeland Security. Entitled "A Renewed U.S. Commitment to International Education," the statement of principles recited the usual talking points of diplomacy, national security, and US economic competitiveness to reassert the United States' commitment to the internationalization agenda as necessary to maintaining its privileged position on the world stage. While the particularities of national electoral tussles have ripple effects on the internationalizing university, I contend that these recent events be read beyond the exigencies of political and policy agendas. What also surfaces as significant here is what Indian student-migrants, like Ani, suggest throughout this book—the United States holds an important place in the educational circuits and imaginaries of neoliberal empire.

The migration of students across US borders has always been linked to the production of the United States as a global hegemony, a point I situate in conversation with the critical analyses of US higher education that have developed in the past few decades. Now known as critical university studies, this field was initially represented by several works that emphasized and denounced the marketization perceived as shifting the agendas and practices of institutions of higher education.[5] While the shifts produced by neoliberal transformations are noteworthy, such perspectives are often premised on a valorization of an earlier golden age of US public higher education, in which the public university is positioned as the ultimate site of serving the public good through the inculcation of US liberal values. Complicating the ways these earlier works glorify an educational access that primarily privileged a culture of whiteness and its benefactors, more recent works have pointed to what this has meant for the educational lives of those marginalized by this history even as US educational institutions adopted a liberal multicultural discourse.[6] Yet, other scholars have sought to push the critique further, arguing against the narratives of crisis that accompany these critical analyses.[7] Research illuminating the entanglements of the US university with the history of and persisting conditions wrought by slavery, land grabs, settler colonialism, gentrification, and war and empire has served as important correctives to the sanitized representations of an educational past that smuggle in an erasure of the kinds of violences and dispossessions that were necessarily part of the racial-capitalist expansion of US higher education.[8] I suggest that to meaningfully explore the encounters of Indian student-migrants at the internationalizing university, their movements across national borders must be tied to these broader histories of violence and exclusion, which have enabled the fraught inclusion politics fundamental to the neoliberal ethos of higher education. Aihwa Ong has contended that, along with other globalizing processes, the internationalization of higher education has "contributed to a kind of crisis of American citizenship."[9] However, I argue that the presence of Indian middle-class migrant youth on American campuses has become important to reproducing the logic of US exceptionalism so critical to the mission of US higher education.

Isaac Kamola's work has added another pertinent angle to these critiques by not only considering the material conditions that have forged the consolidation of US higher education as we know it but by also pointing to the ways that American universities play a crucial role in the production of the imaginaries of global relations of power.[10] Specifically, Kamola traces how the US university moved from being a site of knowledge production linked to the nation-state system, developmentalist discourse, and imperialist interests that constituted Cold War politics to producing the "global" imaginary in which higher education, as well as the world, became constructed as globalized in nature. A valuable implication here is that institutions of higher education are not merely impacted by globalizing forces, but they actually play a crucial role in nurturing the imaginary linked to the material conditions of neoliberal globalization. This book illuminates how Indian student-migrants and their paths serve as a contradictory node in the production of this imaginary.

When considering the place of student mobility and exchange within higher education, the linkages to and shifts in geopolitics that Kamola interrogates are evident. Following the oil crisis of the mid-1970s, which exposed the United States' economic vulnerabilities and contributed to the emergence of neoliberal capitalism, there was a notable discursive shift shaping international education policy.[11] While the rhetoric of defense, diplomacy, and security that informed international education and exchange during the Cold War did not disappear, national policy rhetoric began stressing more explicitly the primary role of institutions of higher education in strengthening the economic power and prosperity of the United States. It is in the context of this shift, along with the contemporary rise of the so-called global knowledge economy that internationalizing higher education surfaced as a vital neoliberal project. The internationalizing university is borne of the global imaginary, but I use it to gesture to how higher education institutions are increasingly institutionalizing specific strategies that contribute to rendering neoliberal globalization as an organizing logic within their agendas. Creating conditions for rising numbers of student-migrants to enroll has become vital to these agendas. There are now five million overseas students in the world. While institutions of higher education across the world seek to attract them, it is clear that the transnational circuits of these migrants are highly uneven, with students moving predominantly from the Global South to advanced industrial nations to pursue their educational aspirations. The United States holds a key place in these circuits as the destination for the majority of the world's overseas students, and specifically, for students from India. As alluded to in Ani's comments, the United States has persisted as a site of longings in the global educational imaginaries of Indian middle-class youth.

The shifts in international education framings that produced the internationalizing university in the United States coincided with the liberalization of India's economy, a transformation that led to a fever-ish questioning of what it meant, in particular, for youth identities and the desires invested in them. A key facet of the celebratory accounts of India's economic liberalization has been the assertion of the emer-gent power of a new and growing Indian middle class. Scholars have discussed how such images of a new kind of Indian offered up ready-made fantasies of the good life to Indian youth, manufacturing consent through notions of good citizenship in the era of liberalization.[12] Edu-cation, which has always played a crucial role in the making of Indian nationhood, became a renewed site of national attention in imagining the potential of Indian middle-class youth and, in turn, India's own rise as a modern global force.

The Indian national dialogue during the liberalization era drew on and reworked existing educational imaginaries to serve a narrative of the political, social, and economic potential of Indian middle-class youth who were purportedly being hindered by outdated educational practices and policies. In doing so, this narrative also enabled a homoge-neous picture of middle-class opportunities and experiences. Significant to this ideological work is the neoliberal assertion of choice being the essential key to unlocking aspirations across what are, in fact, different kinds of life chances among those who aspire toward middle-classness. Entangled in already existing sociopolitical tensions, which are perme-ated by the spread of right-wing Hindu nationalist ideology, contesta-tions of Indian middle-classness have occurred through particular con-structions of choice, deservingness, and institutional failure on the part of the higher education system in India. The articulations between the discourse of India's liberalization and the internationalizing university channel such constructions into the narratives of desiring among Indian middle-class men, for whom educational migration to the United States becomes imagined as a rite of passage to the modern futures they are convinced they are owed.

In some ways, these narratives can be read as a familiar story of as-piration and migration; yet this book suggests it is not a straightforward one. Moving beyond the assumption that these students are merely privileged actors of global neoliberal forces making careful migratory calculations that secure successful overseas education and professional futures in the global knowledge economy, I contend that the racial, gender, and class formations of Indian middle-class student-migrant men locate them ambivalently across US borders and on an American campus, a liminal belonging that inscribes their presence onto the campus terrain as out of place.[13] In analyzing how this ambivalence is taken up in their encounters as subjects of the post-9/11 surveillance state, as part of the labor supply for the university economy, and as the campus's global "other," this book also adds a needed perspective to the recent scholarly attention to South Asian transnationality. In particular, the interventions in this book contribute to scholarship that has highlighted how differences within the transnational class formations of Indian knowledge workers are produced and are made meaningful.[14] Undoubtedly, pursuing education overseas is a privileged stream of migration. At the same time, this book points to how these Indian middle-class men, drawn in by the seductive promises of becoming globally mobile, US educated, and part of the professional elite—markers of successful modern masculinities—enter the transnational educational sphere and are confronted with the intensified unevenness and uncertainties accompanying the global commodification of higher education. Specifically, for many of the young men discussed in this book, "going global" ultimately meant going into debt.

MEN ON THE MOVE

Contemporary scholarship on masculinity has offered important theoretical insight on how idealized constructions of masculinity are formative to the material conditions enabling and enabled by processes of neoliberal globalization. Scholars have illuminated the ways these idealized constructions are produced and aligned with, while also existing in tension with other practices and forms of lived masculinities.[15] For instance, in *Degrees without Freedom*, Jeffrey, Jeffery, and Jeffery analyze how the negotiations of such tensions among young, educated, unemployed or underemployed rural men are largely shaped by the intersections of class, caste, and religious inequalities of a postcolonial, liberalized India. Examining the differing gendered performances that emerged at the nexus of educational aspiration, unemployment, and social stratification, they provide a deeper understanding of the investments in and dissonances of postcolonial masculinities.[16] Tied to the analytical insights of these works, a number of other scholars have considered the ways that the masculine ideals invested in and forged through migration are negotiated through the particularities of places, thus illuminating the contested nature of producing masculinity.[17]

Building on this scholarship and taking inspiration from feminist and postcolonial framings of masculinities, this book attends to the gendered configurations of educational migratory routes. I interrogate how such routes are imagined and produced as a crucial site of masculine becoming among young Indian middle-class men raised in a post-liberalized India, whose arrival on an American campus is imbricated in the geographies of racial capitalism. I consider the ways their desiring for a modern manhood—which they imagine to be possible through accessing transnational mobility, an American education, and the cultures of whiteness embedded in US university life—articulates with the racial and class formations constituting their movement across borders and their encounters with the institution. Influenced by the theoretical traditions of the anthropology of debt, I argue that for these Indian migrant men, the sensemaking that emerged from such articulations is configured by the material, affective, and moral functions of indebtedness. While Maurizio Lazzarato has addressed how debt relations and the production of indebted subjectivities exist at the heart of the neoliberal capitalist project,[18] his analysis fails to consider the ways that differences in social location mean differences in how indebtedness is lived. Following feminist readings of debt that account for this neglect,[19] in this book I explore the raced, classed, and gendered ways that the logics of indebtedness mediating the transnational mobilities of educated Indian middle-class youth come to bear on notions of obligation, belonging, and masculine success.

ETHNOGRAPHIC CONSIDERATIONS

The ubiquity of internationalization projects, and the rising presence of student-migrant populations from Asia on US campuses as an undeniable facet of this trend, became especially evident in the aftermath of what came to be known as the "Great Recession," the 2008 economic crisis that was driven primarily by global financial debt. Immersed in my own academic training in the years that followed the crisis, I found it striking how pervasive the assumptions rendering internationalization as universally beneficial and Asian educational migrants as necessarily elite and wealthy had become. It seemed to me such assumptions effectively functioned to serve the exclusions and erasures of experience wrought by the globalized neoliberal institution. Concerned with this taken-for-grantedness of migratory lives that were increasingly becoming part of the university setting, I was curious what insights could be gained from attending more closely to the encounters between a public university that was especially challenged by neoliberal restructuring and economic crisis and the predominantly nonelite Indian student-migrants arriving on such a campus in growing numbers as a consequence.

This book builds on sixteen months of fieldwork I conducted between 2011 and 2012 at Riverside University. The campus, located in the New York metropolitan region, was grappling with the severe impact of state withdrawal of financial support. At the same time, it was, and still is, a noteworthy destination for student-migrants from the South Asian region, the vast majority of whom are enrolled in professional fields. Importantly, the story of these young people's growing presence on Riverside's campus is tied to the broader history of public higher education in New York, and Riverside's specific creation in the context of the Cold War. Because of a history of political tensions, New York was the last remaining state in the nation to fully commit to public higher education and the creation of a state university.[20] Obstacles included the influence of existing private educational institutions that did not want competition from a public system, class interest, and the widespread discriminatory practices against women and minority populations. Yet, rapid population growth in the New York metropolitan region and the expanding demand for higher education created immense pressure in the state to democratize and build a viable alternative for quality education for the wider public and not merely for the wealthy elite. In 1948, legislation to create a state university system passed and in 1957, Riverside admitted its first students.

Any existing ideological conflicts over what role the state should play in higher education were overtaken by the urgency to generate more scientists and engineers to secure the United States' position as a global power during the Cold War. The creation of Riverside in this context explains the strong emphasis the university placed on developing its resources and departments in the sciences and engineering. However, along with other public institutions across the country, Riverside faced the full effects of the economic crisis of the 1970s. While the demand for higher education continued to grow, New York was met with deep financial troubles. The practices and effects of massive budget cuts, the elimination of academic programs, and widespread layoffs amounted in millions of dollars of loss in educational services within the State University of New York (SUNY) system.[21] The crisis ushered in the neoliberal creep, intensifying the involvement of private actors and bringing in a growing emphasis on efficiency and accountability.

Following the 2008 economic recession, severe cuts in state funding, yearly increases in tuition fees, and the spread of a neoliberal ethos contributed to further neglect of the very student populations that more accessible public campuses like Riverside were established to support. Its embrace of the internationalization project in this context makes Riverside a valuable instantiation of how campuses are negotiating and being transformed by the broader political-economic shifts wrought by neoliberal globalization. Undoubtedly, the drive to open university doors to student-migrants is a key strategy by public institutions to survive austerity measures; in the case of Riverside, this strategy specifically ensures a readily available supply of eligible students necessary for the underenrolled professional fields the university had nurtured during the Cold War. In other words, not only are the large numbers of overseas students arriving predominantly from the Asian region a financial necessity for Riverside University to assure its own institutional presence and survival, but its identity as an academic institution suited for the modern, globalized knowledge economy is dependent on these young people's arrival as well. Such institutional anxieties around its own existence, then, are important to how Riverside turned to internationalization practice. Reflecting the persisting nationwide trend, the South Asian region—India, specifically—is one of the key sources of student-migrants for the campus. Importantly, most of the Indian student-migrant youth at Riverside University were from nonelite, middle-class families; the particular conditions enabling their transnational paths gesture to the significance of classed differences in understanding the migratory routes forged in the context of the internationalizing university.

Like other institutions, these developments at Riverside have implications for the inclusion politics of the university. As a public institution, its origins as a corrective to the exclusionary and elitist nature of higher education in the past further amplify the delicate tensions around inclusion occurring on liberal campuses today. Such tensions emerge as affirmative action policies—which were meant to provide historically marginalized groups with access to higher education but have gradually been dismantled—are replaced with "diversity and inclusion" management on campuses. This shift points to the ways that the liberal multicultural project linked with neoliberal managerialism enforces strategies to regulate the presence of racial difference within its boundaries.[22] Because of the history of this development, scholarship critiquing the empty rhetoric and elision of questions of inequality and inequity these strategies signify has mainly focused on their effects on the experiences of local, racialized student populations.[23] In this context, it may seem disingenuous to include student-migrant populations within the considerations of a university's diversity and inclusion practices because of the different race and citizenship histories involved. However, as the corporate management model of diversity becomes crucial to the branding of universities, the visible and large presence of student-migrants from the Asian region lends itself conveniently to university claims of racial and multicultural harmony. In other words, "going global" and opening doors to growing numbers of overseas students are also being deployed as diversity strategies.

Including overseas-student presence within the rhetoric of diversity was made explicit at Riverside University, as captured in a state of the university address by the school's president, which discussed Riverside's many international students alongside its ethnic minority students as part of its "commitment to diversity." Tying this drive to internationalize campuses to the rhetoric of diversity work suggests that student-migrants, particularly as most arrive from the Global South, are part of the contestations over the terms of inclusion and racial politics on campuses. This book illustrates how, despite Riverside's official rhetoric, a culture of exclusion is reinforced in the relationship between the university and Indian migrant youth, one of its largest and most im-

portant student-migrant populations. Riverside's particular practices of
housing, labor, and policing serve as key sites of regulation mediating
these young people's raced and classed sense of being-in-the-university
and being-in-the-world. Attending to how Indian student-migrants' encounters are implicated in the critical articulations between racialized
othering and the political economy of American campus life, this book
reveals how Riverside is a meaningful ethnographic instantiation of the
seemingly contradictory institutional practices of inclusion involving
migrant youth in the era of the internationalizing university.

My fieldwork at Riverside began in the campus's international student office. As this office was the setting most pertinent to mediating
the relationship between overseas students, the institution, and the
state, I found spending time in the office was critical to illuminating how
the tensions and responsibilities accompanying the growing expansion
of overseas-student enrollments were being managed. However, the
students' presence in the office was highly restricted in the context of
its austere environment as it intentionally shifted to prioritizing compliance. For this reason, meeting Ani here felt serendipitous. Ani, as a
part-time student-worker and overseas student, offered valuable insight
into the routines and shifts occurring in that office. Beyond this institutional setting, though, Ani himself would become my key interlocutor
on the campus as he brought me into the spaces and networks of everyday life that he and his peers were embedded in. This book mainly fo-
cuses on Ani and his friends, a group of middle-class men in their early
to midtwenties who arrived at Riverside University from India to study
in two-year master's programs in a range of professional fields, including engineering, mathematics, business, the sciences, and information
technology. In this sense, they were emblematic of the typical student-
migrant from South Asia. Mobilizing an ethnographic openness, much
of my fieldwork centered on following this group of friends into the
everyday scenes and relational dynamics that made up their migratory
lives. Through encounters in dank apartments, department lounges,
administrative offices, bars, and other settings of their lived experience
as Indian student-migrants, I attended to the acts of placemaking that
emerged from their fraught relationship with the university and their location as ambivalent migrant figures in the United States.[24] The insights
from these ethnographic encounters pervade the analysis in the book.

The social groupings of most of the Indian student-migrants at Riverside University tended to occur along ethnic and linguistic lines. Ani and his friends were predominantly from the southern Indian state of Tamil Nadu; however, their friend group was somewhat distinct as it also included students from other regions of India. For this reason, though Tamil would regularly be heard in their gatherings, English operated as their more inclusive default language to maintain the coherence of this group of friends. Most of these young men were from urban areas and predominantly from Hindu families, except for the student I call Jason, who was from a Christian Tamil community.

When it came to the question of caste backgrounds, by and large, students remained evasive. Throughout my fieldwork, the issue of caste almost never emerged among the Indian migrant youth explicitly. Indeed, when I occasionally attempted to broach the matter in conversations or during interviews, students appeared to become suspicious and to resent me for it. Flustered facial expressions and curt responses back to me always sought to convey that I was being indelicate, as caste did not matter and had no place in our conversations. It is difficult to address something ethnographically that your interlocutors vehemently refuse to acknowledge. Enrollment trends in India indicate that historically marginalized lower-caste and tribal populations, referred to in official state language as Scheduled Castes and Tribes (SC/ST), remain underrepresented in India's system of higher education.[25] Additionally, the caste composition of India's middle classes reveals its predominantly upper-caste character.[26] Even in securing student loans, as most of the Indian student-migrants at Riverside did, the configuration of class and caste produces uneven and unequal educational lending in India. These trends, overall, suggest that Indian student-migrants arriving in the United States are often from upper-caste backgrounds. Naming practices—in which surnames can be, *at times*, a marker of caste capital—also point to how many of the Indian migrant youth I met during my fieldwork were Brahmin or upper caste; some friend groups that formed would be composed of entirely Brahmin or upper-caste students. Yet it is important to note that there were also students present who were not from upper-caste backgrounds. Ani's circle of friends seemed to include both lower- and upper-caste students, though it was never openly discussed, and no one knew exactly which lower-caste categories were represented.[27] In one exchange, Ani became agitated at my interest in learning more about how caste figured into their experiences, indignantly disclosing that he belonged to an "Other Backward Classes" (OBC) community. In chapter 2, I return to the notion of castelessness and how its contradictions work through a narrative of modern becoming among Indian middle-class migrant youth seeking out a US-based education.

While Indian migrant men became my main focus, I purposely pursued accounts from others who were not necessarily directly part of the immediate circle of friends I followed, and especially of those who were positioned differently but were pertinent to deepening an understanding of the racialized, gendered, and classed formations produced in these encounters. For one, while Indian men far outnumbered women among these youth—indicative of the masculinized spaces of the professional fields in which they study—the lives and narratives of Indian women who also migrated for their education weave in and out of these shared social settings. The book's emphasis on masculinity as the enacting of gender necessitates a relational approach to which women and their presence in shared spaces are pertinent.[28] To the extent they are a part of this setting, but also to examine more closely the gendered nature of the relationship between mobility, indebtedness, and education, the perspectives of Indian migrant women appear in particular discussions and contribute to my analysis.

I also intentionally sought the perspectives of Pakistani, Bangladeshi, and Indian Muslim student-migrants, students who were almost never part of the spaces of sociality created by the Indian youth I followed. Among the large numbers of Indian migrant youth arriving on the campus, the presence of Muslim student-migrants was sparse, partly indicative of India's own structural inequalities that constrain its minority Muslim student population's access to educational opportunities.[29] I met and interviewed a couple of these youth who did come to study on the campus; their reflections on how their positioning as part of the Indian Muslim minority and a globally persecuted religious population figured into their experiences of educational migration inform the analysis and accounts shared in the book.

Students from Pakistan and Bangladesh were, by far, much smaller in presence on the campus than Indian student-migrants, and most were in doctoral programs using doctoral funding they had received in their departments. This meant that the circumstances of how they were able to migrate and the conditions under which they studied at the university were not the same as Indian migrant youth. This contrast is meaningful in highlighting the particularities of the political-economic realities of the latter. Especially important, however, is what the accounts of the students from Pakistan and Bangladesh offer to understanding the differences that both religion and national identity can make in the racialization linked to the post-9/11 surveillance state. To instantiate these distinctions in experience more closely, chapter 3 includes an extensive exchange with Imran, a doctoral student from Pakistan. Recalling some of his experiences with surveillance as a student-migrant, Imran's accounts are emblematic of how the particularities of war-on-terror geopolitics mean differing experiences of the excesses of state surveillance among student-migrants. It is both because Imran is Muslim and because of the ways that Pakistan has been situated in the geopolitical relations of the war on terror that he offers a different tale than what Indian student-migrant men had to endure. His account, then, provides a valuable *comparative* glimpse that reveals more about the constellation of privilege and marginalization that Indian student-migrants, in contrast, move through.

In addition to factoring in women and non-Indian migrant men studying in graduate programs, I have threaded into my analysis formal semistructured interviews I conducted with Indian student-migrants in undergraduate programs and pertinent faculty, staff, and leaders of student organizations. While all ethnographic endeavors are necessarily partial truths, the perspectives of other actors positioned differently in relation to the university community work to deepen insights, presenting important points of relation and contrast, as well as other nuanced layers through which I analytically read the dynamics and encounters this book examines.

Though attending to the everyday lives of Indian student-migrants is a crucial way to center accounts that are often marginalized, it is important to note that this project moves beyond following individual migrant stories. The inquiry necessarily involves turning a critical ethnographic lens on how student mobilities figured into the production and sustenance of the neoliberal university itself. I emphasize, then, the *encounters* between Indian migrant youth and the university to delineate the spatial and temporal boundaries of the project. Following these young people into the different institutional settings that were integral to arranging their arrival and presence as student-migrants, I remained with them until the time of their graduation, the crucial moment that signified when the university was no longer expected to bear any responsibility in its exchange with these students. This abrupt ending that students faced in their ties to the internationalizing university was accompanied by the angst of facing precarious futures; it is these uncertainties that lie at the heart of the analysis of chapter 5. I draw, overall, on the methodological sensibilities of institutional ethnography,[30] seeking to uncover the cultural logics that are produced in the linkages between transnational migration, the educational institution, and late-stage capitalism. As such, my fieldwork also included reviewing and analyzing a range of institutional documents, national security policy reports, and archival materials.

Finally, I want to make a more explicit note on my location in this project, a consideration that is undeniably tied to my family's own experience of migration to and settlement within the US-based Indian diaspora. Though we did not arrive through educational migratory routes, education was a crucial refrain of imagined possibilities in our family narrative of migration. The persistence of that refrain was always curious to me as our arrival in the 1980s through family reunification policies was a last resort for my family—a consequence of my father's place in postcolonial India's generation of men who were educated in technical fields considered critical to India's national development but who still faced chronic unemployment. In this sense, there are resonances between my family's own migration history and the material conditions, longings, and disillusionments produced in the articulations of Indian postcoloniality and US exceptionalism that are discussed in this book. Finding my way to and through this project was fundamentally informed by these aspects of my personal biography. Ultimately, not only was I moved to scrutinize the very institutional lifeworld in which I had become immersed as an academic[31] but I also had become preoccupied with the ways in which such educational institutions configure, reproduce, and fracture the desiring forged in the nexus of migration and education. These intellectual preoccupations, along with my position as an ethnographer, an academic, and a middle-class diasporic Indian woman, influenced my complicated presence in the spaces I shared with my interlocutors, and thus, are also formative to the analysis found in this book.

CHAPTER OUTLINES

In India's postliberalization era, studying overseas is understood as a key educational strategy of the so-called *new* Indian middle class, and "Western" nations are often the desired destination. In *Paradise Redefined*, Vanessa Fong argues that the pursuit of a generalized, Western, developed citizenship served as a key motivation for the decisions of Chinese overseas students in her study.[32] Yet, I contend in this book that the United States, specifically, plays an important role in the global educational imaginaries of Indian middle-class youth. To make this argument, I begin the book with a historicization of the ties between the consolidation of US higher education, the migratory circulations of Indian student-migrants, and the rise of the United States as a global hegemonic power. Chapter 1 reveals how the transnational movements of Indian student-migrants to the United States have always been embedded in the geopolitics that linked the US settler-colonial project with the emergence of the postcolonial state of India.[33] It is in that linkage that migration for an American education became imagined by Indian youth as an invaluable route to pursue the desire for Indian modernity. Attending to two crucial periods of US immigration history, the exclusionary era of the early twentieth century and the period following the passing of the 1965 US immigration policy, chapter 1 sketches how Indian educational imaginaries, forged through (settler) colonial, postcolonial, and imperialist entanglements, positioned a US-based education as the site of contestations over student-migrants' transnational obligations to and longings for an Indian modernity in earlier historical moments. In tracing how those contestations were cast through particular global configurations of race, nationhood, labor, and surveillance, the chapter illuminates that the pertinence of these configurations to the encounters between Indian student-migrants and the internationalizing campus in the contemporary age of neoliberal globalization is not new or incidental. This history gestures to how US exceptionalism has been tethered to the story of Indian educational migration to the United States, the resonances of which continue to mark the preoccupations, subjectivities, and notions of obligation that emerge in the current moment of the global neoliberal order.

Beginning the exploration of these resonances, chapter 2 attends to the attachments that mediate the movements, practices of placemaking, and futures of Indian student-migrants at Riverside University. The chapter specifically offers these young people's reflections on why they migrated and what they imagined for themselves with their degrees in hand, illustrating how the educational migratory routes of Indian youth today still serve as pathways of longings that far exceed the sole pursuit of an educational degree. Drawing on a Deleuzian conceptualization of desire,[34] chapter 2 explores how acts of desiring serve as a productive, compelling force, which draws these young people into the transnational educational sphere. Filtered through classed, gendered, and upper-caste invocations of deservingness, choice, and the invincibility of middle-classness, Indian student-migrants reveal how the desire to become modern selves continues to serve as the animating force setting these youth across national borders to pursue their education on an American campus in the United States, which persists as the imagined site of this becoming. Here, I include a discussion of the tensions around Indian higher education and its affirmative action policies, known as the reservation system, and how the investment in an Indian secular modernity that was part of those tensions informs these young people's articulations of modern becoming. Educational migration to the United States as the vehicle enabling the transformative process of becoming modern in the age of neoliberal globalization, one that they imagine as not available to them in India, is integral to how these middle-class students construct notions of successful masculinities. Indicative of the neoliberal ethos and marking a shift from the nation-state and national-development centered narratives prevalent in the colonial and post-colonial periods, these young men assert themselves as knowing, calculating migrants who tailor individualized dreams and are in control of their destinies.

At the same time, the chapter points to the ways that their desiring to be modern "men of the world" is entangled in interrelated webs of obligation formed through market-based student loans and kinship ties, as well as nation-state interests. The relationship between global capitalism and the desiring machine that informs the global educational landscape translates the obligations attached to Indian student-migrants' transnational mobility into a cultural logic of indebtedness, a notion of owing and being owed, that becomes woven into these young people's sensemaking. Revealing important linkages between economic forces, power, and social ties, one crucial insight that the anthropology of debt literature has offered is that indebtedness is not a purely economic matter; rather, the material realities of debt must be situated within the moral tensions that produce logics of indebtedness.[35] Here, I specifically draw on David Graeber's analysis of varying moral logics of exchange to interrogate how notions of reciprocity, obligation, and debt figure into the moral calculus of my middle-class participants. Chapter 2 also introduces invocations of sacrifice as a meaningful emic perspective that illuminates further how indebtedness is part of the affective structure of transnational paths of Indian middle-class students. The contemporary phenomenon of educational migration may seem like an unusual place for meditations on sacrifice. However, I contend that it is a noteworthy feature of the classed refrain in these young people's migratory narratives, serving the self-fashioning of Indian middle-class youth whose negotiations of their positioning as migrants are, at times, implicitly reconciled as the acts of sacrifice or suffering necessary to enable their transformation into modern figures of the neoliberal moment.

To consider how the cultural logic of owing and being owed mediates the placemaking practices of these young people, the next chapters move more deeply into the different settings constituting the students' migratory lives. Chapter 3 specifically takes up the ways that the consolidation of the post-9/11 surveillance state figures into their transnational encounters. While, on the one hand, the erosion of state support for public higher education contributes to institutional interests in increasing overseas-student enrollments, the aggressive deployment of security measures after the attacks of September 11, 2001, enabled a strong and lasting presence of the surveillance state to regulate these same students' paths. Indicative of the evolving modes of power accompanying the shift from the disciplinary society to societies of control that Gilles Deleuze had predicted,[36] chapter 3 examines how the residual effects of the post-9/11 policy mandate to "institutionalize the imagination" come to bear on the experiences of student-migrants arriving through the racial geographies of the war on terror. In this chapter, I emphasize accounts shared by Pakistani and Muslim student-migrants to highlight that religion and national origin produce important differences in how the post-9/11 surveillance state is experienced. Relatedly, I introduce how the ideological and geopolitical underpinnings of the war on terror resonate with India's own religious politics, specifically Hindu nationalism's rise to and consolidation of power since the 1990s. I contend that these resonances effectively produce "Muslim-looking" as an especially important racial sensemaking category mobilized by Indian migrant men.

Moving through various sites shaped by the existence of the surveillance state, both official and unofficial—visa offices, airports, campus ceremonial rituals, multicultural displays, and the bureaucratic routines of the international student office—chapter 3 considers how the rendering of migrant figures as racialized subjects reflects a newness linked to post-9/11 security regimes while also revealing the persisting racial logics of earlier nationalist and imperialist discourses. The racialized and gendered constructions of the terrorist threat that accompany the bureaucratization of post-9/11 surveillance produce a compliant student-migrant figure. Though in conflicted ways, students interpret surrendering to the watchful gaze of the surveillance state as an obligation of their circumstances; doing so is part of what they imagine they owe in exchange for a US-based education. The discussion in this chapter necessarily includes a closer examination of how the public university, in its own pivot from forming as a Cold War institution to positioning itself as a globalized one, is implicated in the ideological and bureaucratic work that the maintenance of the surveillance state requires, highlighting that remembering 9/11 is an important facet in producing the global imaginary discussed by Kamola. Even as the public university transitions into the "internationalizing" university, partly as a means to survive the withdrawal of state support, university life continues to be deeply entangled in serving the ideology of US exceptionalism that sustains the "imperial university."[37] Chapter 3 alludes to the dissonances that entanglement produces for young Indian student-migrants, thus, contributing to creating ambivalent spaces for their (un)belonging.

Capturing the ordinary scenes and routines that constitute student-migrant life on campus, chapter 4 interrogates how Indian migrant youth at Riverside negotiate this ambivalent positioning. Practices of housing, part-time labor, sociality, learning, policing, and social networks emerge here as everyday threads, revealing that the campus is a location of unstable reterritorialization.[38] This chapter will also return to how the racial effects of state surveillance appear in other modes for these young people. Drawing on the insights of migration network theory, the experiences explored in chapter 4 illuminate the ways that Indian student-migrant networks extend into and become a crucial facet of belongingness on campus. The acts and expectations of sociality, care, and reciprocity that emerge from these networks form a moral economy that exists alongside their encounters with campus segregation, exploitative labor practices, and racial profiling. Together, these experiences gesture to a fraught politics of inclusion between these students and the university, informing how students reconcile their desire for a US-based neoliberal modernity with their location at the margins of university life. This is particularly significant as many institutions of higher education point to the growing presence of student-migrants from Global South locations, such as India, as serving national demands for more diversity on campuses. Taking up and contributing to existing scholarly insights on South Asian raciality,[39] I contend that for the Indian migrant youth themselves, the racial and class sensemaking that surfaces from their everyday life is partly premised on market-type calculations about what kinds of promises were broken and which debts were not paid, including by the university itself. Chapter 4 concludes with a discussion of why the students I befriended recognized the exclusions that constituted their campus encounters but did not work collectively to improve conditions, a consequence of a middle-class moral calculus that effectively serves the neoliberal project of the internationalizing university.

Chapter 5 attends to the anxieties of the young men as they approached graduation and faced uncertain futures.[40] Burdened with debt, Indian migrant youth confront the possibility that the "cluster of promises" that was attached to their transnational circulations may not materialize as they imagined.[41] At the same time that a logic of indebtedness (and the imagined acts of sacrificing or suffering that are tied to it) mediates their sensibilities of becoming modern subjects, it also grooms them for the volatility of the global neoliberal economy. Here, I will specifically discuss the role of "consultancies" using "body-shopping" practices to funnel some of these graduating youth into the IT industry as precarious, flexible, and indentured labor. Certain that they were the ideal migrant subjects, the Indian migrant men at Riverside sought to make sense of the university's disregard for them, as well as their struggle to secure stable work in their fields and remain in the

United States. Those final days on campus forced a reckoning with their gendered and classed anxieties about successful masculinities, which manifested through competitive frictions with one another, the uncertainties of their role in supporting existing or future households, and the precarity of being drawn into the global knowledge economy as indebted migrants.

The epilogue returns to and reflects on what is at stake, and for whom, in the encounters between these youth and the internationalizing university project. In a moment when "going global" is declared an essential modern facet of university life while the United States continues to hold an important place in the educational circuits and imaginaries of neoliberal empire, understanding ethnographically the lifeworlds of Indian student-migrants, central figures in this development, underscores how the answer lies in the long-existing ties between higher education, racial capitalism, and US global hegemony. I suggest that the political, social, economic, and environmental upheaval the world faces today necessarily means that we must take more seriously what possibilities for radical transformations of university life exist on the horizon and to what ends. Building on the insights offered by recent radical scholarship seeking to push the boundaries of critical university studies, the concluding remarks reflect on the complicities involved, including among student-migrants, in the exclusions of the internationalizing university. Yet, it also offers a way forward by considering what conditions would have to exist to make possible the kinds of solidarities that are needed among those who are dispossessed by the globalized campus, so that there may be a move toward a more meaningful, liberatory notion of the inclusive, global university.

1 · Traces of Empire

In January of 2011, US Immigration and Customs Enforcement (ICE) agents raided the property of Tri-Valley University (TVU), an unaccredited higher education institution located in Pleasanton, California. The university had been under investigation for fraudulent activities involving the illegal issuance of student visas. The case was the largest of its kind for federal agents, ultimately leading to the TVU president's arrest and conviction. The media coverage of the case was limited in the United States, and much of it focused on the potential of fraud among the growing number of for-profit educational institutions.[1] Yet, there was a subtext to this controversy that was directed at the students who had migrated across national borders to enroll in the university, almost all of them coming from India. Though the university was generally condemned as a "sham," several of the students were forced to wear GPS trackers and many faced deportation.[2] Debate on the culpability of the Indian students themselves followed.[3] Were the students naive victims of the scheme or active participants who were exploiting the student visa program? This questioning attempted to reconcile contradictory representations of these young people either as educated and desirable or as scheming potential threats to national security. Adding to the suspicion was that the enrolled students were scattered throughout the United States, most working full-time low-wage jobs off campus, an act strictly prohibited on the student visa.[4] Their willingness to pursue this more checkered educational route for the promise of being able to work while studying in the United States foregrounded the complex raced and classed dimensions to student migrations from India in the contemporary period. The concept of Indian youth migrating for their education easily resonates with dominant, long-standing tropes of South Asians embodying inherent cultural values that make them more ambitious, hardworking, and naturally inclined for educational success and upward mobility. In other words, they are emblematic of the good and desirable migrant. In this context, the suspicious readings of the Indian students at TVU may appear to be anomalous or unusual. Yet, while the TVU incident is a more egregious instantiation of the kinds of exploitative forces that have emerged with the neoliberal drive to internationalize, the ambivalence around Indian student-migrants' positioning revealed in this controversy has, in fact, always been a part of the story of student migration from India to the United States.

To attend to this point, I start this story by considering the presence of Indian student-migrants in two key moments of immigration history—the exclusionary era of the early twentieth century and the period following the 1965 Immigration and Nationality Act. In historically tracing the circulations of Indian student-migrants across US national borders, this chapter illuminates how the paths of these migrant figures have been entangled in the transnational educational histories of US global and settler expansion. At the same time, as education has always served as an important domain of struggle around third-world modernities, the movements of young students into the emergent center of global power were also significant to the formation of an Indian nation. In this way, Indian educational imaginaries, produced in the geopolitical nexus of the settler-colonial and imperialist formation of the United States and the anti- and postcolonial struggles of India, positioned a US-based education as the site of contestations over Indian student-migrants' transnational obligations to and longings for an Indian modernity. Importantly, the transnational channels of education in these earlier historical moments forged a sense of obligation that centered nation-building, but the liminal nature of Indian student-migrants' journeys shaped their political alignments in unexpected ways. In tracing how those ambivalent negotiations were cast through particular global configurations of labor, racial exclusions, nationhood, and surveillance, this history gestures to the long-existing interests tethered to US exceptionalism that have necessarily been part of Indian educational migration to the United States, the resonances of which continue to inform the subjectivities, horizons of desiring, and notions of indebtedness among Indian migrant youth

encountering the internationalizing university of the current global neoliberal order.

EARLY TWENTIETH CENTURY: UNITED STATES
AS ALTERNATIVE SITE FOR INDIAN MODERNITY

During the early years of the twentieth century, as the British Empire
struggled to maintain its control over its colonies, the United States was
expanding its own global power and influence. Recognizing how con-
solidating a higher education system would play a vital role in this expansion, the United States passed the Morrill Act in 1862, through which
large tracts of land were granted to various states by the US federal government as funding to invest specifically in higher education. As scholars have argued, this policy development was only possible through
the direct seizure and transfer of Indigenous land to existing and new
educational institutions.[5] In other words, by dispossessing Indigenous
communities to offer a technical education in agricultural production,
engineering, and military tactics to (mainly white) settlers, the Morrill
Act was a state technology of US expansion and settler colonialism.[6]
Yet, in spite of the violence it entailed, the Morrill Act is often praised
for its role in ensuring a nationwide system of public education that was
accessible to larger segments of the US population, purportedly reflecting an American brand of modern liberalism dedicated to ideals of equal
opportunity and access that were fundamental to the narrative of US exceptionalism already circulating both at home and abroad. This context
set the stage for the trickling in of Indian student-migrants to the United
States in the early twentieth century, which was closely tied to the Indian nationalist struggle for independence from the British Empire. The
settler-colonial imaginary of the United States extended an alternative
site of Western (capitalist) modernity made available through educational routes; Indians could form a Western-educated class that could
eventually realize a modern, industrialized, and independent India, a
vision of the future that was increasingly being embraced by Indians in
that historical moment.[7]

The movement of Indian students across borders began with the
British Empire's own calculated efforts to use education as a way to
maintain its imperialist hold over India. The British commitment to creating an English-educated Indian elite that would be loyal to the Brit-

ish led to what historian Tamson Pietsch, coincidentally, refers to as the trend to internationalize the education of Indians.[8] Regardless of the intended motivations, encounters with widespread racism and financial hardship during the students' studies in England fueled growing Indian nationalist sentiment as well as collective resistance against the British Raj. As Harald Fischer-Tiné contends, "The radical brand of Indian nationalism was not merely the outcome of the travel activities of a few elite 'Indian patriots.' . . . It would hardly have been conceivable without the existence of a much larger number of Indian students studying abroad."[9] In 1909, concerns about controlling the "problem" that the Indian student-migrant population posed were exacerbated by the assassination of a government official by an Indian student-migrant.[10] The subsequent tensions that accompanied being portrayed as threats rather than subjects loyal to the British Empire led many Indian youth to redirect their pursuit of a Western education from the colonial center to the United States.

Because of its history of resistance to British rule and its growing reputation for technical education, which was widely perceived as crucial to building the industrial infrastructures necessary for a modern Indian nation-state, the United States was considered the most viable possibility of studying beyond the reach of the British Empire. As such, a small but steady stream of Indian students began entering the United States, part of an overall rise in migrants from the Asian region at the time.[11] By 1914, there were approximately ten thousand South Asians living in the United States legally.[12] Of these, the vast majority were labor migrants providing the kinds of labor needed to support US expansionist projects.[13] While Indian labor migrants outnumbered Indian student-migrants in the United States, the presence of the latter was indispensable to shaping a collective attachment to an imagined independent Indian nation, laying the groundwork for a US-based Indian diasporic consciousness.

This important role despite Indian students' relatively small presence was partly due to being a highly organized population, a consequence of the lessons learned by the earlier experiences of the Indian student community in England. The US-based Indian student organization Hindusthan Association of America (HAA) provided Indian students with support, resources, a social network, and a shared media outlet called the *Hindusthanee Student* (HS). The stated mission of HS was to offer a platform from which "India could be interpreted to America and America to India."[14] Serving as a kind of cultural translator to what was readily understood as a white America, HS published issues that often included explanations of the Indian social context.[15] For instance, editors would occasionally publish bibliographies of readings meant to counter orientalist representations of Indian society, offering instead "the true picture of Indian life."[16] A collective anxiousness to create a positive global image of Indians was reflected in the publication's rhetoric and subject matter, which were often nationalist and anticolonial in design. Student members used HS as a platform to garner support for the nationalist cause, appealing to popular sentiments around progress and modernization at the time in the United States by suggesting British subjugation was the sole factor preventing Indian society from the kinds of advancements made possible in the United States. As such, the turn to the United States as an idealized diasporic site to pursue an anticolonial, nationalist vision of Indian modernity through educational migratory routes occurred simultaneously through an implicit denial of and complicity in the anti-Indigenous and anti-Black subjugation that have necessarily been part of the settler-colonial logics of the United States. The HAA furthered this erasure through its ties to the Indian nationalist agenda by actively encouraging more Indian middle-class youth to migrate to the United States for their education. Contrasting the treatment and conditions students faced in England, HAA argued for the importance of a pool of US-educated Indian youth to India's future. Studying in the United States was depicted as a meaningful alternative that would serve Indian middle-class aspirations for upward mobility through a Western education, as well as develop the human capital necessary for India's modernization. Framing "America" as the civilizational embodiment of an alternative vision of a modern, independent nation offered the discursive material to mobilize Indian migrants around an identity that would help sever ties to their British colonial masters.[17]

In this way, Indian students' presence in the United States served as a crucial part of the overseas resistance to British colonial rule, but it did so by legitimating the entwined liberal, capitalist, settler-colonial narratives of US exceptionalism and modern educational opportunity. The ambivalence of this positioning soon led to particular contradictions for Indian student life in the United States that were grounded in class difference, racial exclusion, and state surveillance. One noteworthy facet of the Indian students' experiences that reflected these tensions was their involvement in low-wage labor while pursuing their education. Their participation in low-wage work was critical to forging the cross-class connections essential to the militant Indian anticolonial resistance in the United States, but it also ultimately captured the attention of the US white settler population and the US state.

STUDENTS, SELF-SUPPORT, AND CROSS-CLASS CONNECTIONS

According to historian Ross Bassett, student migration from India in the earlier decades of the twentieth century required extensive support from kinship and patronage ties, indicating that Indian migrants arriving through educational routes during this time were predominantly from educated, upper-caste families.[18] At the same time, financial challenges were not uncommon for these student-migrants; unlike in England, however, students in the United States at the time were encouraged to participate in wage labor as a means of supporting themselves, often referred to by student-migrants as "self-support." The practice of self-support facilitated the solidarity between the two populations that became crucial to the US-based Indian resistance against British rule: workers and students. Yet, the complexities of this cross-class dynamic required negotiating tensions predicated on settler logics that would ultimately contribute to a more fraught experience of Indian diasporic belonging.[19]

Student-migrants practicing self-support meant they found themselves working alongside uneducated Indian laborers and farmers—waiting tables, washing dishes, cleaning, working in canneries, or spending their summer vacations and holidays picking fruit or doing other farm-related work.[20] Middle-class Indian students engaging in menial labor in the United States was a significant point of contention for Indian nationalists, reflecting the different and at times conflicting ideologies that informed nationalist visions for a future independent India. Some Indian nationalists, including those involved in HAA, encouraged self-support, portraying the practice as specific to US modernity and progress. They suggested it would enable students to navigate difficult financial circumstances, interact with American people, and experience the particular US capitalist ethos of work while struggling to attain educational success.[21] More ardent nationalists—former student-migrants themselves—also linked self-support with the leftist ideologies inspiring some of the nationalist rhetoric at the time.[22] In the India-based *Modern Review*, which regularly discussed student life abroad, a series of articles specifically addressed the question of self-support.[23] For instance, Sarangadhar Das, a former US-based student-migrant and radical nationalist, penned the *Modern Review* article "Why Must We Emigrate to the United States of America?" as a critical response to Shiv Narayan's piece, which discouraged Indian middle-class youth from pursuing their studies in the United States.[24]

While Narayan argued the rightful place of the Indian educated class was at home in India, leading the nationalist cause rather than toiling in the United States, Das accused Narayan of seeking to "usher in the Indian bourgeoisie who will exploit the proletariat."[25] Das connected the US capitalist narrative of hard work and individual responsibility, the Indian nationalist model of "Swaraj" (or self-reliance), and the Marxist emphasis on class struggle to persuade Indian middle-class students of the benefits of self-support to the nationalist cause. According to Das, low-wage work nurtured self-sufficiency in student-migrants, suggesting that doing so was characteristic of and enacting the nationalist spirit of sovereignty and self-determination. Implicit in this insistence that both menial labor and technical education are important to these young men's migratory experiences in the United States was an assertion of an alternative Indian masculinity as a crucial basis to resist British subjugation. Moreover, Das argued, it would allow student-migrants to gain a unique sense of class struggle that would contribute to an Indian nation mobilized around the working masses. Indeed, the presence of an Indian educated class within the borders of an emergent global power working alongside and forming alliances with working-class Indians was a formidable threat, serving as the basis of the unique cross-class solidarities that shaped the efforts of the US-based radical Indian nationalist organization, the Ghadar Party.[26]

Still, such cross-class connections were ripe with tension, illuminating the contradictory ways that the Indian educated class in the United States positioned itself and managed its delicate ties with Indian laborers. Students often expressed sentiments that were indicative of their conflicted, classed apprehensions regarding their role in Indian nationhood. In his inaugural address at the 1915 International Hindusthanee

Student Convention, K. D. Shastri suggested some of the hostility Indians were beginning to face in the United States was due to the behavior of uneducated Indian laborers. As he explained, Americans "have been largely led to misunderstand us as most of our adventurous fellow-countrymen who arrived in this country happened to be illiterate and unassimilable."[27] Capturing a common portrayal of Indian students' positioning in relation to Indians overseas, Shastri asserted students serve as an alternative and more ideal image of Indians in the United States, one which embodied the possibility of Indian modernity and a closer and more positive relationship with America. This perspective on the significance of students was echoed regularly. In the February 1916 issue of HS, the HAA editorial board wrote that students were crucial to awakening "the slumbering millions back home and [to] rous[ing] them to activity . . . to develop an opinion which will guide and shape the future of India."[28] Student-migrants were constructed as an indispensable part of the struggle to garner respect from the world's emergent global power for the Indian people and an Indian nation. However, tensions around their positioning in the United States deepened as Indians and other Asian communities faced mounting class and race hostilities. For student-migrants, confronting this reality led to a reworking of the place "America" held in the nationalist desires of Indian diasporic imaginings.

US EXCLUSIONS AND THE "TIDE OF TURBANS"

The United States' extensive expansion and settlement efforts were accompanied by a national identity crisis that hinged on the shifting and persisting racial logics of national belonging, a crisis borne of US settler-colonial maneuvers rooted in the racial capitalism of "Manifest Destiny" ideology, anti-Indigenous and anti-Black violences, and the exploitation of migrant labor. While the resistance to (British) colonialism that was fomenting among Indian student-migrants neglected to account for the ways that US liberal thought was intricately linked to such colonial violence itself, economic downturns in the United States during this time directed white settler hostilities toward the Asian migrant presence.[29] The rising resentment among white populations over the competition of Asian labor contributed to racial depictions of Indians as a "tide of turbans"[30] and to widespread local violence. This period of hostility was directly linked to evolving racial categories produced by the state, which led to the emergence of several quota-based and exclusionary immigration policies, making the country an unwelcoming destination for migrants, particularly from the Asian region. In 1910, the Immigration Commission Report stated explicitly that East Indians "are a filthy, ignorant, and despised race, and are considered the least desirable immigrants in the State."[31] With the passing of the Immigration Act of 1917, the entry of individuals from the "Asiatic Barred Zone," including from India, would be prohibited for the next thirty years, reflecting one of the most exclusionary pieces of immigration legislation in US history. The reality of race riots, labor conflicts, and the implementation of these discriminatory policies exposed the seeming contradictions between the liberal ideals Americans espoused and the student-migrants' direct encounter of living in the United States. They had to reckon directly with the exclusionary racial logic in which US settler nationhood was grounded.

Concerned about how the proposed legislation excluding Asian migrant populations would affect not only laborers but also Indian students, the Indian student leadership agitated for more favorable conditions for themselves by again distinguishing and emphasizing the desirability of student-migrants.[32] It was an opportune time to do so. The effects of the First World War had afforded the United States the chance to cultivate itself as a dominant presence on the world stage that would be distinct from European powers and serve as a geopolitical counterweight to the Soviets, who were already being deemed a possible threat to US capitalist expansion. In this context, international education and exchange were increasingly being recognized in the United States for their potential as a mechanism of geopolitical influence, and therefore, they started cohering, as Chay Brooks describes, as a "civilizational force" that could more systematically circulate the myth of US exceptionality across the world while cloaked in a rhetoric of peace and cooperation.[33] As such, while the period of the late nineteenth and early twentieth centuries in the United States was marked by isolationism and xenophobia, foreign students were one of the excepted classes identified in the proposed immigration restrictions during this era. However, accompanying this exception was the significant caveat that students were forbidden from engaging in work while they studied.[34] Indian student leadership took issue with this new regulation as it would mean the end of self-support practices. The restriction indicated the serious threat that students working alongside laborers posed. The clause ensured only wealthy Indian students who could afford living and tuition expenses could enroll in school; therefore, they would not serve as a demographic challenge to white labor. It also helped prevent the cross-class solidarities among Indians that contributed to the radical Indian nationalism that had taken root in the United States.

Beyond their connection to Indian labor, Indian students' direct involvement in the more militant activities of the Ghadar Party ultimately caused them to be a crucial concern for the US state. As the US government began to realize that challenges to British imperialism also had implications for its own imperialist interests, the HAA, associated with nationalist activities, eventually came under government surveillance and scrutiny.[35] These circumstances, mirroring the repression Indian students encountered in England, reflected how educational migration was a site through which a globally circulating discourse of exclusions mediated by racial capitalism facilitated collaboration between the two nations and their imperialist projects. For the Indian educated class, this growing repression reinforced the urgency of using the Indian presence in the United States to mobilize Indian migrants and help establish a free Indian nation that they could return to as their own. However, in 1917–18 the so-called Hindu Conspiracy trial in San Francisco led to a number of convictions of Indian nationalists, including prominent student activists, such as Taraknath Das. The trial was a jarring moment for Indian student-migrants, one that revealed their uneasy positioning as the embodied personhoods of both threat and ideal migrant.

As transnational agents, student-migrants played an invaluable role in circulating across borders the nationalist narrative of an independent and modern Indian future, for which the United States as diasporic location held a privileged place. Yet, the confluence of exclusionary legislation, state surveillance, and high-profile convictions of this period brought Indian student-migrants into a direct confrontation with the racial-capitalist logics masked by and undergirding US exceptionality. In that confrontation, one which signaled the "out-of-place" settler-colonial *spatial* modality that framed Asian migrants as perpetual outsiders within,[36] the United States shifted in the collective Indian diasporic imagining from an alternative site offering a route to a modern India to yet another global setting of subjugation in which the struggle for Indian modernity was threatened. Decades later, the transformations of the world order that included the Cold War, the creation of newly independent postcolonial nation-states, and the rise of the United States as a global hegemony led to a second vital historical conjuncture in which Indian students' border crossings for education served as a crucial transnational site of struggle for Indian modernity and nationhood. As key changes were made to US immigration legislation and an independent India faced its postcolonial insecurities, the Indian student returned as an important migrant figure symbolically embodying the potential and angst of Indian modernity, for which the United States was positioned as a productive location yet again.

POST-1965 IMMIGRATION LEGISLATION: POSTCOLONIAL POLITICS AND STUDENT LOYALTIES

The aftermath of World War II and the emergence of the Cold War deepened higher education's involvement in securing the United States' position on the world stage as a military, political, and economic superpower. This period is often heralded as the golden age of US higher education, during which military and other federal funding were channeled into expanding universities' institutional capacities and enrollments. As Europe experienced the destabilization of its own academic institutions due to the devastation of World War II, the United States attained a more formidable role in asserting itself as a center of knowledge production. This also meant more widespread and systematic efforts to enhance the international dimensions of higher education. The moralizing rationale of international peace and mutual understanding that dominated the rhetoric around international education in the interwar period was gradually supplanted by "soft power" approaches that drew higher education more directly into matters of foreign policy and national defense.[37] Further, as the United States began its long-standing struggle with the Soviet Union to gain strategic influence over the newly independent nations of the Global South, a core feature of Cold War politics, it recognized the importance of educational policies to this power struggle; educating the elite of the Global South would be a key strategy in nurturing US global hegemony. The expansion of educational aid schemes, policymaking, and exchange programs that encouraged student mobility was a facet accompanying the call during this period to move from "the provincial and insular mind to the international mind."[38] Along with establishing area studies departments, international relations programs, and foreign language centers, the federal government also offered significant funding provisions that pumped financial aid into higher education to specifically target the advancement of science and technology fields, recognized as important to the United States' competition with the Soviet Union. However, these fields were not adequately being filled by US citizens.

This served, partly, as the catalyst for the remarkable shift in the United States' stance toward immigration policy, reflected most prominently in the momentous passage of the 1965 Immigration and Nationality Act (INA). Essentially abolishing the national origins quota system, the new legislation's system of preferences prioritized family reunification and migrants who could fulfill the needs of technical fields.[39] Because of these priorities, it was assumed that the legislation would merely lead to the expansion of the white demographic through immigration from European nations, while simultaneously fostering a more benevolent image of US empire by opening its doors to the rest of the world during a period in which the nation, and the liberal capitalist model of progress it was peddling, were being depicted internationally as exclusionary, isolationist, and hypocritical.[40] It was never intended to lead to the influx of non-white immigrants and the radical transformation of the racial composition of the United States that ultimately occurred.

These changes were reflected in student migration as well. While in the early part of the Cold War student and scholar exchange primarily occurred between the United States and Western Europe, the 1960s and 1970s witnessed a transformation in student mobility, now characterized more from the Global South to the North.[41] Unlike in an earlier period, the immediate years after the passage of INA witnessed much larger numbers of South Asian immigrants from the professional and technically skilled classes. Educated Indians were especially appealing to the United States. This was not only because South Asia was a valuable battleground in the ideological and strategic dimensions of the Cold War but also because the Indian educated class typically had English fluency and the training and skills needed in technical fields, an effect of the Nehruvian development model. Despite his anticolonial and anti-imperial sensibilities, the first prime minister of India, Jawaharlal Nehru, uncritically reproduced the hegemonic Western model of modernization in his national educational policies by emphasizing the importance of cultivating a pool of science, engineering, and technology talent, often gendered as an arena for men, and minimizing the significance of the arts and humanities.

However, the Indian labor market was unable to adequately absorb its educated classes, and this became an aspect of India's postcolonial struggle to carve out its own nation-building path to modernization. As this challenge coincided with the US interest in receiving students and labor in technical fields that would expand its influence globally, higher education served as the primary migratory route from India to the United States in the initial period after 1965. By 1970, students were almost two-thirds of all Indian migrants in the United States.[42] Educational migration to the United States, once again, was imagined as the channel to attaining the potential of an Indian modernity. As a consequence, however, students' transnational movement carried with it a postcolonial angst about India's global image, a sentiment famously captured by Prime Minister Indira Gandhi's words: "We project an image that India is out with the begging bowl."[43] Tied to the legacy of colonial racism, the desire to unravel the racialized image of India as impoverished and inferior remained in India's psyche. This also weighed heavily on the social life of Indian students. As in an earlier era, Indian student-migrants' hope to assert a more refined, educated, and modern version of Indian identity to a Western audience led to the formation of cultural clubs and organizations.[44] These organizations offered a cultural and social outlet for the Indian migrant community and served as a forum to explain and represent Indian society to Americans.[45] However, even as this vested interest in student-migrants as transnational cultural ambassadors—exemplary figures of the educated class embodying an Indian modernity—existed, the particular developmental logic of the postcolonial era contributed to anxieties about whether the movement of crucial forms of human capital, such as student migration, would be a problematic "brain drain" that would only serve to perpetuate the unevenness of the global order.[46] Therefore, while the desire for a Western education received in the world's rising superpower was invaluable to the Indian national imagination, the decisions and futures of student-migrants, by nature engaged in a transient type of transnational migration, were an important national preoccupation for India. The question whether they would neglect their responsibility to the modernization of the newly independent nation became a key concern. This anxiety was not lost on Indian students. Seeking education in the United States was as much about their own individualist middle-class ambitions to improve life chances as it was about turning back to a home they left behind and acting on their nationalist sense of obligation to help India arrive as a modern nation.[47]

Still, the transitory nature of their positioning fostered complex transnational dynamics that were filtered through the sociopolitical transformations occurring within the United States and across the world at the time. The United States had hoped not only that the presence of student-migrants from Global South nations would contribute to the technical academic and professional fields the US state was investing in more significantly to continue advancing its military and economic prowess but also that the student-migrants' circulations across national borders would enable the reassertion of the ideological premises of US exceptionalism and its influence over postcolonial nations. Moreover, the arrival of non-white students from overseas served as a potential counter to the fraught politics of racial difference that was increasingly becoming a source of tension both on and off campuses. After all, their presence as academically ambitious figures, coincided with, and arguably fed, the emergent master narrative of the "model minority" trope that was being used to typecast US-based Asian populations with the intention to divisively quell growing critiques of the United States as racist, exclusionary, and unequal. For these reasons, student-migrants from Asian postcolonial nations, in particular, represented ideal, desirable migrant subjects for the United States. Yet, at the same time that institutions of higher education became more deeply entangled in the United States' quest for global dominance, American campuses were also becoming crucial settings for the volatile social and political upheavals of the 1960s and 1970s.[48] In the broader geopolitical context of Third-Worldism (reflected most notably in the 1955 Bandung Conference and by the Non-Aligned Movement), as well as the various liberation struggles and solidarities that were occurring from within and across US borders, some of the Indian student-migrants who were arriving on American campuses were drawn into the radical activism occurring around them.[49] Indian student-migrants, liminal subjects transiting between a postcolonial India and the settler-colonial United States, perhaps, were dangerously close to recognizing the contention by Tuck and Yang that the "anti-to-post-colonial project doesn't strive to undo colonialism but rather to remake it and subvert it."[50] It is precisely when these students' political commitments do not align with the agendas of nation-states that they are marked as undesirable and suspicious, as they were in the earlier period of the twentieth century. Interestingly, in this second historical moment, the new Indian nation's political angst figured prominently in how these tensions unfolded. When Indian student-migrants' activities moved beyond solely social and cultural exchange, their presence on American campuses was of great concern, particularly for the Indian postcolonial state, which increasingly became the target of the students' political activities. Echoing the internationalist sentiments of the existing movements both within and outside of the United States, Indian students used their position as educated migrants to address the political problems in India by voicing solidarity with the mass movements occurring locally and globally.[51] Organizations like the Committee of Concerned Indian Students and the South Asian Students Association regularly organized and wrote about the failures of the Indian state, its acts of repression, and the influence of US "imperialist aggression."[52] Such publications not only circulated among the Indian population in the United States but were also sent to India for free as a reflection of students' commitment to forging transnational political subjectivities.[53]

STATE OF EMERGENCY AND SURVEILLANCE OF STUDENT-MIGRANTS

During this period, a galvanizing issue was the state of emergency (1975–77) declared by the Indian Prime Minister, Indira Gandhi, which led to widespread protests and demonstrations among Indian student-migrants.[54] Criticizing the government through political writings and staged protests, Indian students expressed vociferous overseas opposition to the Emergency.[55] India's own educated youth protesting the Indian government from the United States was a noteworthy humiliation for the Indian state, raising the issue of student-migrants' loyalty and responsibility to the postcolonial Indian nation. During demonstrations, many students, feeling vulnerable about their temporary visa status and fearing retribution, covered their faces with cardboard masks and paper bags to protect their identities.[56] Such fears were not unfounded. In 1976, during a meeting with the Subcommittee on International Organizations on Human Rights in India, the organization Indians for Democracy, whose membership included overseas students, testified to the various acts of intimidation Indian government officials were using against Indian students.[57] In their April 1977 issue, the leftist student publication *India Forum* published a report chronicling the various measures and actors involved in this intimidation, surveillance, and infiltration. The report, created from investigative research compiled by several staff members, is a testament to Indian students' suspicions of and encounters with the extended transnational reach of surveillance by the Indian state.

According to the report, Indian officials warned students "to either 'patriotically' defend Indian Government policies from American criticism or stay strictly apolitical (i.e. conduct only social-cultural get-togethers and show Hindi film fantasies)."[58] The report discussed in depth an especially egregious act by the Indian state in which government officials actively and intentionally interfered in the Berkeley-based Indian Students Association (ISA) elections to destabilize the leadership.[59] Indian student collaborators sympathetic to the government, essentially serving as agents of the state, not only collected and reported information on their politically active peers but also forced another election, causing immense internal turmoil for the ISA. Unsuccessful in overturning the more politicized leadership of the organization and concerned the political activities among Indian students would spread even further, a key Indian diplomatic official, K. Pratap Rao, held a meeting with US-based students studying on Government of India scholarships. Rao warned the students that the Indian government was monitoring their behavior and demanded they cease any further political participation in ISA. He pressured them by vowing to report their identities to the government, as well as revoke their scholarships. Demonstrating that these were not empty threats, the Indian government withdrew the scholarship of Anand Kumar, an Indian graduate student who was actively involved in Indians for Democracy and served as a vocal opponent of Emergency policies.[60]

Reflecting the national insecurity around India's global image, this confrontation with the Indian postcolonial state exposed the underlying expectation that loyalty to the Indian nation was a debt owed by Indian student-migrants in return for their education abroad. Students' encounters with the aggressive policing of their political interventions that emerged during the Emergency were important to their long-distance negotiations of belonging. Even as Indian student-migrants recognized the complicities and violences of the US state, the attempts to bring students' conflict with the Indian state to an American public through the US-based human rights hearings and through their own collective political writings underscored how the United States figured into these negotiations in fraught ways. In the 1977 *India Forum* report, Indian students strategically alluded to US exceptionalism in their condemnation of the Indian state's acts of intimidation, writing: "the fact that they should be used on American soil cannot be tolerated by freedom-loving people anywhere."[61]

As in the earlier twentieth century, ideas of obligation among the post-1965 generation of students centered the nation-state in longings for modernity, but the transnational paths that brought them to American campuses led to productive tensions in how they negotiated that obligation. As these youth were positioned ambivalently across national borders, the sentiments of obligation, loyalty, and betrayal that emerged from the hostilities between the Indian government and student-migrants were a conflict over both the collective postcolonial vision of a modern Indian nation and the terms on which those outside of its territorial boundaries could engage with that vision, or its undermining. While Indian migrants traveling through educational routes were expected to be compliant figures, their entanglement in the interlinked circuitries of US global hegemony and Indian postcoloniality actually meant that the educational legacies attached to Indian migrations included fostering a political consciousness grounded in a culture of resistance, as shifting and contested as it may have been, that was anti-imperialist, anticapitalist, and internationalist in character.

Though post-1965 students initially assumed they would return to India, the lack of economic opportunities back home, the disappointment in the failures of the postcolonial state, and the United States' desire for immigration based on skill and education drove many students to seek long-term settlement after graduation. The settlement of these students, along with other Indian migrants arriving through subsequent waves of professional and technically skilled migration and family reunification provisions, meant that the United States held a more

permanent place in the collective imaginaries forged by Indian transnationality than in earlier historical periods. This context of permanent
settlement is important to understanding contemporary student migration from India. Not only does it explain the collective amnesia regarding student-migrants' historical role in forging political solidarities,
which were formative to US-based Indian diasporic consciousness, but
it also points to how US exceptionalism continues to configure the conditions of aspiration embedded in Indian educational imaginaries.

Migrants of color who settle in the United States are invaluable fodder
for the liberal capitalist narrative of the model minority, which persists
in holding currency in the popular imagination despite long-standing
critiques. Offering a paradigm of the hardworking Indian leaving one's
home country to pursue education overseas, student-migrants, in particular, contribute to the reified image of the more desirable and deserving racialized migrant "other."[62] Their trajectories serve as a valuable
link between the Indian national desire for modernity represented by
an American education and the US exceptionalist logic that educational
and economic success in the United States are determined solely by
meritocratic principles, not by racial and class inequality. Yet, as the ex-
traordinary circumstances of the TVU incident that opened this chapter
lay bare, there is an ambivalence accompanying educational migratory
routes in the current context that continues to position the figure of the
Indian student-migrant uneasily in the discourse of the good-versus-
bad migrant. As an entire industry centered around internationalization
emerges and the United States is receiving the largest numbers of Indian
student-migrants in its history, how does that ambivalence come to mark
the ordinary, everyday worlds of the predominantly middle-class Indian
youth migrating to study at an American public university campus that
is being reworked by the corrosions of late-stage capitalism? How do
these young people reconcile the contradictions of migration regimes in
post-9/11, neoliberal empire? The following chapters illuminate how, in
Indian student-migrants' encounters with the internationalizing university, the particular obligations and longings mediating their migratory
lives continue to be formed in the shadows of US exceptionality and its
concomitant relations of racial exclusion, labor, and surveillance that
have been a part of the educational circuits linking the settler-colonial
and imperialist project of the United States and the postcolonial project
of India. At the same time, while a deeper desire for becoming modern

subjects found in those interlinkages persists among these youth, in the current era of globalized education, that desire works in tandem with a logic of indebtedness that is not *solely* articulated through an obligation to nationalist and nation-building interests, as was the preoccupation in previous historical conjunctures of Indian student migration. Through a discussion of the conditions that compelled Indian middle-class youth to move across US national borders and onto a US campus in the context of the global neoliberal order, I turn to these considerations next.

2 · Debt and Desire

In *Cruel Optimism*, Lauren Berlant writes that desire is "a cluster of prom-ises" holding out the possibility of a becoming that is worthy of the good life. For young people located at the intersection of global processes of migration and education, two critical sites of generating such imagined possibilities, what kind of desiring takes place? This chapter takes up this consideration by starting with a necessary question: What are these young people chasing as they set out across national borders to arrive on an American campus? Below, snapshots of students recounting their intentions point to the longings, both educational and otherwise, that were attached to their consumption of an American education and that contributed to setting their transmigrational lives in motion. Formed in the interstices of postcolonial and liberalization discourses, these long-ings are constructed through particular classed and gendered notions of deservingness, choice, potential, and global savviness, revealing a noteworthy pivot from the historical moments explored in the previous chapter. Still, their accounts illuminate the persisting, collective desire to become modern subjects, a possibility imagined as being located else-where from home, located in the United States on an American campus. In other words, the United States remains centrally positioned in the global educational imaginaries among these migrant youth. At the same time, threaded through these young men's articulations of the desiring that animated their migration are allusions to the significance of the ed-ucational market, kinship ties, and the nation-state. The second part of this chapter teases out how these threads are, in fact, three crucial inter-

related domains of obligation through which these young people negotiate their desire for modern selfhood. Mapping out how this desire works
through such webs of obligations, this chapter points to indebtedness, a
sense of owing and being owed, as a meaningful cultural logic produced
from the transnational lives of Indian student-migrants.

DESERVING OPTIONS

Summer had officially arrived and the afternoon sun, beaming down on
Williams Apartments, struggled to dissipate the bleakness that seemed
to always hang over the housing grounds. A complex of indistinguish-
able, low brick buildings with beige shingles and brown roofs were set
in blocks adjacent to one another. In front of this labyrinth of buildings,
a scattering of cars waited between uniformly painted white lines. A
wooded forest, characteristic of New York suburbia, stretched out across
the backdrop. The quietness of Williams in the afternoon hours was occasionally punctured by leaves rustling, a car pulling away on the gravel,
or brief exchanges between neighbors. The complex was unimpressive,
and one got the sense that it was developed in haste, a forgotten corner
hidden away at a distance from the campus. What did grab an outsider's
attention immediately was that its residents seemed to be almost entirely young students from India and China.

Williams is where I spent most of my time during fieldwork, visiting
and hanging out in the cramped dorm-style apartments of the Indian
graduate students I befriended. Rohit, whom I met during one of the
many evening "drinking parties" held by the young men in the apartments, also lived at Williams. Agreeing to let me interview him, he invited
me to come over that afternoon. I made my way across the now-familiar
grounds, passing two Chinese students dribbling and tossing a basketball
in the court the Williams residents shared. Though students from China
and India were the two largest overseas-student groups on the campus
and at Williams, the ethnic division was evident, as they hardly inter-
acted with one another. When it came to the small basketball court that
they were forced to share, however, there seemed to be a tacit agreement
between the two groups of students on the scheduling of its use. In the
afternoons, the court belonged to the young Chinese residents.

Rohit was leaning near the glass porch doors of the first-floor apartment of his building; he was wearing track pants and a white T-shirt,

and his thick black hair was left unkempt. He was slowly smoking a cigarette, watching the Chinese students on the court with disinterest. He
noticed me as I walked up and started puffing on the cigarette faster. I
had heard of Rohit long before I met him. He was tall and athletic with
a light complexion, and the Indian women I knew would often name
him as the most attractive at Williams. He was popular among his male
peers as well—over the weekends, he would move effortlessly between
the various parties he was invited to by friends, taking advantage of the
free alcohol available to him at each one. Rohit was also known for having a fondness for smoking marijuana, a reputation he was uneasy about
but sheepishly accepted when his friends messaged him several times to
come smoke with them during my visit with him.

The sound of the bouncing basketball echoed behind us as Rohit took
his last few drags of the cigarette and exchanged some pleasantries with
me about the weather. Flicking the cigarette remains against the wall,
he led me up the narrow concrete stairs of the apartment building where
he was staying after he graduated. Rohit had not yet found work, but
his popularity among his classmates served him well, allowing him to
stay in one of their apartments for free until he did. As with most students I spoke to that summer, our conversation seemed to naturally start
with talk about work after graduation. I asked him if he was worried at
all. Leaning the blue plastic chair he was sitting on off its back legs, he
pursed his lips and shook his head no with a confidence that was wan-
ing for many of the other students who were also still struggling to find
work. Rohit assured me he was certain he would find something. For the
time being, he was working as an unpaid research assistant for a faculty
member whose projects Rohit believed would strengthen his résumé.
The professor had also held out the vague promise of possibly turning
the position into paid work after Rohit completed the project.

During our conversation, Rohit mentioned his class background a
number of times; asserting his middle-classness was important to the
explanatory narrative for his migration. For instance, he admitted that
the United States held an allure for him because, as he put it, "I'm from
a lower middle . . . well, not lower, but middle-class family. So that was
always in my mind. Okay, I have to go to the US because the life is good,
and all that." As if to expound on how this figured into his trajectory,
Rohit made a point of highlighting educational concerns as the key
consideration. At Riverside, Rohit was studying mathematics, a subject

he had always loved. Back home, he was not able to pass the entrance exam for the elite, competitive Indian Statistical Institute (ISI), one of the few institutes offering undergraduate math programs in India. Rohit explained what this meant for him: "There are no good math programs apart from those couple of colleges. And you can't even imagine how hard it is. It's crazy. My main motive was to study math, so there was no option back in India. I gave the ISI [exam] in undergrad. In India you cannot have a graduate degree unless you have an undergraduate degree in the same subject. It's not that easy to change streams. Here, it's pretty easy." Rohit was referring to the highly competitive, examination-based process for entrance into India's elite educational institutes, a vestige of Nehruvian planning that steered education to serve the specific purposes of industrialization. The culture of high-stakes examination is deeply entrenched in India, playing a critical role in determining what educational and professional streams young people can enter and, ultimately, what kind of upward mobility is possible for many Indian youth. The centrality of the exam system is, indeed, high stakes, contributing to a billion-dollar test preparation industry and, at times, to student suicides. For Rohit, not receiving the scores necessary meant that a degree in the academic subject he longed to pursue was a path closed off to him. His undergraduate education was in engineering instead, and it would prove too difficult for him to return to studying mathematics at the graduate level in India. His father implored him to be pragmatic and take the exams for a graduate degree in business school in India; Rohit complied with his father's request but did not pass those exams either.

Rohit reinterpreted his failure to meet the scores on the competitive entrance exams as the failures of an outdated mode of educational practice that limited opportunities for young people like him. Alluding to this inadequacy, Rohit lamented, "I didn't have any option. I mean, I would have stayed if I had any options but there weren't any options." This repeated utterance of lacking options was a familiar refrain among Indian middle-class youth, one that surfaced more within the liberalizing context. For instance, Nikhil, a 22-year-old engineering student from Punjab, indicated a similar reason for his migratory decisions. As someone who struggled academically in India, Nikhil was not able to receive entry into any graduate programs or secure work after his undergraduate education. He portrayed the situation as hopeless, alluding to how it kept him from his potential as a young middle-class man who was willing to study, work, and succeed at upward mobility but was apparently prevented from doing so. When Riverside accepted him as a graduate student, it was the opportunity he needed, and he believed he deserved.

The larger story of higher education in India is important to the transnational lives of young people such as Rohit and Nikhil. As was explored in the previous chapter, education was always positioned as an invaluable vehicle to a new and improved India. Yet, the perceived failures of India's Nehruvian nationalist vision for modernizing the young nation framed India's existing institutions as inadequate to meeting the educational aspirations of a new generation of youth desiring the revised promises of modernity peddled by the liberalization project. Essential to this narrative of an inadequate educational system is the aspirational sentiment of having potential. The discursive shift accompanying India's liberalization had effectively framed the nation as exemplary of the neoliberal success possible in the era of the global knowledge economy. While a whole new generation of Indian youth was positioned as the key to India's emergence on the global stage, middle-class Indian men imagined themselves, specifically, as the intended bearers of its possibilities. Yet, how can they reach this rightful potential to which they are entitled when they are locked out of their own nation's elite educational institutions or cannot find work after receiving an education? In other words, they believed they were being denied what they deserved as aspiring young men.

The idea of deservingness was a recurring undertone in the reflections of the Indian student-migrants I met, which was not only indicative of classed and gendered attitudes but, I would suggest, casteist ones as well. The Indian youth at Riverside were overwhelmingly silent on their caste backgrounds. Despite this resistance to address caste explicitly, the pertinence of caste to the discourse and practice of Indian higher education is, in fact, undeniable. Rather than seeking to determine individual students' caste identities, I want to consider here how upper-casteness mediates the collective narratives accompanying the transnational circulation of student-migrants from India. References to lacking options to pursue educational passions that these students felt they deserved are entangled in national debates on caste that have made Indian higher education a battleground in the postliberalization era.

India's affirmative action policies, often referred to as the reservation system, have been particularly contentious. The reservation system was incorporated into the newly independent nation's constitution to ensure educational and employment opportunities in the public sector for India's most marginalized groups using quotas. Though these quotas were originally focused on the lowest caste and tribal categories, or Scheduled Castes and Scheduled Tribes (SC/ST), in 1990, the state implemented the Mandal Commission Report's recommendations to extend these quotas to the broader category of "Other Backward Classes" (OBC) groups. OBCs are considered disadvantaged groups existing in between upper-caste and SC/ST populations. The massive anti-Mandal protests, riots, and violence that had followed attacked the decision as antithetical to the modern liberal values of merit and efficiency, framing reservations, instead, as handouts to those who did not qualify for, and therefore, did not deserve, the opportunities. This classed, casteist narrative of reservations as handouts had become ingrained in the postcolonial public discourse on higher education, but such arguments were further amplified as neoliberal forces transformed the educational landscape in India. In 2006, when a second Mandal Report led to the implementation of OBC quotas within central educational institutions, including the prestigious Indian Institutes of Technology (IITs) and Indian Institutes of Management (IIMs) responsible for producing an Indian global elite, the subsequent protests not only recycled the narrative on merit but also made assumptions about how such a move would only jeopardize India's own rise as a modern global power in the neoliberalization era.

A number of scholars have highlighted how these developments point to the necessity of understanding caste as a constitutive, contradictory feature of the assertion of a secular, modern India.[1] Certainly, the insistence among the Indian student-migrants I met to appear casteless partly reflects a broader, commonplace reaction that is especially asserted among upper-caste Indians anxious to deflect global attention away from the caste system in India. However, as Satish Deshpande has argued, the language of merit and claims to castelessness have also become part of the postcolonial common sense that positions upper-caste Indians as the natural bearers of merit and a secular modernity, while lower-caste populations are reduced to caste itself.[2] In this sense, framing meritocratic values as superior to the principles embedded in reservation policies is fundamentally about narrating who is truly deserving of the promises of education in the global knowledge economy, and who is not; even as caste is not named, the latter is often read as India's poorer, lower-caste communities. I understand Rohit's and Nikhil's comments on lacking and deserving options through this caste-laden narrative of merit that circulates in the debates around Indian higher education. In *The Caste of Merit*, Ajantha Subramanian offers an incisive analysis of how upper-caste IIT graduates transform their caste privilege into claims of being meritorious subjects.[3] One feature of this process is upper-caste IIT elite's fetishization of mass examinations as a purely modern rationale instrument, which Subramanian argues allows for a masking of the extensive, historically accumulated caste capital that nurtured their routes to these elite institutions. Through this caste erasure, exams are positioned as ultimately transcending caste, illuminating who is truly deserving of success and inherently dispositioned to succeed in elite technical education.

While nonelite student-migrants like Rohit and Nikhil may have borrowed from the narrative of deservingness that emerges from the anti-reservation position, they also revealed their own contradictory stance to merit as dictated by mass examinations. In other words, they were not willing to make sense of their own failings to pass national exams and their other academic struggles as simply a matter of not having the natural abilities to meet meritocratic standards, a claim the privileged "IITians" in Subramanian's study worked to assert. Instead, for the Indian migrant youth at Riverside, their notion of limited options was implicitly class- and caste-inflected commentary about what they are rightfully owed, yet apparently refused due to outdated educational policies and practices, including the rigid parameters set by India's entrance exams and the restricted availability of seats in elite institutions assumed to be caused by quotas.

In this way, young Indian middle-class (and often, upper-caste) men's resentment of India's perceived failures to deliver on promises of upward mobility and the status of truly modern subjects has played a part in propelling them into the transnational educational sphere. Contrasted with India as a location of no choices is the United States; American higher education is deemed capable of doing what Indian higher education cannot. An escape from India's exclusionary high-stakes examinations and caste-related educational policies, the United States is, instead, understood as a liberal, secular site where flexibility and opportunity in educational paths are made available, where merit is recognized as tied to hard work, and where these young men would be able to secure the kind of professional careers they believed they were destined for. In other words, if India's reservation system and national exams discounted them, transnational mobility and an American education promised to recoup for them the status linked to educational success. For many of these Indian youth, then, pursuing one's deserved futures and potential for becoming modern figures through educational desires is only imagined as occurring on an American campus. In their analysis of desire, Deleuze and Guattari argue against existing psychoanalytical frameworks predicated on the assertion that a sense of lack was at the heart of the workings of desire.[4] Rather than the notion that an inherent incompleteness or absence within the making of a subject produces the act of desiring, Deleuze and Guattari posited that desiring is, in fact, a principal productive force of capitalist relations that subsequently generates constructions of lacking. This insight clarifies the significance of the narrative of "no options," which is at once an articulation of desire in the service of the global project to neoliberalize education while named through an assertion of an incomplete becoming. In what is constructed as worthy choices, who is deserving of them, and where those choices are located, this desiring meaningfully links India and the United States in the educational imaginaries of these young people once again.

GLOBAL STANDARDS: MEN IN THE KNOW

I turn next to another common explanatory narrative among the Indian student-migrants at Riverside, but one that highlights the privileged and distinct place that the IT sector has played in the global knowledge economy, particularly within the context of a liberalized India. Kalyan exemplified this distinction in his conversation with me about the decisions that figured into his arrival at Riverside, in which he articulates calculations around global educational standards in the IT field. Through naming such calculations, Kalyan, like some of the other young men I befriended, worked diligently to portray himself as a strategic and rational actor. In the discussion that follows, I suggest that this kind of self-portrayal is also partly a preoccupation with and performance of a successful masculinity.

When Kalyan, a computer science student from Hyderabad, India, agreed to chat with me about his time at Riverside, he asked if we could meet over drinks at Andies rather than at Williams. Andies was the perfect slice of classic American sports-bar culture, serving as an escape from the Indian students' usual routines of socializing at Williams Apartments. Exposed brick walls, dimmed lighting, dark wood tables, and leather seating made up the bar's decor. Countless large TV screens, ostentatiously hanging from the walls, televised different American sporting events occurring throughout the day. Sports jerseys were framed and showcased proudly around the bar, including those of Riverside's own sports teams. Riverside students and local residents drifted in to drink, eat, watch, and chat about the games playing on the screens. As at most of the bars and restaurants in the area, the patrons and service staff at Andies were almost exclusively white Americans— Kalyan and I were the only exceptions.

Relaxing a bit with each sip of his drink, Kalyan shared about the life he left behind in Hyderabad. What was particularly striking throughout the conversation was Kalyan's constant assertion that it was his sharp understanding of global standards in education and training that served as the key factor in why he left. The unique role that India has played in the IT boom and the ways in which it has served to produce an upwardly mobile Indian transnational class has generated in young IT students, such as Kalyan, the conviction of their own inevitable success. Hyderabad, in particular, had received significant attention in recent years because of its rise as India's so-called next Silicon Valley.[5] Xiang Biao offers an incisive analysis of the place of Hyderabad in the emergence of the IT industry and what he calls the production of "IT people."[6] Kalyan's upbringing and education occurred in the midst of the elevation of Hyderabad. He was slightly older than most of the other students because he had worked for an investment bank for three years after he graduated from one of the National Institutes of Technology, considered a second-tier of prominent Indian public institutes for engineering and technology. With a prestigious education in the IT field, Kalyan was able to secure a high-paying job in India immediately after graduation. Yet, he longed for more; specifically, Kalyan wanted to attend graduate school overseas. Biao's argument that a noteworthy feature of the social status afforded Hyderabad's IT people hinged on their ability to be globally mobile is pertinent here. Despite his enviable professional success after receiving his education, Kalyan's position did not offer him the crucial status of globality; truly successful IT professionals' lives existed across national borders, after all. Internationalization and the global education market forge another route to this desired status, and the American campus figures prominently as the site affording it.

As if to illustrate that he was already deserving of the status, Kalyan was eager to flex how his choices around education were globally inflected and precise. The United States is "the best place to do computer science," he insisted. Keen to demonstrate how knowledgeable and measured he was, Kalyan reiterated in a matter-of-fact tone, "Maybe for industrial engineering, Germany is the best. But for computer science, it's the US." Therefore, the United States was the place he needed to be. Kalyan continued by rattling off names of highly prestigious American academic institutions, admitting that Riverside was not his ideal choice but that he had not received admission into the others. Still, he was confident that it did not matter in the grander scheme. Suggesting there existed an international division of intellectual specialization in the knowledge economy, Kalyan saw traveling to and receiving a computer science degree from any US institution as enough to establish his educational status as "the best."

Though many of the young men I met expressed that the intended purpose behind their migration was to enhance their education and training, they also sought to assert themselves as an already valuable form of human capital, an assertion performed through particular kinds of gendered dispositions. Masculine identities as globally authoritative figures were actively performed through their articulations of decision-making around their movements across borders. In Kalyan's case, the late-stage capitalism discourse of IT's power in transcending national boundaries articulates with a masculinist sensibility that his own aspirations and destiny should and do lay beyond such bounds. This was further illustrated when Kalyan brought up his father, who was vehemently opposed to Kalyan's plan to go overseas for his education. His father was concerned that this decision not only would mean Kalyan walking away from a stable and well-paying job but, more importantly, the potential of Kalyan "becoming westernized." Tossing back his beer and shaking his head with a laugh, Kalyan dismissed his father. The fear of Western adulteration echoes a persisting and prevalent Hindu nationalist talking point, but for Kalyan, his father's ideas of cultural erasure were outdated, a relic of an earlier postcolonial anxiety about purportedly "Indian" values that Kalyan believed were no longer relevant.

Kalyan juxtaposing his father's fear of cultural loss in the face of Western norms to his own fearlessness, superior insight into the way the world operates now, and global-mindedness was an exercise in highlighting and enacting a supposedly more modern masculinity, one that transcended older nationalist preoccupations. At the same time, Hindu nationalists, under the Bharatiya Janata Party (BJP) leadership, have actively worked to frame the contemporary neoliberal ethos as entirely compatible with the masculinist promulgation of a pure (read: Hindu) Indian nation.[7] In this sense, unlike his father, Kalyan knew that making savvy global calculations and acting on them were important to the kind of future he felt he deserved, and he believed this served as no threat to his identity as an Indian man. This contrast between Kalyan and his father recalls Smitha Radhakrishnan's argument that Indian IT professionals' privileged positioning in the global knowledge economy enabled them to serve as critical actors in the cultural production of the modern Indian subject in the contemporary era.[8] Through what Radhakrishnan refers to as "cultural streamlining," they can simultaneously navigate the kinds of normative professional practices expected of them in other global locations while confidently asserting appropriate forms of difference embodying "Indianness," which was filtered through an upper-caste Hindu nationalist ideology. Kalyan's dismissal of his father's postcolonial anxieties gestures to his sentiment that he already had the modern dispositions and sensibilities to participate in such cultural practices. His middle-class aspirations to be part of this transnational class of Indian IT professionals drew him into the circuits of educational migration and were narrated through constructions of a desirable masculinity appropriate to the modern economy—student-migrants, such as Kalyan, were men in the know, men on the move, men of the world.

In their own ways, then, the accounts of Rohit, Nikhil, and Kalyan reveal a rendering of decisions as well-calibrated calculations, conveyed as an effect of the inherent global sensibilities expected of the idealized rational migrant man of the neoliberal moment. Reflecting on this point is not to discount that these students were, in fact, quite knowledgeable about global educational standards and made decisions accordingly. Due to the privileges of class, caste, gender, and educational backgrounds, their trajectories were set apart from those of Indian youth who do not easily access the kinds of social and cultural capital necessary to navigate foreign educational contexts. Most of the young men at Riverside who I befriended were tapped into networks that offered knowledge into the workings of educational systems both at home and abroad well before they moved overseas. Without access to such privileged networks, students who may wish for similar opportunities can be lured in by the more predatory and fraudulent practices of the international education industry, as was seen in the Tri-Valley incident described in chapter 1. Still, the accounts here of Indian student-migrants' idealized self-portrayals as rational, globally minded, and shrewd decision-makers regarding educational opportunities also illuminate the relational dynamic between the project to neoliberalize education and the making of modern selfhood among young Indian men.

"IT'S THE AMERICA THING": THE CONSUMPTION OF AMERICAN YOUTH SOCIALITY

Students also expressed the ways their intentions were intertwined with other youthful longings. For instance, during our conversation, Kalyan had confessed that he was also moved by the wish to experience the kinds of romantic possibilities enabled by American youth culture. The freedoms associated with American dating practices were appealing to him, something he wanted to engage in and that he believed would be part of the kind of consumption of experience he would access through the sexualized cultures of whiteness understood to be embedded in the American campus. The longing and expectation to connect with the whiteness of US youth culture were partly an expression of proving one's own manhood through a racialized ideal of hetero-masculinity. Here, I want to turn to the students' sharp awareness of how expectations about American youth culture, in fact, figured prominently in their desire to migrate as young men.

One night, a large group of us from Williams decided to go to Andies for an evening out. Some of the women in another clique had agreed to join us, and the young men hoped to use the night out as a way to get closer to them. The dimly lit bar was busy when we arrived. Clusters of mostly white youth dressed casually in jeans, T-shirts, button-down shirts, and Riverside sweatshirts were chatting as they leaned on the bar or stood around in different sections of the room. We grabbed a few high-top tables by one wall, and Ravi, an engineering graduate student, entertained everyone with his antics. The young women in our group started dancing in the corner to the pop music playing from the speakers placed throughout the bar while Ani and another friend, Arjun, stood nearby, teasing and flirting with them. Occasionally, the white patrons would look over at us, whispering to each other about Ravi's eccentric dancing, which was being goaded on by the other men in our group for their own amusement. Even in that crowded space, we were set socially far apart from the white patrons. Yet, as usual, for the Indian students, it was a nice enough change from their social life at Williams. More than that, the bar setting of Andies served as one of the few spaces in which the students could experience a proximity to American youth sociality that was not readily available to them on campus.

I was sitting at one of the high-top tables chatting with a young woman who had joined in the outing when Jason, Ani's roommate, noticed us and came over to sit to my other side. Jason was often cautious, even moody, around me, but that evening, he was talkative, something he tended to be after a few drinks. Like Ani, Jason was a materials science engineering student from Tamil Nadu. With that shared background and a shared bedroom in their Williams apartment, the two had become close friends. Jason asked how my research was progressing and then proposed an arrangement where he would provide me with a formal interview in exchange for a bottle of rum. He chuckled, amused by his own research-for-liquor bartering. With slightly slurred speech, Jason demanded, "Anyway, what more do you want to know after spending all this time with us?" I told him I was still learning about what led them to make the journey. Jason waved his hand at me dismissively, "Oh, you know, it's the 'America' thing. That's probably the answer they all give you." He insisted this was not his own motivation before continuing:

I wouldn't know how to put it, the America thing. Everybody talks about it. Americans even talk about it. You see in movies how these people, they're like "oh, it's America!" You talk about independence and freedom and all the parties and what they have. . . . The whole country looks like it's a party place. And for anyone from a different cultural background, especially from India, I don't think people have seen this kind of independence. At least, that's what we think when we're there. When you come here it's not exactly what we thought it would be. . . . But it is famous, right? It's in the news all the time.

Jason's depiction of the United States as a carefree and exciting "party place" was widely echoed by the other students I met; as he predicted, many did point to how the desire for the consumption of such cultural experiences was folded into their migratory decisions. These preoccupations stand in contrast to the "flexible citizenship"[9] negotiations of transnational professional elites whose privileged positioning in the global economy enable them to serve as the cultural ambassadors of a "rising" India. While such elites seamlessly navigated overseas locales and confidently asserted a brand of Indian identity appropriate for global consumption,[10] the young people from the segment of Indian middle class arriving at Riverside yearned to newly access a direct experience of American youth sociality (often read as whiteness) and the symbolic capital it is imagined as offering. I point to this distinction not only to reflect the heterogeneity of classed experiences among transnational knowledge mobilities but also to highlight the persisting role the United States plays in the classed and gendered configurations of Indian youth identity formation.

For most of the student-migrants I met, it was their first time traveling outside of India and their first direct encounter with the United States, but the portrayals of a liberated lifestyle as being at the heart of American youth culture were cultivated long before they arrived. Such representations circulate globally in a number of ways. Jason astutely recognized the influence of the media and entertainment industries. Indian student-migrants at Riverside regularly demonstrated how much they attended to the lives depicted on screen. They would often ask me to list my favorite American films and television series, and when our dinner gatherings would occasionally lead to "movie charades," I was proven to be vastly inadequate in my knowledge of recent Hollywood films in comparison to the Indian students. They were as at ease with discussing Hollywood as they were with discussing Indian cinema and would excitedly share their favorite classics. They often referenced the *American Pie* movies, the first of which was released in 1999. Portraying the exploits of young, American, and exclusively white students, *American Pie* was a telling example of the depictions of white, heteronormative, hypersexualized youth culture in the United States that some of the Indian student-migrant men sought. Similarly, highly successful and popular television sitcoms, such as *How I Met Your Mother* and *Friends*, were also cited as students' classic favorites. Both are situated in one of the most cosmopolitan and exciting cities in the world, New York, and scenes almost always portray a life of youthful freedom. Characters pass leisurely time with friends, making jokes, playing pranks, and reflecting on and pursuing romantic interests. Though there is usually more socializing than work portrayed, the characters always achieve their professional aspirations no matter how impossible they may seem. Hollywood screens offer compelling tales of American lives easily weaving together upward mobility and the thrill of youthful adventure.

It was not only Hollywood, however. In the wake of India's liberalization, the Indian film industry has consistently centered on elite Indian characters, generating imagery of enormous wealth and lavish, jet-setting lifestyles and revealing Indian stories that effortlessly intersect with the material, social, and cultural life of Western locations. This was not lost on the Indian youth I befriended, who articulated the ways that Indian cinema had also marked the horizons of their desire for American youth culture. Ashok, a recent graduate from the biomedical engineering field at Riverside, spoke extensively about the connection he drew between portrayals in contemporary Indian cinema and educational decisions:

So, the natural progression from [school] is to go on to the next stage of life which is more attractive than what you have or what you would have in India. And US has always been the dream for most of us. Almost all Bollywood movies that you watch, all the classy ones, are shot here. No Shah Rukh Khan movies are shot in Bombay or the slums. It's like a dream that people sort of put in your mind and you grow with, right? There were a couple of movies that really hit me hard because of the things that you see can be done in US. They show you very attractive lifestyle and all, right? You start imagining what it would be to go on to the next stage. Especially when you start realizing how crappy things are around yourself in India, and you see how beautiful life is elsewhere when it is shown to you. So the natural progression after you finish your undergrad is to come to America. Coming to America was not a goal. It was a passion, I guess, that I had to pursue.

Echoing Jason's reflections, Ashok's comments here point to the pronounced role film and media play in fueling acts of desiring among

Indian middle-class youth, conditioning them to covet the imagined lifestyles of the United States. This narrative stands in contrast to the lower middle-class youth in rural India who Shakuntala Rao interviewed and who expressed their growing sense of disconnectedness from these same film representations.[11] The fantasies portrayed were alienating for Rao's interlocutors, who could not imagine their lives reflected or captured on the Indian screen. For my friends at Riverside, however, the fantasy of entering into the lifeworlds of the Indian global elite, depicted through transnational media connectivities, felt attainable; they did not have entry *yet*, but they believed it could and should be theirs. When students shared these accounts, they never explicitly named American citizenship as a necessity to that future, though nearly every student I met intended on remaining in the United States to work after graduation. What was more important was achieving the possibilities of the kind of truly unbounded *transnational* lives of the characters they watched on the film screens. Further, for this segment of Indian middle-class youth, arriving on an American campus seemed like a "natural progression," the appropriate setting to start such lives for themselves.

Such ideas cannot be disentangled from the global circulations of the "American Dream" discourse. As Inderpal Grewal has argued, embedded in it is the "search for a future in which the desire for consumption, for liberal citizenship, and for work came together to produce a specific subject of migration."[12] Of course, the entertainment industry was only one medium for these circulations; the students noted how their existing social relations, networks of families and friends, also played a central role in reinforcing this idealized image of American life. For instance, in Ani's earlier allusion to traveling to the moon, he had drawn a direct connection to his uncle's return visits from the United States, which highlighted material possession as important to masculine mobilities: "Coming to America was always a dream of mine. When I was small, my uncle would come back from America, and he would have nice things and talk about how good it was here." Rohit admitted that receiving an American education was imbued with a status for his own community:

> For example, we are neighbors. And if your kid is going abroad for studies, like it's kind of a status symbol nowadays in India. It's the latest norm. People think that it doesn't matter what kind of schools

or marks he gets. If he's going to US, he's smart. People don't care if you studied from Columbia, UPenn, or some shitty university. For example, in my case, if when I go back to my grandparents' place, no one even asks me what field I'm studying. They'll just be like, okay, he just came from New York. He just came from US. So, it's a big thing.

Jason also complained how he felt immense pressure from his friends to pursue his studies in the United States even though he wanted to carve out a unique globalized path for himself that would offer him a freedom from his social ties, perhaps both a youthful longing and one that reflects neoliberal sensibilities:

I wanted to get out of India, just to get some exposure, you know. And it's fun to go out of the country. In India, wherever you go, you have people there. And I wanted to get out of that. Go to a completely strange place, start anew. I didn't think about if it was going to be difficult. I didn't want to come here. I applied to Singapore. I got through. Then I spoke to my friends, and they all washed my brain. And then I had to change my direction. Friends here in the US, and relatives, and a couple of friends back home also. So it was this big hype that most students who go to the US to study end up in really good jobs, which is the first thing. That's the first priority, right? You finish your undergrad there in India and then you go to the US. That's like the pathway. You know how it is in India, right? Education is like a big turn on if you're in a bigger institution.

Jason may have wanted to forge his path abroad as independent from social attachment, but the reinforced pressure from those social networks to make responsible calculations about the education and work opportunities that are tied specifically to the United States was too great. For many of these student-migrants, entering the transnational educational sphere meant a balancing act between their expectations to consume idealized youth experiences and the expectations of being and becoming men. Jason's friends and relatives reminded him that securing work after graduation would be an important turning point in this becoming and had to be the "first priority" in an education overseas. Also, echoing both of Ashok's and Rohit's sentiments, Jason deemed moving from an

Indian education to an American one as *the* pathway, and he believed that distinctions between American institutions hardly mattered to these students' networks—the notion of a "bigger institution" is conflated with any American institution. Thus, landing at Riverside University, which is not a prestigious, elite American institution but a moderately ranked and predominantly commuter public campus, still held out the chance to chase the curated fantasies of status, upward mobility, material wealth, and the freedoms of American youth culture conjured up by family, friends, and film industries.

Such expectations are actively fueled by university marketing schemes. The neoliberal transformations of the higher education landscape have meant aggressive marketing strategies that not only emphasize curriculum and job prospects but also promise the exciting sociality of American campus culture. That the latter has become an especially compelling feature was evident recently when the COVID-19 pandemic forced many American campuses to move courses online and to temporarily suspend residential activities. Uproar and debate among students, their families, and the general public followed, intimating that it was precisely the in-person, direct *experience* of American campus life that justified the exorbitant tuition costs characteristic of US higher education institutions.

The explanatory narratives of Indian middle-class youth at Riverside suggest that the "cluster of promises" produced specifically by the circuits and seductions of US neoliberal empire continues to be centrally part of the stories of their educational migration. Formed and circulated by media and entertainment industries, kinship and other social networks, and higher education marketing practices, such promises of possibility within US borders are a productive and compelling force that draws middle-class Indian men desiring modern selfhood into the transnational educational sphere. Chapter 4 will return to these considerations as students attempt to reconcile their expectations of American campus culture with the routines of sociality, work, and learning that emerged for them at Riverside. Whether articulated through invocations of deservingness, choice, global savviness, or American youth sociality, the United States holds an important place in these middle-class migrant men's imagined horizons of possible becomings. India could not be the site of their arrival as global modern subjects, but an American campus could be.

This also highlights a crucial classed distinction from the transnational routes of wealthy Indian elites, for whom studying abroad can often mean enrollment in expensive and prestigious American institutions. For these students, traveling to and living in the United States are experienced as an unremarkable elite practice, but this is not true for the student-migrants described in this book. It is noteworthy that for most of these youth, Riverside was where they ultimately landed because the tuition costs of a public university made it a more affordable option than US private institutions where tuition fees are exorbitant. Still, even with the lower tuition fees at Riverside, traveling to and attending an American university were only viable for many of the youth at Riverside because of the availability of educational loans. Attending to the significance of loans to Indian student-migrant trajectories, the next section begins an exploration of how the relationship between capitalist forces and the desiring machine unfolding in the global educational landscape is produced through particular webs of obligation for these youth. Market-based student loans, kinship ties, and the nation-state constitute these spheres of obligation, mediating these young people's desiring for a particular classed and gendered notion of modern selfhood that is attached to their pursuit of a US-based education.

MIGRATION ON LOAN

> Getting loans is so easy these days. My father works in a bank. He gave out so many educational loans. My father, he tells me like, you wouldn't have even heard about the university and no one knows about the university, it's a very small university. I think because now the Indian economy is driven by the middle-class people, okay. Those are the main consumers. So now, Indian middle class does have a lot more power than they used to back in the '80s or '90s or something. Like if someone wants to go abroad for studies, they can't just stop them. If you have enough property, if you can show you have enough money to pay back the loans, no one can stop you.
>
> ROHIT

Opening our discussion on student loans' role in educational migration, Rohit's comments are important, revealing how commercial loaning practices are not only a financial consideration here but also figure centrally in the classed desires and anxieties of Indian middle-class youth aspiring to study overseas. As noted, the vast majority of the student-migrants I met financed their education at Riverside through the use of student loans. While student debt has reached the point of crisis in the United States,[13] the provision of loans for higher education is a relatively new development in India. The growing availability of student loans through the current system of predatory commercial bank loaning was a consequence of economic liberalization, the global expansion of the education market, and the rapid decline in public funding of higher education. Paralleling the deepening influence of structural adjustment programs on India, a number of national committees offered up market-driven recommendations as solutions to the crisis in Indian higher education. Among the strategies recommended was the call to make student loans more available. This was part of an important discursive shift regarding educational development that had occurred, reinforced by neoliberal reform and the priorities set by influential international organizations. Specifically, the increasing emphasis on developing primary and secondary education worked in tandem with the assertion that higher education was actually a private good meant to benefit individual students, qua consumers, and not national development; thus, the state should not have to be responsible for funding the sector. In reimagining the state's relationship to the higher education sector in this way, commercial-bank-issued student loans were presented as the perfect solution for the growing demand for higher education. Debt, then, is the "resource" that appears in the place of state planning around educational development. Not only was responsibility shifted from the state and placed squarely on individual students' shoulders but expanding the availability of student loans was promoted as a means to make higher education more inclusive.

Education has now become one of the sectors of priority lending by commercial banks in India. In 2001, the Reserve Bank of India (RBI) ordered banks to adopt the "Model Education Loan Scheme," a set of uniform guidelines developed by the Indian Banks' Association to expand the issuance of student loans. Under this scheme, the scope was extended to include educational programs both in India and abroad, emphasizing in particular, technical education fields that were perceived as offering secure jobs with higher incomes after graduation. Similar to other national contexts, loan amounts and recipients were linked to the repaying capacity of students, mainly determined by what kind of income potential was predicted to be part of their futures. Since the establishment of the loan scheme, student loans have grown more than tenfold.

The emergence of commercial lending as a crucial source of financing higher education is inherently tied to moral claims about the deserving subject. One determining factor outlined in the RBI guidelines is the idea of the "meritorious student," a morally ambiguous term through which lenders (and the public) make claims about who deserves higher education, who deserves credit to finance it, and who is worthy of promising futures. As elsewhere, classed backgrounds and social networks play a significant role. While no security was required for smaller loan amounts, any loans over approximately five thousand dollars would require collateral. Though some students were able to manage financially at Riverside without requesting that amount, the high cost of travel, tuition, and living standards in New York meant most of the middle-class students at Riverside sought loans exceeding that limit, and families would have to offer assets that equaled the amount of the loan as security. As growing numbers of middle-class youth receive student loans, there have been widespread reports that poorer students from SC/ST backgrounds often have a difficult time borrowing for their education because of these conditions;[14] further, when they do, they struggle to receive the income to help them pay it off, leading to rising default rates. Thus, despite claims about wider inclusion, the growth of lending for educational purposes reflects and reproduces the leveraged fault lines of caste and class in India.

Given this context, how do we read Rohit's comments? As he correctly suggests, these new lending options have affected who can now move overseas for their higher education. Rohit's family is part of a segment of the middle-class population in India who was not previously able to fathom sending their own children to pursue educational degrees abroad in the United States due to financial constraints. However, the expansion of the student-loan scheme now positions them as the ideal and deserving borrower. Not part of the wealthy elite but having enough assets for collateral, these students and their families, who are typically not from SC/ST backgrounds, are recognized as precisely those worthy of the promises exchanged in this lender-borrower relationship. The centrality of student loans to securing educational paths also reinforces the neoliberal discourse of the student-as-consumer. Expressing a sentiment widely shared among Indian student-migrants at Riverside, Rohit raised the notion of an invincible, unstoppable middle class by pointing to how their access to credit opened the door to educational consumption overseas. In other words, student loans are framed as unleashing Indian middle-class youth's potential as student-consumers, enabling the pursuit of their desire to be globally mobile, modern subjects, a transformation promised by an American education and which may have otherwise remained elusive.

As if to make a distinction from his own path in which loans were part of his necessary, pragmatic decisions to seek out the options he deserved as a good student-consumer, Rohit shared, with a hint of a moralizing tone, how student loans could serve other longings beyond educational interests:

> With my younger brother, it's a different case, because he doesn't study at all. He asked my father, "Okay you sent [Rohit], but why didn't you [send me]?" He's still in first year, but he's already talking about, like, going to US after he completes undergrad. He flunked in two subjects. How can he talk about that? His motive is not to study. His motive is to come here and party. He thinks of US as a place where everything is good—no one has to worry about anything. Not only him. Most of the students they think like that. They come here because of that. Like I know people who couldn't get a job. They didn't do anything. After undergrad, they stayed at home. "Let's just go to the US. Take a loan because that's the easiest way to go to the US." And you also have the option of earning money after that. Because if you have a graduate degree, you can still earn money. That's not the case in India.

Students widely conceived of receiving student loans as a liberatory act, one that set in motion their move across national borders to pursue their longing for connection to an American campus and American life. Of course, accepting bank-issued loans directly tied to a student's ability to secure sufficient income shortly after graduation is high risk. The impersonal and legal nature of this kind of market-based obligation binds these student-migrants to particularly unstable and perilous financial circumstances if confronted with the possibility of not securing stable work, much like the widespread reality indebted students in the United

States are confronting today. Obligated to repay Indian banks the full amount along with the cost of any incurred interest, a relation of material debt figures centrally in these young people's migratory trajectories. As Cavallero and Gago argue, debt has an ambivalence of its own, at times turning on the possibility of mobility and at other times fixing in place, but always functioning through commanding and exploiting an obligatory relation to future work.[15] I return to discuss this point in chapter 5. Still, student loans and other financial considerations were also interrelated with another important form of obligation—the involvement of kinship ties in students' migratory lives. Next, I explore how students experienced this involvement, and how it deepened a logic of indebtedness in their sensemaking as student-migrants.

THE TIES OF KINSHIP: RESPONSIBILITY, RECIPROCITY, SACRIFICE

As migration studies scholars have argued, kinship ties play an invaluable role in forging the transnational migrant networks that shape who gets to migrate and how migration patterns are formed and reproduced.[16] In the accounts shared above, the young people at Riverside alluded to the presence of kinship, both real and fictive, in the expectations and decisions they made in their migration. That involvement was certainly important to the economic aspects of their transnational mobility. As mentioned, most students at Riverside received loans large enough that they required some form of collateral, assets that were provided by their families back home. This often meant that until the student debt was paid off, or the students could find work that secured enough income to send money home, students' families in India were deferring other middle-class economic activities. Selling their house, travel and other forms of leisure, or supporting younger siblings' educational goals all had to wait. This waiting, in which middle-class families participate in and support their children's aspirational choices by suspending others through calculations about collective kinship futures, was a formative temporal dimension to these young people's migratory lives and conditioned their affective ties between home and abroad. To capture the significance of those ties, students would often invoke the notion of sacrifice. While it may have been a path they felt they deserved, they expressed that their education at Riverside involved sacrifices—sacrifices of human capital, money, time, property, leisure, well-being of parents, and futures of siblings translated into loss, struggle, or suffering because of them. When Rohit alluded to it, he suggested that sacrifice was part of the Indian ethos of care, part of the ways obligation to one's children and their education is expressed by family: "I don't want my father to pay back the loans because he has paid for everything. Now they have suffered because of me. Because of me they can't do anything. In India, they will sacrifice. Now I'm in the condition to work and pay back, and pay loans and send some money over. You know how much sacrificing your parents are making? And no one is earning that much. Here, the pay scale is huge. Compared to India, it's huge."

The sentiment of sacrificing is a familiar part of the migrant narrative, one that captures the risk-taking practices involved in those seeking economic security and upward mobility through migration. What is noteworthy in Rohit's explanation here is that with the obligation of fatherly care expressed through an act of sacrificial loss, Rohit felt an implicit expectation to reciprocate that care in some form. This is not to suggest that acts of reciprocity are necessarily acts of sacrifice but that they are shifting and interlocking logics. In their seminal work on sacrifice, Hubert and Mauss explained that sacrifice is simultaneously an act of obligation and love, as well as an act of self-interest. If one gives, "it is partly in order to receive."[17] Sacrifices always come with an understanding that something more valuable will be returned. Many of the young men I encountered shared Rohit's anxiety, experiencing this expectation of return as a sense of burden, both a moral and material debt, which they felt a responsibility to alleviate as soon as possible. This can be read as both a genuine wish to return what they sensed they owed their families and also as a key part of how they measured their success as educational migrants, and as men.

Temporality figured into these considerations as well. As noted earlier, Jason's kinship networks were also crucial to his move to the States. His friends and relatives convinced him that securing work after graduation was far more likely in the United States, and they also assured him that funding opportunities in an American graduate program were more readily available. This kind of advising from his kin networks is what led him to change course and start the application process over. When he was not able to secure funding from a program in the United States, however, Jason felt he had already invested too much into the process to change his mind again: "So, I already wasted like eight to ten months. And I didn't want to drag it along again. I have to think about my parents. They are the ones who are funding me. So this was my only chance. I thought, okay, well, let me just go then. I came here." His indecisiveness around whether he should pursue an American education also led Jason to being out of work for almost a year. His preoccupation with not wasting time is noteworthy, alluding to the kinds of demands these men felt were part of their trajectories, the expectation that choices around educational aspirations, migration, and their futures should occur through smart, precise calculations. Wasting time meant they were delaying their own timeline in becoming successful men abroad. This sentiment, for Jason, also shaped how he experienced his obligation to his parents. Though he insisted it was not due to any explicit pressure from them, Jason felt indebted to them. Both his parents had worked for the local electrical company, his father a human resources manager and his mother an administrative assistant. They went to great lengths to secure the kind of education and professional future abroad their son desired. Jason confided that for his overseas studies his parents spent the entirety of their savings, which they had initially intended for other financial needs. To cover the remaining costs of his move, they borrowed money from other relatives, to whom they were now financially indebted. Jason attempted to convince his family to allow him to acquire student loans instead, believing it would limit the financial sacrifices involved and the burden of repayment would be his alone. Dismissing the idea, his parents reassured him, "You don't worry about the money, we'll take care."

Yet, Jason did worry. His parents' financial risk-taking revealed the central place that educational aspirations have when middle-class families take stock of collective futures. With this fetishization of educational degrees is the sentiment that parents have a duty to sacrifice and carry the burden of ensuring its possibility. His mother and father were intentionally vague with Jason to shield him from that burden, but their strategies for financing his education overseas also entailed potentially relinquishing other kinds of futures for their family, including for his younger sister. Jason understood that something was inherently expected in return from him: "I want to put [the money] back as soon as possible. I can do it earlier if I stay here and find a job. If I go back home, I can still do it but it's just gonna take a longer time. Plus, I have a sister. And my dad is retired. There's no income from his side." He was anxious to recoup the savings and borrowed money he sensed he hijacked, particularly since his sister expressed a longing for a graduate education overseas as well. His parents had no savings left, and they were now in debt to their relatives. All of it was now conditioned on his education at Riverside, and his work and financial circumstances after graduation. Jason's role as the elder brother needing to pave a path for his sister's education as soon as possible also figured into his calculations of his own masculine success. He felt an urgency to catch up, to not waste time again. His family was waiting on him to contribute meaningfully to their lives and their futures.

Jason's situation was further distinct from other students because he had several relatives who had settled in the United States, creating connections for him to first- and second-generation family in the Indian diaspora. His sensitivity to the dissonance in transnational care that he saw as part of his relatives' permanent settlement complicated his sense of obligation to kinship networks:

> I've seen most of my relatives, the earlier generation of people who came here for studying. They all found jobs here and they settled down. And I know all the parents. They're all back home there. Now they're all old. I know how the situation is there at home. Two old people sitting at home alone. It just doesn't look good. You cannot see your parents when they fall sick. You're not with them to take care of them. And when I think about it, I don't want to see my parents like that. I would want to go back, at least. You feel bad. I know all these cousins of mine—I know they feel bad too but just can't do anything about it right now because they have a family here. Their life is here. They have a job, they have kids, and the kids are all Americans. It's all messed up, and they wouldn't want to come back. It's sad. It's very sad.

Stressing this point, Jason recounted a specific instance involving one of his cousins who had settled in the United States and whose mother had fallen seriously ill in India. The cousin did not visit until his mother's death was imminent. Jason believed it was disgraceful, remarking, "It was sad. And you don't know what's going on in the parents' mind. Is this what they wanted to see when they sent him out to study? I don't know." Reciprocity within kinship networks was essential to Jason's framing of the educational migration path. He interpreted his responsibility to their involvement as emerging from but also laying beyond a bond of gratitude.[18] In his eyes, his cousin had failed to meet the responsibility to reciprocate, through expressions of love, care, and attention, to the kinship networks that enabled his cousin to study overseas. His cousin's failure to fulfill this obligation to his dying mother back home was the ultimate moral failure.

I want to share one final account in relation to the integral involvement of kinship ties in the arrival and presence of Indian student-migrants on an American campus. Unlike the direct experiences of students shared above, this was a commonly accepted and circulated rumor conveyed to me during a conversation among a few friends one evening in Williams Apartments. A few of us had gathered in Ani and Jason's cramped bedroom, chatting at the end of a day of scheduled classes and part-time jobs. Bored, we started brainstorming ways to break the monotony. I was the only one with access to a car, so my presence often allowed for coming up with outings off campus without the students having to incur the cost of doing so. The young men landed on grabbing food at a chain family restaurant, a trademark of the suburban social landscape. Jason went off for a shower while Ani used the half bathroom to change his clothes, put on cologne, and gel his hair. With any trek outside of campus, the men would take their time to groom and ready themselves. I waited in the bedroom with the other friends, Arjun and Mital. The two twin beds Jason and Ani slept on took up much of the space in the narrow room and served as the main seating arrangements. We sat facing each other in close quarters at the edge of each bed, chatting and gossiping about dating, part-time work, and travel. They were both Tamil students, part of the reason they were in a friend group with Jason and Ani. Mital was studying business at Riverside, and he often enjoyed inquiring about the economic aspects of my research project. Whenever he found an opportunity, and whether I asked or not, he would instruct me about the intricacies of finance or debate me on the virtues of capitalism. This is how we wandered into a discussion about the financing of education overseas. They reminded me that overseas students are required to prove their financial ability to pay tuition fees, which had to be demonstrated through liquid assets covering the complete term of their enrollment. We talked about the pervasive use of student loans, which both students needed for their own arrival and enrollment at Riverside. "Actually, some guys have other ways," Mital shared in dramatic, hushed tones, wobbling his head from side to side. "Other ways?" I asked. Encouraged by my curiosity, Mital and Arjun passed on rumors of peers who deployed other arrangements to get past the requirement of demonstrating the necessary assets.[19] As rumor has it, some families seeking to avoid incurring debt ask for and collect the total amount necessary for their son's education from a number of relatives. Then, they temporarily deposit that money into their own bank account. With the money now technically in the account, these families are able to present a bank statement to the university that demonstrates they do have adequate financial means. Arjun added that having relatives or family friends who worked in the bank, or family members making a carefully placed bribe to one of the employees, can also be an effective means to secure a printout of the bank statement, even when the necessary amount is not, in fact, there. Of course, youth and their families must make the right calculations, such as knowing how long to leave the collected money in the account before returning it to relatives, in the event the university requests additional statements.

On the one hand, such strategies require access to well-resourced and well-connected social networks; through forms of giving and receiving, they enable the kind of cooperation needed to facilitate a more supported route for those who move across borders.[20] At the same time, the practices described are risky and implicate those networks in fraudulent acts that transcend national borders. Their transnational networks materialize in ways that can create fraught attachments between those who migrate and those left behind, adding another layer to these student-migrants' burden of debt to their kin. Mital and Arjun had gone on to suggest that the desperation of these families to send their children to study in the United States made them part of the problem of India's corruption, a dominant narrative about the nation's failures and backwardness. Incurring student-loan debt meant taking personal responsibility and, thus, was framed as more legitimate than these other strategies, which middle-class youth like Mital and Arjun believed made for migratory routes that were fraudulent and morally compromised.

Whether providing collateral for student loans, spending life savings, borrowing money from relatives, paying bribes, or committing fraud, the involvement of kinship ties in educational migratory paths through collective risk-bearing acts formed key webs of obligation for Riverside's

Indian middle-class migrant youth. Though such acts, grounded in family, friendship, and community, were crucial support for their education, these students experienced them as a burden, a debt that accompanied their migration that had to, in time, be paid back. In most cases, this meant the return of financial contributions, but it also implied other kinds of reciprocity, whether that was enabling the educational migration of younger relatives or committing to forms of care for their elders. David Graeber's analysis of debt addresses how obligation has come to be understood as relations of debt historically.[21] As Graeber suggests, the prevailing disposition to understand obligation in these terms in the contemporary era is the consequence of a shift in a broader moral ethos, in which any kind of human relationship is conceived of as a form of exchange. This is a feature particular to middle-class sensibilities. The role of student loans and the supports provided by kinship networks contributed to these young men taking self-conscious inventory of what they were owed and what they owed in return, thus configuring a governing logic that shaped how they registered the experience of educational migration. As I discuss later in the book, the notions of sacrifice, duty, and individual responsibility that are part of this logic of indebtedness were formative to how the students made meaning of their encounters on campus, their anxieties over their futures, and how they imagined themselves as men who succeeded overseas.

RETURN, NATION, AND A MATTER OF HOMELAND?

What is the pertinence of the nation-state to how Indian middle-class student-migrants, as a transnational population, experience indebtedness in the contemporary moment? The earlier historical periods discussed in chapter 1 illustrated how educational migration from India to the United States was always entangled in their respective postcolonial and settler-colonial nation-building projects. In particular, there was a shared sentiment that student-migrants had an obligation to remain loyal and contribute meaningfully to the emergence and development of a modern Indian nation. As was noted, the transnational attachments of technically skilled migrants have been an important point of contention in the "brain drain" debates, questioning whether the migration of the educated, professional class was, indeed, detrimental to the national development of places like India that were already ravaged by the effects of colonial rule. Even today, the presumption that this migrant population owes something to their sending nation informs various existing international education programs funding studies overseas that specifically require students to return after graduation and work for a predetermined number of years as part of their obligations to development efforts back home.

Still, the theorization of transnationality that emerged from these debates has since pushed migration scholarship to move beyond the home/host nation paradigms and to understand lives as being made and maintained across national boundaries. "Brain gain" and "brain circulation" surfaced as key concepts capturing these critiques, pointing to practices such as remittances, development of professional networks and foreign investments, and even the return of successful professionals and their families as indications that skilled migration does not have to amount to a loss of human capital for sending nations.[22] As part of these debates, the argument that the significance of the nation-state has weakened due to the consolidation of global capitalism has been widely critiqued. Despite this, universities and their internationalization projects are constructed as sites of transcendence of national borders in the neoliberal moment. Older discourses involving student mobility persist and certainly contribute to this conceptualization, such as the premise of student exchange as fostering diplomacy and mutual understanding between nations. At the same time, the pervasive market-based discourse emphasizing consumer choice and opportunity really drives the sentiment that internationalization projects and, particularly, the rising movement of students across borders produce modern subjectivities that are not linked to nation-building imperatives.

In many ways, this shift is reflected in Riverside's Indian student-migrants' considerations of obligations that tie them to India. None of the youth I met arrived through government funded programs; absent mandatory requirements of government financial support, there was hardly any suggestion of a sense of responsibility to the Indian nation that was part of earlier historical periods of Indian student migration. Most of the Indian students I met, particularly the men, intended to stay in the United States after graduation to secure work so they could manage their debts, achieve the professional success they imagined as their rightful destiny, and attain a sense of masculine autonomy. This is not to suggest that some students did not want to return home. For instance, Priyanka—Jason's girlfriend and the only young woman who was regularly part of our friend group—described her desire to return as missing her loved ones and "a matter of your homeland—where you grew up, what you're used to." Of course, any wish she had to return to India hinged on her ability to pay off the student debt she owed, which she recognized would be harder to do working in India. These kinds of references to longing to be near friends and family back home tended to be shared more by the young women than the Indian men, alluding to the different gendered expressions of emotional ties and considerations of autonomy, mobility, and obligations to kinship networks.

However, wanting to return after graduation is not the same as feeling a responsibility to contribute to national development efforts. Navin, a first-year computer science student, was possibly the only Indian student who explicitly remarked that returning to India would also mean returning something owed to the Indian nation: "It might sound silly to you, but I think I owe something to my country. I see the state of people over there and I feel bad. So, I want to go back, give back something." Navin's impression that his feeling of obligation to Indian national development would seem absurd to me suggested his suspicion that it may be perceived as an outdated allegiance to India. Pointing to the continued presence of widespread poverty in the country, he articulated his embodiment of valuable human capital as tied to an emotional sense of obligation to contribute to the Indian nation and its prosperity.

Yet, Navin's sentiment was not commonly shared among the Indian youth. To emphasize this, I offer a noteworthy point of contrast found in the perspectives shared among the Pakistani students I had befriended. Unlike most Indian students, Pakistani students made explicit references to their sense of an immense social obligation to their home nation. Ahmed, for instance, was a PhD student who expressed his wish to return to Pakistan in classic brain-drain terms, as a commitment to improving economic conditions back home: "At the moment, I do want to go back, because I feel like back home there's more use of a person like me than most probably here. I can sort of like have my own company on the side—give some people employment opportunity as well. And I think I can do a good job at it back home."

Saleem, another doctoral student from Pakistan, asserted that commitment as strengthening the nation's educational resources and as part of a cycle of obligation among Western-educated nationals: "I sort of feel a sense of responsibility in going back and contributing. In the sense that we have in Pakistan a growing academia. And when I was in Pakistan, and when I did my undergrad, I got to study from some really good people who were really passionate who came back from US. From MIT, Stanford, and they sort of really inspired, you know? So I also felt that when you sort of go back and you teach or do research, there are lots of opportunities to contribute." Saleem's reference to being taught by US-trained faculty who returned home illustrates how this sentiment of owing is forged collectively among Pakistan's transnational educated class, an act of reciprocity paid forward from one generation to the next. In this way, the sentiment of an obligation to Pakistani national development figures into the ways these Pakistani students imagine their futures. However, most Indian student-migrants seemed to disregard such concerns of the place of return and nationhood as part of their shared responsibility, a difference, perhaps, pointing to the unevenness of economic conditions among South Asian nations.

How do we make sense of this disregard when brain migration debates take for granted skilled migrants' relationship and obligations to nation-building? Of course, the Indian state continues to be formative to these students' migratory routes, exemplified by the state's direct involvement in mandating and regulating the availability of student loans that enabled educational migration for most of these youth. Still, for Indian middle-class students, longings to become modern subjects were not necessarily entangled in a discourse of building the Indian nation through the state, as was the case in previous historical conjunctures. The construction of a "new" Indian middle class hinges on this turn away from an obligation to the Indian nation-state to a market ethos that emphasizes self-discipline, autonomy, and individual responsibility as key values of the modern subject.[23] Indian student-migrants' resentment at the Indian government's inadequacies in facilitating their class aspirations, as was noted earlier, nurtures a desire for autonomy from the Indian nation itself, an autonomy they partly seek through transnational mobility. At the same time, the coming chapters show how such detachments from nationhood are not the entire story. Sareeta Amrute has explained how the reframing of the Indian middle class does not necessarily mean a total erasure of the development discourse; rather, she argues, the emphasis on individual, entrepreneurial accomplishments is imagined as still being in service to a modern India.[24] Echoing this point, the coming chapters suggest that the nexus of desiring and indebtedness among the Indian middle-class youth studying at Riverside revealed how their self-fashioning as successful men overseas continued to be entangled in anxieties about the Indian nation and its place in the world. Further, the consolidation of the surveillance state in a post-9/11 context also ensured that considerations of the state, nationhood, and empire persisted in other ways as critical to their migratory journeys, shaping how Indian student-migrants mobilized a logic of owing and being owed.

3 · Institutionalizing the Imagination

One of the more frightening aspects of the Sept. 11 attacks is that the hijacking suspects were men who were living and learning in the United States, using student visas to hide in plain sight while they plotted an attack.

"HOW CAN WE KEEP TERRORISTS OUT OF AMERICA?,"
GOOD MORNING AMERICA

When a group of nineteen men, mostly from Saudi Arabia, hijacked several commercial planes and flew them into the World Trade Center and the Pentagon in a coordinated attack on September 11, 2001, it struck at the heart of US empire and marked a crucial historic moment. What emerged since, midwifed through the discourse, policies, and practices of the Bush Administration's "war on terror," has been an era of renewed, aggressive US militarization abroad and an ushering in of the national security surveillance state. In some quarters, "9/11," as the event came to be known, drew scrutiny to the complicity of American universities in this rise of US militarization.[1] As the war on terror grew to include the invasion and military occupations of both Afghanistan and Iraq, universities became important settings of anti-imperialist and antiwar critique and dissent, including against the institutions themselves and the kinds of war-profiteering projects from which they were, and continue to be, benefiting. Yet, on another front, university campuses were also a critical site of post-9/11 regulation because their commitment to internationalization and increasing overseas-student enrollments was implicated in those events. It was revealed that several of the 9/11 hijackers had been issued student visas or had used educational aims as justifications for their entry and residence in the United States. The *Good Morning America* quote above reflects the alarm this had caused for the American public. The reality that an attack of this magnitude on US soil was carried out by individuals who actually infiltrated national borders legally, including disguising themselves as overseas students or using education as a ruse, became a feature of the national moral panic that ensued. It unsettled the existing national discourse around undesirable immigration, which typically centered on the notion of illegality. It was further disorienting to American nationalist sensibilities, for which the pursuit of education and learning is usually part of the moralizing narrative of chasing the American Dream.

This particular revelation had tremendous implications for the student visa process and the presence of overseas students on American campuses. This was primarily captured with the momentous passing of the Uniting and Strengthening America by Providing Appropriate Tools Required to Intercept and Obstruct Terrorism Act of 2001, more popularly known as the USA PATRIOT Act. The Patriot Act was responsible for formally authorizing extensive powers for the government to conduct racialized surveillance and searches, access records, confiscate property, and detain noncitizens merely by labeling targeted individuals and groups as suspected domestic terrorists. The legislation was drafted and rushed through Congress, being passed into law within a month of the September 11 attacks. It was widely criticized, including by the American Civil Liberties Association (ACLU), which condemned it as a serious attack on US constitutional freedoms. Regardless, the Patriot Act dictates national security practices in the United States to this day and has served as crucial legislative justification for various kinds of surveillance schemes that have come to define our contemporary political moment.

With the recognition that the student visa process and international education played a role in making 9/11 possible, the Patriot Act's Title IV, "Protecting the Border," along with the Enhanced Border Security and Visa Entry Reform Act passed in 2002, called for a major overhaul that would ensure the systematic and ongoing collection of information on overseas students. These policies drew from earlier proposed legislation that was rolled out after the first attack on the World Trade Center in 1993, a bombing for which six men were convicted. One of these men was a Jordanian national named Eyad Ismoil, who had arrived in the United States on a student visa. In 1996, the Illegal Immigration Reform and Immigrant Responsibility Act (IIRIRA) mandated the creation of a program that would require any educational institution that hosted overseas students to collect and report information on those students. Yet, the Immigration and Naturalization Service (INS), the department managing immigration-related issues at that time, was vastly unequipped to handle the massive restructuring and reorganization that this would have required. It was only with the events of 9/11 that student visa reform was turned into a national security priority.

When the INS released the legal statuses of the hijackers, it was clear that the majority arrived legally in the United States, with at least two issued student visas. Regardless of their visa statuses, however, several were attending flight school, taking English classes, or presenting themselves as overseas students to those they met.[2] The backlash against the INS and its handling of the foreign student program grew when it was learned that two of the hijackers who had trained in flight school and had applied to change their tourist visas to student visas received letters confirming that they were approved six months *after* the 9/11 attack. In May 2002, the Office of the Inspector General published a report admonishing the INS for its incompetence: "The INS's foreign student program historically has been dysfunctional, and the INS has acknowledged for several years that it does not know how many foreign students are in the United States. In addition, the INS lacks accurate data about the schools that are authorized to issue I-20s, the students who obtain student visas and student status, the current status of those students, and whether fraud is being perpetuated in the foreign student program."[3] The report goes on to suggest that the events of 9/11 were a direct spark for more security-minded restructuring of the foreign student program: "Since September 11, 2001, the INS's focus on foreign students has changed dramatically. In the past, the INS's philosophy has strongly favored admitting foreign students, viewing them as relatively low risk. After September 11, tighter regulatory controls have been proposed to make it more difficult for aliens to obtain student status and to more closely scrutinize persons entering the country who might later attempt to become students."[4]

The language of risk has been crucial to post-9/11 policy discourse. Through evocations of American vulnerability and betrayals of the nation's trust, the conceptualization of the terrorist subject as perpetual risk provided the needed legitimation for what Giorgio Agamben calls the "state of exception," the post-9/11 surveillance state.[5] Rather than being an exceptional measure, the extension of state powers to suspend legal and civil protections is increasingly becoming the normalized form of governance in the contemporary period. Justifying such a state of exception is often done through the paradigm of "risk," which does not refer to the catastrophe itself but to the anticipation of the catastrophe.[6] As is seen here, this question of risk was also adapted to reframe the ambivalence of overseas students' presence as particularly suspicious and high risk. The report offered several recommendations for accountability, since "the foreign student program is highly susceptible to fraud."[7]

Indicating how the fragmentation of the agency's overall administrative structuring was partly to blame for these failures, one of the recommendations called for more coordinated efforts.[8] The government repeatedly returned to the message that "the terrorists exploited deep institutional failings within our government," and that the attack could have been prevented with more unified efforts and sharing of information among government agencies.[9] In 2002, the passage of the Homeland Security Act initiated a massive reorganization of federal government agencies. This reorganization included the creation of the Department of Homeland Security (DHS), which represented the consolidation of twenty-two federal agencies and programs, including the absorption of INS and the making of the US Immigration and Customs Enforcement (ICE). The restructuring led to the full implementation of the Student and Exchange Visitor Program (SEVP), which had originally been proposed in the IIRIRA. As will be explored later in this chapter, the establishment of the SEVP program caused a tremendous shift in the work and ethos of international student offices on US campuses.

THE *NEW* TERROR: THE CALL TO "INSTITUTIONALIZE THE IMAGINATION"

The 9/11 Commission Report released in 2004 by the National Commission on Terrorist Attacks upon the United States offers insight into the discursive work that contributed to this shift. The five-hundred-page document is a remarkable text because of its unusual blending of bureaucratic writing conventions and evocative literary prose. The effect was not only a captivating, detailed narration of the events of 9/11 but it also worked to assemble the collective emotional dimensions expected of that narrative. The otherwise ordinariness of the day of the attacks, the stunning betrayal of the nation's trust, and its patriotic resilience and fortitude in the face of catastrophe were all part of this affective messaging. Most importantly, the report's storytelling style functioned as a dramatic reminder of the threat of "the new terrorism."[10] While fundamentally drawing on already existing constructions of particular racialized subjects and their home nations,[11] the report insisted that it was a "new" threat created by the resentment found predominantly among Muslim populations who were envious of the United States' emergence as the sole, successful global power at the end of the Cold War era. Echoing the messaging of the "clash of civilizations" discourse prevalent after the events of 9/11, the Commission wrote: "America stood out as an object for admiration, envy, and blame. This created a kind of cultural asymmetry. To us, Afghanistan seemed very far away. To members of al Qaeda, America seemed very close. In a sense, they were more globalized than we were."[12]

According to the report, 9/11 merely exposed that resentment, which may have been foreign but had infiltrated and made its way onto American soil. Americans and their government, due to their own naivete, failed to recognize this supposed hatred of "the American way."[13] Unsurprisingly, the report's release had coincided with the implementation of the Patriot Act, which had led to mass detentions and deportations of individuals of Muslim, Arab, and South Asian descent, including the extrajudicial detentions of foreign nationals at the Guantanamo Bay prison. It also accompanied the follow-up to the occupation of Afghanistan—the very unpopular invasion of Iraq that brought into the national lexicon the "shock and awe" campaigns that were premised on the Bush administration's fallacious assertions of the presence of weapons of mass destruction in the country. In other words, the report served as compelling propaganda for domestic and international state surveillance, militarization, and racialized state exclusion in the post-9/11 climate.

In the context of the claim to a new kind of threat, the Commission contended that what was urgently needed was what they identified as the "institutionalization of imagination," a call to weave into the folds of bureaucratic power the imagining of new and different ways that terrorism against the United States could occur. The allusion here to the pervasiveness of terroristic possibility and the need to open the national imagination to conjure up what those possibilities may be effectively exploited Americans' collective racialized fears and imperialist anxieties. In this way, along with accelerated US military expansion, mass detention and deportation, and state repression, the post-9/11 era has been characterized by the deep and enduring transformations of the workings of bureaucratic structures necessary to the consolidation of the surveillance state. For those involved in the international education industry, the report's call to "find a way of routinizing, even bureaucratizing, the exercise of imagination"[14] meant a bureaucratic reimagining of the student-migrant as a risky, suspicious figure, particularly those linked to regions racialized as the breeding grounds of terror. In this context, the migratory routes of young people traveling from South Asia to an American campus necessarily included racialized encounters with such routinized exercises of bureaucratic reimagining. Resonating with the considerations of earlier historical periods discussed in chapter 1, this chapter suggests that the post-9/11 context is another historic moment in which migrant youth who cross borders in the pursuit of education are situated ambivalently as morally good and nonthreatening and as possible threats to imperialist interests.

Below, I consider how these student-migrants experienced the effects of the bureaucratic power of national security policy. Recounting their experiences with the student visa process and with travel, students expressed conflicted, ambivalent ideas as they attempted to construct the meanings of those experiences, define the contours of their legitimacy, and make sense of it as a feature of their everyday lives as student-migrants arriving through particular racial geographies. Their reflections reveal how practices of surveillance are tied to racialized and gendered constructions of threat through which the compliant student-migrant figure is produced. While "Muslim-looking" racialization is central here, a consideration I return to shortly, the hypervigilance of (Muslim) religious identity and ethnonational origin within the context of the war on terror also translated into key differences in the magnitude of student-migrants' encounters. Serving as an instantiation of such differences, I include in this chapter an exchange with Imran, a Pakistani overseas student I had befriended. Following this discussion, I describe Riverside campus scenes and rituals, both commemorative and routine, that form part of the ideological backdrop to the practices of state surveillance of student-migrants in the post-9/11 context. By exploring how the "institutionalization of imagination" mandate of the surveillance state configured pertinent formal and informal spaces within the public university campus, I point to crucial instantiations of the university's continued role in supporting US imperialist interests. Illuminating this facet of the neoliberal university working in tandem with geopolitical realities, the chapter offers insight into the conditions under which obligations to the nation-state continue to be an important consideration in the placemaking practices among Indian student-migrant youth in the contemporary moment.

VISAS, TRAVEL, AND THE SUSPICIOUS STUDENT-MIGRANT

Students' initial reflections on the possibility that the US state saw them as potential threats to security often explained it away as an ordinary and unimportant aspect of their lives. National security regulation "doesn't matter to us," said Ashok. "I've just accepted it as part of my international experience." Echoing this sentiment, Kalyan remarked, "Well, if you're going to go to a country, then you need to follow their rules. They need to keep themselves secure. If you don't like it, then you should leave." Such views among the students were common, often articulated through conservative sound bites and rationales that the United States had a "right to protect" itself. These assertions would be accompanied by a reminder to themselves and to me, that, as student-migrants, they were just visitors. As foreign nationals and racially marked subjects, they believed the United States had no obligation to care for them. Drawing on the logic of owing to reconcile the presence of the surveillance state in their lives, these young migrants came to accept their surveillance as part of the exchange for an American education.

Yet, with the increased stringency of the F1, or student visa, application process in the post-9/11 policy climate, particularly for those from regions of geopolitical interest to the United States, students recounted the difficulties that arose for them and their friends. While some who experienced visa application issues were reassured by friends and acquaintances that it was common and would just be a temporary delay, others recounted being devastated, helpless, and anxious as they were not sure what would happen—many had attached their professional aspirations to studying overseas. Undoubtedly, Muslim students and students from nations with a large Muslim citizenry were especially affected. Saleem, the Pakistani PhD student in computer science mentioned in chapter 2, faced such a long delay that he was prevented from starting in his first fall semester as he intended. The uncertainty of the situation caused him immense anxiety.

Beyond the ways they emotionally grappled with the obstacles to the visa process they encountered, students also revealed how they made sense of the justifications for those obstacles. Take Nasir, for example. Nasir was an Indian Muslim student from Madhya Pradesh who had enrolled in the master's program in computer science but was initially rejected for a student visa by the consulate, supposedly because he posed a "threat to permanent immigration." This had been frustrating for Nasir, who had previously listed a number of reasons why he hoped to return to India within a few years of graduation. He especially wanted to return because he was close to his family and did not want to be separated from them for too long. When I asked him why they would, then, be under the impression that he would permanently settle in the United States, he replied, "You better ask them why do they think like that. . . . I told them that I'll come back to India. The second time, they asked me the same thing and I told them the same thing and they gave it to me. You never know."

Though he said one can never know with this process, Nasir actually moved into an extensive discussion to sort through the reasons he and some of his other friends would have their applications rejected. In doing so, he further expressed his lack of clarity on why such rejections occurred. Throughout our conversation, he would suggest various possible explanations, trailing off between each when he recalled friends' experiences that were not feasibly captured by those explanations. As the targeting of Muslims by the United States had by now become globally acknowledged, the first explanation Nasir ventured was tied to his own positioning as a young Muslim man, though he framed it as not knowing "whether this was a coincidence or not." Pondering out loud what the different possibilities could be, he indicated he was still not clear on whether his religious identity was an important consideration. He tied this doubt to the rejections several of his Hindu friends back home had also received: "At the same time, my other friends who were not Muslims, their visas were also rejected. A lot of my friends. In fact, two of my friends had their visa rejected. One of them had thrice, and one of them has had twice. And they were not Muslims, they were Hindus, right?"

Frowning and looking pensive, he contemplated further, newly aware of his own dissatisfaction at not knowing why. He moved on to a range of other possibilities—changes in US administration policies to prioritize job security for American citizens, preferences for more academically competitive overseas students, or the potential intellectual threat students from abroad enrolling in specific professional fields are seen as posing because of the suspicions generated by foreign policy and the US state. Each possible reason he contemplated seemed to lead to a dead end when he remembered how other friends' situations disproved one or the other. Nasir reiterated, "I really don't know why. But I think from the past year or so the visa thing has become a bit more difficult. That's what I feel because, again, I can feel it empirically."

These "empirical feelings" Nasir refers to were the sense he tried to find in stories shared and circulated among students and their friends about a process that simultaneously felt specific and systematic as well as arbitrary in design. In other words, the routinization of reimagining student-migrants as suspicious subjects reworked the student visa process, but that process is accompanied by a feeling of arbitrariness. That feeling, produced by the uncertainty over the reasons behind decisions, as well as the authority visa officers have to permit, delay, or prevent students' overseas educational pursuits, recalls Elizabeth Freeman's conceptualization of the chrononormative. As Freeman explains, it becomes a technique of normalizing temporal experience, in which "institutional forces come to seem like somatic fact."[15] The sense of bureaucratic contradiction underlying the arbitrariness *felt* had a further important effect. Nasir complained, "The visa officers are above everyone in the US. They're even above some of the government officials, I feel." The seeming unpredictability of their decisions led students like Nasir to conclude that American visa officers were not only powerful but powerful in ways that were distinct from the state, as much as they constitute a component of its apparatus. This imagined displacement of state involvement in producing the racialized other of national security is a meaningful and disciplinary effect of state power itself. Nasir understood the visa rejections he and his friends received as indicative of the suspiciousness their otherness embodied, but his contradictory "empirical feelings" did not offer any clear picture of what kind of threat he and his friends represented. Was it a civilizational threat? A threat to American political and economic power? This uncertainty is productive of and for the surveillance state. The arbitrary power to deem particular student-migrants as suspicious and a potential risk imbues the entire visa process with an indispensable ambiguity, hailing young men whose paths are implicated in particular geopolitical relations as racialized and gendered compliant subjects even before they arrive on an American campus.

Air travel was also a site of such negotiations. One of the most visible changes after September 11 occurred within the airline industry; it experienced massive economic loss from which it never fully recovered and underwent profound transformations in its security regulations. Airports and air travel have been permanently shifted into highly securitized spaces, and the damage to commercial flight culture meant pervasive suspicion, racialized fears, and frustrations attached to the punitive measures accompanying the changes. Airports were now characterized by a heavy presence of Travel Security Administration guards, explosive detection canines, long lines of agitated passengers, body scanners, signage and announcements declaring "if you see something, say something" (suggesting that good citizenry involved personally engaging in surveillance), and mandatory "random screenings" that, in fact, regularly profiled and targeted specific racialized individuals. This new ethos of hypersecurity has rendered airports permanent sites of systematic profiling and discrimination.

Most Indian student-migrants were keenly aware of the post-9/11 hate crimes, state surveillance, and racial profiling that were occurring in the United States, stories that had made their way across the globe. Coinciding with national security legislation, the modes of state and popular violence that characterized the period after 9/11 constructed the terrorist threat as fundamentally a racial figure, embodied by Arab, Muslim, and South Asian populations, a reflection of the emergence of a post-9/11 racial construct, the "Muslim-looking person."[16] For this reason, families and communities back home collectively had concerns involving students' travel overseas, worrying over markers like names and facial hair that could create trouble for them in airports. Recognizing how Indian men were also implicated by the configuration of a racialized masculinity that lay at the heart of the terrorist threat, many families urged their sons to, at least, shave their beards before traveling. Several of the Indian men shared accounts of being pulled aside for additional security screenings while traveling in airports. When asked why, most had no clear idea, and as with Nasir's attempts at understanding visa officers' decisions, they could only speculate. On more than one occasion, non-Muslim Indian students explained that having facial hair probably made them "look Muslim," and therefore made them seem more threatening in airports. For these Indian men, being "mistaken" as Muslim was the only way they could justify being seen as suspicious subjects. Their invocation of "Muslim-looking" as a racial sensibility links how they make meaning of their racialization within the United States with ideas of Indian nationhood that echo the anti-Muslim premise of Hindutva ideology promulgated by India's ruling class. Emerging as a formidable political force since the 1990s, right-wing Hindu nationalism's ideological underpinnings were grounded in the notion of the pure Indian (read: Hindu) nation, whose glory could only be restored by protecting it from the perpetual threat of the foreign enemy within, almost always read as the Muslim figure.[17] In the aftermath of 9/11, Hindu nationalists deepened their consolidation of power as India strategically aligned with the United States in the global war on terror.[18] Global Islamophobia structures these linkages, pointing to how "Muslim-looking" not only became a readily available racial category for both popular and state violence in 9/11's aftermath in the United States but also became easily summoned in Indian youth's sensemaking of their own racialization as transnational migrants. I will return to the Indian student-migrants' racial framing of "Muslim-looking" in the next chapter.

Though many of the student-migrants indicated that this kind of racial sensemaking was part of the negotiation of various aspects of travel, religion and national origin served to make such sensemaking more pertinent for some than others. Because of its porous borders with Afghanistan and its political and economic vulnerabilities, Pakistan, in particular, has had a significant though conflicted and tenuous place in the geopolitical landscape of the war on terror. The accounts shared below by Imran, a Pakistani student-migrant who was working on his PhD, offer a glimpse into how this produced differences in the ways South Asian student-migrant youth experienced state surveillance. Having become friends despite his lack of connection to Indian student-migrants or Williams Apartments, where I spent most of my time, Imran and I agreed to meet in the Student Union, the hub of student life at Riverside, to discuss his experiences. We took a few minutes to catch each other up on our lives, watching and enjoying the hum of campus activity around us, which was punctuated faintly by the Muslim call to prayer. That the call was permitted to be part of the campus's soundscape resonated with the appearance of multicultural and religious tolerance the university sought to maintain.

As a student-migrant from Pakistan since the age of seventeen, Imran actually had been in the United States longer than most of the students I met and had come to accept surveillance, tracking, and questioning as a routine, normal, and even justifiable feature of his life. Because of his extended education in the United States, Imran felt a deep responsibility to remain connected to Pakistan and his family back home, which meant he made efforts to return to Pakistan a few times a year. In the context of the post-9/11 surveillance state, this kind of commitment to fly back and forth as a young Pakistani man studying overseas in the United States translated into suspicious activity. In the decade following 9/11, travel by young men like Imran was specifically impacted by the special registration program called National Security Entry-Exit Registration System (NSEERS). The program had compiled a list of countries that were framed as the highest "threat" and required any foreign nationals from those countries to register when entering and exiting the United States. As both Pakistan and Bangladesh were placed on the high-threat list for the NSEERS program, student-migrants from these South Asian nations confronted additional tracking at airports to which Indian students were not routinely subjected. Imran's movements across US borders overlapped with this program, and during that period, his travel experiences involved a grueling, time-consuming process of security checks that included three security screenings and many hours of interrogation, while also being processed by biometric technologies.

Even with the eventual termination of NSEERS,[19] Imran continued to be subjected to a "secondary" screening that would still last anywhere from two to three hours. These screenings also meant the added scrutiny of anything that supposedly was not straightforward, even otherwise innocuous details, such as a layover in Washington, DC, as Imran returned to Pakistan. Imran shared that during interrogation, agents would reveal that they had also accessed and monitored his credit card accounts, purportedly to determine whether he was financing terrorist organizations. Like Nasir, Imran was conflicted when recalling such practices: "And they know everything pretty much. They know every single transaction I've made on my credit card. So, I understand why they're doing it. But it just puts a sense of restriction on you. Not really like you're being watched but more in the sense of that you're just being monitored in some way or the other. Yeah. Again, I don't mind that at all because I think that I understand the purpose of it, right?" Though he faltered when remembering and reflecting on such details, Imran repeatedly offered justifications for these acts of state monitoring of his transnational travels, reasserting that it was trivial and probably for his own protection anyway. Collecting and mining data as a means to anticipate and chart subjects' moves prior to those moves even occurring are important techniques of what Deleuze argued is the contemporary shift toward control societies.[20] The sense of the omniscience of the state and the dubious distinction between being monitored but not necessarily "being watched" are desired, controlling effects of the surveillance state, leading young men like Imran to ultimately reconcile it as their obligation to the greater purpose of national security. Importantly, Imran rarely alluded to his own status and racialization as a Pakistani national; in fact, he insisted that this hypersecuritization was fundamental to the student-migrant experience: "I'm an international student. I can't come in and go out as easily as someone else would, right?" It was with this understanding that he casually noted to me that travel through American airports had also regularly led to strip searches for him:

I'm a painting minor as well. So I take paints and these boards, and these weird things like palette knives. And, so very often I get, you know, strip searched. I think I'm actually a very nonaggressive person [*Imran laughs*]. Like that's one of the things that I've sort of maintained. If it's not completely going against my rights, I think it's okay. I mean, I understand the reason why they did that as well. I was going through the scanner and it was still beeping and I had everything off. So they were like okay, let's step into the other room, you know. I don't know if it was particularly because of bias or something like that, but I don't feel it was something too bad. I think it was okay.

Imran worked through this moment of being pulled into a private room to be stripped and searched through the linked logic of transparency.[21] The state here needed to literally see all of Imran to know for sure that he did not embody potential violence and that he had nothing to hide, his body included. He gestured to a range of performances occurring within this exchange at the airport that helped him re-sort his notions of bodily privacy and surveillance. The officers' politeness, the reasonable doubt of deviance cast by the warning alarms of the monitoring technologies that scanned Imran, and his sense that others were subjected to the same process all offered a perceived sense of objectivity. While he expressed doubt on whether profiling was involved, these aspects of the experience suggested to Imran that it was not a violation of his rights, making his encounters with strip searches as a function of national security reasonable and ordinary. When I suggested that strip searches are extraordinarily invasive practices, Imran was dismissive and intent on convincing me to accept the banality of these acts. "You're making a big issue out of something that is really not an issue," he insisted. In his account, Imran had also mentioned his dual training in painting, as well as alluded to his "nonaggressive" disposition. Both references suggested how these security performances in airport travel were entangled in his own delicate balancing act of student and terrorist suspect. In Imran's reckoning with his own relation to the world as a brown Muslim man traversing borders, there are reverberations of orientalist constructions, in which South Asian masculinity embodies the dual comportment of docility and threat.[22] Located ambivalently in this way, young men like Imran are interpellated by the "state of exception" ideology and participate in their own making as docile subjects. The airport was one node in their movements from a particular postcolonial "there" to a particular settler-colonial "here," where the settler-consumerist desire for a Western education was exchanged for absolute and literal transparency, which was expected and demanded. While non-Muslim Indian men also had to negotiate racialized and gendered border practices that deemed them as risky subjects, I share Imran's accounts as a Muslim, Pakistani student to demonstrate how geopolitical considerations and the centrality of Islamophobic politics can inform the degree and nature of those encounters.

Though masculine anxieties were part of many of these young men's negotiations, the students' invocations of bureaucratic arbitrariness, mistaken identities, protection, and transparency helped normalize the excesses of state surveillance practices as part of their exchange for an American education, effectively garnering their consent and producing docile migrant subjects in the process. Yet, the war-on-terror policy mandate to institutionalize the imagination did not only figure into these students' lives through the process of acquiring visas and travel. It has had a profound impact on campus culture as well. I turn next to the informal and formal spaces of post-9/11 inclusion practices that emerged at Riverside University to consider how the casting of student-migrants arriving from South Asia as ambivalent figures of the post-9/11 world has informed their relationship with the institutional life of the American campus.

CHANGES AT THE OFFICE: FROM HUMAN TOUCH TO SURVEILLANCE

In considering how the bureaucratizing of imagined threats worked its way into the campus culture, it is the international student office that serves as the central setting. When the backlash against and scrutiny of INS's national foreign student program led to significant systemic changes in INS's management, universities' international student offices were pulled in closer to the work of the surveillance state. The strict enforcement of a surveillance program that routinized the surveillance of student-migrants became crucial to the inner workings of the office, and at Riverside, it profoundly transformed the office's bureaucratic culture, priorities, and work. With the establishment of SEVP, the agency's duties were laid out, such as certifying educational institutions, overseeing the implementation of policies, and detailing how universities must track and report on their nonimmigrant students. Part of the "mutual commitment or shared responsibility with the educational community to maintain support and cooperation"[23] included the implementation and administration of the Student and Exchange Visitor Information System (SEVIS), an automated, web-based tracking system that serves as the program's key technology to monitor and report on students. To maintain this program, student-migrants are required to pay a fee as part of their costs to enroll, which at the time of implementation was $200 and has now increased to $350. Enforcing such a measure is a clever, built-in mechanism that ensures these students' consent to their own surveillance by requiring them to pay for it themselves.

It became the responsibility of universities and their international education programs to enforce and administer the regulations of the new SEVP program, which included the routine monitoring, tracking, and reporting on overseas-student populations to the DHS. The DHS even gave formal titles to international student advisors, designated school officials (DSOs), as part of the restructuring of their duties. Their primary role now was to compile data on students and report to SEVP through SEVIS. These reporting responsibilities are elaborate and time-consuming, particularly at Riverside, with an advising staff of four tracking a growing foreign student body that was already well over three thousand students. Moreover, the new regulations required specific time constraints on reporting that also shaped the nature of the office's work. For instance, within thirty days of starting an academic program, new overseas students must report to the university, at which point the DSO-advisor must register the student in SEVIS. If this does not occur within the allotted time frame, SEVIS will automatically terminate the student record, leaving the student with only two options—apply for reinstatement or leave the United States immediately. This temporal element is significant. Post-9/11 organizational restructuring ensured that the information maintained by databases like SEVIS is accessible and shared by multiple government agencies engaged in national security activities, including the Federal Bureau of Investigation, Customs and Border Protection, the United States Citizenship and Immigration Services, the State Department, and the Compliance Enforcement Unit. As such, not entering data within given time frames or adhering to other compliance regulations can have serious consequences.

At Riverside, compliance requirements for post-9/11 federal regulations combined with the rising enrollments of overseas students created both philosophical and operational tensions for the international student office. This was, perhaps, most symbolically captured in the decision by the new chair overseeing the international programs at Riverside to change the name of the center: what used to be called "International Services" is now called the "Visa and Immigration Office." Of course, the name change reflected the broader post-9/11 shift requiring universities' international student offices to play the main role in administering national security regulations involving overseas students. Two competing discourses, claims made through (neo)colonialist and surveillance productions of knowledge and authority over the otherness that these students represented, were integral to the tensions that accompanied this change in names. Situating the Visa and Immigration

Office within this context illustrates how it is a governable site produced through the ideological particularities of the US imperialist project; I consider this below.

I walked through the tiled white corridors of the old building to make my way to the Visa and Immigration Office. Several offices constituting the International Academic Programs sat on one side. On the other, windows alternated with framed posters. "The Serengeti" with an image of an elephant, "India" with an image of the Taj Mahal—facile representations meant to capture other parts of the world. Outside the front door of the Visa and Immigration Office, a red banner hung from a stand welcoming visitors in different languages. This sparse and low-budget office decor feebly gestured to a bureaucratic attempt at seeming worldliness and cultural exchange. Inside, the shuffling of paper, light clicking on a computer keyboard, and faint sounds of office chatter could be heard. Dana, the talkative receptionist, was on the phone; holding the phone receiver in one hand while scanning the screen in front of her, she explained routine procedures to the person on the other end. She smiled and waved as I took a seat in one of the stiff purple armchairs. A few Chinese students were sitting and waiting patiently under the harsh overhead lighting of the office, their gazes locked in front of them on the beige-colored divider separating them from the receptionist's desk. The exchanges in this office were almost entirely about processing legal paperwork or checking on the legal status of overseas students. This meant a workday consisting mostly of data entering, searching for files, and showing and sharing with each other various documents. When I walked in that day, the usual quietness hung over the office. Throughout the day, students would trickle in and out, quietly picking up or dropping off paperwork. While they sat in the waiting area, one of the staff members—a DSO-advisor—would walk to the front desk, pick up a clipboard, call out a student's name from the visitor list, and silently lead the student to an office in the back. Typically, the student would leave the advisor's office within fifteen to twenty minutes. The almost willfully impersonal undertones of this routine were reminiscent of a hospital waiting room.

By this point, most of the staff in the office seemed to be adjusting to my presence. Ani worked here part time, and he and his friend, Ben, the building's tech support student-employee, would regularly tease me for expressing interest in what they saw as mundane and uneventful office work. They saw me sitting there again that afternoon and, as they walked by, joked, "observe me walking out." I laughed. It was an unusual sound in the quiet and sterile office, and it coincided with the DSO-advisor named Mildred walking out right then from a small, fluorescent-lit room located across from the director's office. It had a large window on one side to peer in from the office hallway. Members of the office referred to this room as the "SEVIS room" since much of the SEVIS-related paperwork was stored there.

Holding some papers with both hands, Mildred shot me a fleeting, suspicious glance when she heard me laugh. She walked over to sort through the files behind the receptionist's desk, look for more paperwork, and talk to Dana. Over the months I spent observing the center, Mildred would alternate between recognizing and then ignoring me, and not recognizing me and assuming I was one of the South Asian overseas students. Showing the papers to Dana and instructing her to process them, Mildred began talking loudly about the student for whom the papers were being processed. Shaking her head and rolling her eyes, Mildred complained, "Yeah, she didn't do it right. She's from Liberia. I've told her so many times what to do. She just gets confused easily. She's Liberian. Let's just say, she gets confused really easily. So now this needs to be fixed." The regulations and accompanying paperwork were tedious and complicated. On many occasions, I had witnessed Mildred not only demonstrate a lack of patience with students who were not familiar with the procedures but also reference their national or ethnic backgrounds as some kind of cultural explanation for their lack of understanding. Her regular condescension and unfriendly demeanor toward students from overseas suited the generally cold and sterile atmosphere of the office; her attitude was not uncommon among some of the advisors.

Sonia, whom I was waiting to meet that afternoon, was a stark contrast to Mildred. Sonia's frustrated voice called out from the SEVIS room in the back. Presumably referring to a SEVIS entry for a student, she yelled across to another advisor's office, "Does it still say master's? They're not accepting it!" The elaborate paperwork required for security and border control to confirm the legal statuses of the students was intricately tied to processing other aspects of student life, such as healthcare and registration. Even minor errors could lead to students falling out of status, which could have big consequences. Sighing, Sonia came out to the front desk a few minutes later. Greeting me with a smile, she asked if I wanted to grab lunch from one of the food trucks parked outside. We walked to the back of the building where the trucks were parked, picked up our lunches, and went to talk in the nearby Student Union. In her early forties now, Sonia had been working in the international education field for over a decade. Having originally arrived as a student from eastern Europe many years ago, she had always felt she understood what the students she advised now were experiencing. Over lunch, she spoke passionately about the importance of working with and supporting them, but when I brought up the post-9/11 security regulations, she became quiet. Sonia looked down at her half-eaten sandwich and then around the cafeteria at the students gathering in different places, chatting, eating, and taking their breaks. She tucked her blond hair behind one ear and let out a sigh before she described to me how she saw the apparent shift in the nature of the work at the office.

For Sonia, 9/11 marked the creation of different categories of international education advisors. There were those, like her, who were part of the industry much earlier, and there were those she referred to as "post-SEVIS advisors" who "don't know any other system because they came after SEVIS was established." According to Sonia, the name change of the office, in particular, was a move to make explicit that the office's older values of cultural exchange and services were now replaced by security concerns and issues of legality. This, of course, altered the nature of the relationship between the office and the students, reducing it merely to things related to "their legal paperwork, and then sending them away." Sonia went on to complain how the office was incredibly understaffed for an overseas-student population numbering in the thousands. For her, this harmed what she imagined as the more righteous mission of international education services. As she argued, "Yes, we can talk about security, but there is no human touch. We are not actually helping anyone." Sonia's frustrations captured how the intersection of post-9/11 national security regulations with the university's market-driven practices to enable increased overseas-student enrollment was creating pressures on the office. The loss of the "human touch," she explained, was the worst part of the shift away from providing social and emotional support for overseas students:

We used to have cultural shows, public safety orientations. We would be the ones welcoming them at the airports! But now we

don't pick them up anymore. You know there are students who eat
one meal a day because they no longer have a graduate assistant-
ship? But they're so invested in getting their degree they try to stick
it out. I know about these things because I've done it for a long
time. Students are isolated on the campus and many get depressed.
The international programming here is not giving them the support
that they need. Instead, we are always in front of the computer doing reporting.

Sonia's allusion to some kind of an old guard, one that once cared for
and had the knowledges of the actual needs of overseas students on
campus, in contrast to the new guard that included advisors who arrived
with the contemporary post-9/11 emphasis on security and surveillance,
was not uncommon. Rachel, the director of international student services, referred to it as "a calling."

When I had started spending time in the office, Rachel was caught
up directly in the turmoil occurring there. Within a few months into the
academic year, she had been demoted, and the new chair of the international programs, John, turned Rachel's work responsibilities as director over to the coordinator of the study abroad programs, Jenny. As part
of this demotion, Rachel was also forced to relinquish her office and
move to a lower floor, an obvious and effective move to isolate her and
erase her role, presence, and views from the center. While John's decision was partly due to personal conflict between the two of them, the
aggressive maneuver to push Rachel out was justified by and reinforced
a message about the office's new alignments to prioritize national security compliance.

Rachel was crushed by the demotion, calling the events "bizarre" and,
in a way, she was relieved to have me as an outlet to share her discontent.
Uncomfortable with discussing the changes with the rest of the staff and
the chair nearby, however, she asked we talk outside. I followed Rachel
out and to a bench near the back of the building. Having felt the immense
tension hanging over the office, I uneasily took a seat and looked over at
her, waiting for her to take the lead. Rachel was a woman in her fifties,
tall with short, graying hair framing her face. Consistent with her usual
professional office attire, she was wearing a dark pantsuit that afternoon.
She took a seat next to me, maintaining the calm composure of someone who seemed long socialized into white-collar professional conven-

tions of demeanor. But her expression was conflicted, a combination of pain and pride. Like Sonia, Rachel suggested that the biggest loss with the shift was the loss of personal connection. Partly to explicate this and partly to defend her practices as the former director, she offered up examples of how the narrow push for efficiency altered the nature of the office's relationship to its students. For instance, student-migrants wishing to travel out of the country and reenter the United States were required to acquire "travel signatures," which confirmed that they had maintained a valid status. Previously, the office would request a letter from the student's department faculty verifying the student's progress and status, a measure that was not actually required by the federal regulations and was now eliminated by the office's new leadership. Yet, Rachel insisted that it enabled advisors to reach out to faculty and stay informed about students' academic situations, which could help them advise students more accurately. If a student's GPA had fallen under the required minimum, for instance, it would be risky to travel out of the country. In other words, though taking additional steps meant more work for the staff, it was valuable to do because it kept the staff more engaged with overseas students. As a result of occasional, passing exchanges between some of the office staff, I learned that they shared Rachel's sentiment; the work culture of these offices in the past meant a lack of technological resources, additional labor and time, and more challenging coordination, but they were still nostalgic for what they saw as more meaningful work. Now, under the hyperscrutiny of the state that emerged after September 11, they were being turned into mere technicians.

In this sense, these advisors imagined themselves as crucial brokers in student-migrants' lives; as caring mediators, they were meant to facilitate the cultural and social transition of overseas students to American cultural and university life. Rachel had worked in the international education field for over twenty years and so, like Sonia, pointed to 9/11 security compliance as a key rupture in their roles on campus. As Rachel put it, "I think the biggest shift post-9/11 was you could no longer allow regulatory issues to sort of take a secondary position as related to the functions of the office. That constant duty to have this reporting relationship with the government." Rachel lamented these changes. She continued, "For those of us who have been in the field for a long time, this work, it's almost like a calling. Really, like a missionary. It's not just a job. Even before SEVIS, there was compliance. But now the office has been stripped down to that level." Rachel's curious evocation of religious connotations—a calling like that of missionaries—is a telling gesture toward the imperialist ideological work of international student offices, which has a long history.

As international education has been forged in the belly of US empire, both complicit in and as reaction to the aggressive campaigns of US global expansion, programming focused on services for overseas students must be understood within this context. As was noted previously, the very emergence of international education as a field occurred in tandem with US foreign policy and geopolitical considerations. Underlying the range of narratives that framed earlier agendas of international education, such as peace, exchange, and understanding, has been a mission to proselytize about the virtues of American power masked by the secular gospel of liberal democratic ideals. In other words, the presence of international education programming on American campuses was a soft power exercise, peddling the benevolent imperialism of the United States. Through sanctioned and sanitized notions of educational exchange and cooperation, international education professionals laid claim over knowing and influencing the experiences of student-migrants. Rachel's reference to the earlier discourse and practices as missionary in design illuminated quite aptly how the crusading mission was to serve an imperialist imagination. Following her metaphor, the advisors' role as pastoral stewards of the salvation embodied by a secular modernity that American education promised had to be done with a nurturing sensitivity to the work of ensuring the cultural and social "adjustment" of overseas students arriving from the Global South. The rhetoric of human touch and a calling mobilized by Sonia and Rachel, as well as Mildred's racial attitudes toward overseas students, were reflective of the evangelical discourse of salvation and notions of racial and cultural superiority on which the image of benevolent US imperialism depended. They may not have recognized it, but they were complicit stewards of American empire.[24]

The staff's attachment to this mode of knowing and managing the student-migrant's presence on campus was part of the turmoil they were now encountering as the office moved toward a surveillance-based model. Other advisors I had spoken with offered vivid analogies of how they were experiencing their compliance responsibilities. Nicki described her role as advisor as directly related to state surveillance:

"Well, really, we end up doing [the government's] dirty work. We're the ones who have to track [overseas students]. But it's hard because, what do we represent? We are not immigration officers. Not police officers. After 9/11, we did act like that though. There are other, new ways the tracking is getting expressed. They're working on it. The students are going to be tracked even better—all the holes, the gaps, they're going to be closed. That circle is going to be closed. It will definitely affect us. We're [the government's] facilitators, right?"

Caught up on the frontlines, or the "dirty work," of post-9/11 governance, Nicki pointed to how the neoliberal logics of efficiency meant more refined, perfected surveillance of the students. She also lamented how this would mean the entire erasure of the staff's roles as cultural brokers and advisors, replaced instead by the bureaucratic policing and enforcement work associated with immigration officers. Another advisor, Terri, shared this frustration with the shift in roles; combined with the overwhelming caseloads, she suggested it was leading to the weak assimilation of student-migrants. Asserting her authoritative knowledge of the student-migrant experience, Terri explained, "Sometimes I'll have a student who comes in here and they've been in or at Riverside for four years, and their English is absolutely atrocious. Atrocious. So there's no steps. It's because of the McDonald's of international students service. You see students come in and come out."

While some of the Visa and Immigration Office staff lamented this shift, others were aggressively working to herald in a new moment of efficiency and surveillance. The tensions this caused were hardly subtle at the office. John, who had taken over the leadership of the office and other international academic programs within the past year, defended his move to demote Rachel and replace her with Jenny as necessary to the new priorities of documentation, efficiency, and elimination of what he considered unnecessary social and cultural services. Jenny, an ambitious young woman with a business background, echoed these priorities; she often described in minute detail the procedural and administrative changes they were making to achieve this goal. For instance, it was with this shift that John and Jenny gutted the international student orientations, cutting them down from a three-day welcoming event to a three-hour information session on visa procedures and processing of students' documents. For John, the longer program was an inefficient use of the staff's time and labor. As he explained, indelicately, "All those staff were sitting there, listening to the orientation for three days. They all had to work for weeks to prepare this orientation, sitting around having sandwiches and talking." This is also why he made the decision to change the name of the office from International Services to Visa and Immigration: "So that I could tell everybody, if this didn't have anything to do with the visa or immigration, leave me and that whole office alone and let them work on what they should be doing. And we sloughed off orientation, graduations, dinners, trips, host families. Sloughed all of that. Which I really don't think are our concern."

Jenny pointed to how this was aligned with Riverside's broader efforts for "shared support services." She was referring to the university-wide effort started in 2010 as a response to the massive budget cuts Riverside faced. Under the direction of the powerful corporate consulting firm, Bain & Company, Riverside announced its intent to implement measures that would streamline its operations, cut costs, and generate new revenue streams with the purpose of a more efficiently run campus. As part of this university-wide restructuring, Bain & Company proposed shared services as a business strategy that would consolidate a group of administrative departments into shared support centers in order to streamline and centralize student support. This turn to corporate tactics to drive efficiency was indicative of the evolving neoliberal ethos at the university in the face of austerity measures. There was strong criticism of this development on campus. The university president admitted in a meeting with the Association for Graduate Students (AGS) that this maneuver would, indeed, involve department closures and job loss. Moreover, it would diminish the specialized student support and services that specific departmental administrative staff were offering. The intentional elimination of the social, cultural, and emotional dimensions the other advisors saw as valuable to their roles echoed this concern.

In addition to this restructuring, John and Jenny were systematizing the transfer of all documentation into electronic format and automating communication with students, measures that Jenny explained were a means to also ensure that students took responsibility for their own tracking, an expectation of post-9/11 regulation. In other words, they had fully embraced the federal mandate on these offices to function as a surveillance hub on campus, linking it directly to more efficient operations of the office itself. This emphasis on efficient bureaucracy, procedure, and even students taking individual responsibility in their tracking is consistent with neoliberal values; in this way, the market-driven shift occurring on campus was working in tandem with the national security state to produce the self-regulation of the office.

The effects of this emphasis were not lost on some of the student-migrants I befriended. Ravi, a graduate student in the electrical engineering program, alluded to how it played out for him on one occasion. Once permitted to enter the country to attend university, students on F-1 visas are responsible for following procedural protocols, including completing pertinent paperwork, paying the SEVIS fee, maintaining a GPA of 3.0 at the graduate level, and enrolling in and completing a full-time course load. Not complying with these requirements can threaten a student's legal status, an issue Ravi faced when he did not have enough time to complete some work for one of his courses his first year, causing him to take an incomplete: "The F-1 status is a pretty tricky thing, maintaining that. So I was told my F-1 status is under siege if I don't get that 'I' cleared. And I was told this very, very late. Even after I got the 'I,' I didn't get an email or something. Few days before my F-1 status would be relegated, they sent me an email that it's under danger, you have to register for extra credits if you want to keep it up." The email came from the department coordinator who, according to Ravi, wrote in "an alarmed tone and didn't even give me the options—she didn't tell me what to do." However innocuous the situation that led to Ravi's incomplete coursework, Ravi did not have the luxury to fall out of the parameters defined by national security legislation. After meeting with various faculty members and Visa and Immigration Office advisors, Ravi eventually sorted out how to save his F-1 status. The whole experience was stressful for him, not only because of the potential consequences of falling out of status but also because of how the Visa and Immigration Office managed it: "Every moment they kept saying this, 'You'll be deported. You'll be deported if you don't do this, that's all.' They just don't look at you as people or something. You're like a record, all right? So unfeelingly, they're like talking like computers. 'So if you're gonna crash, you're just going to have to hit the brakes.' You know? 'There's no way. That's it. You're gonna go to jail!' Like that [*Ravi laughs*]. You get the idea, right?" Ravi was surprised by this reaction since he had more gentle, pleasant exchanges with other advisors at the office previously. The moment the question of losing his legal status arose, the more that gentle face to the office seemed to disappear. The staff's alarmed tone, the lack of compassion, and the "talking like computers" indicated their simultaneous investment in algorithmically *knowing* him while also distancing from him and positioning him as an outsider to the university community, all of which emerged to coincide with the underlying racialized logic of state surveillance—that Ravi, a foreign national arriving on campus through particular racial geographies of the war on terror, came to constitute a national security threat concealed by his purported educational pursuits. He potentially embodied the suspicious activities that, in fact, had led to the establishment of the surveillance measures.

As stringent post-9/11 security measures and their accompanying discourses were carried into the already existing bureaucratic spaces of a public university facing state defunding, a contentious struggle over the meaning, agenda, and managerial practices of international education work at Riverside emerged. The nexus of surveillance and austerity produced a site of neoliberal governance at the office as it made its way toward a leaner and more efficient bureaucracy. The internal tensions that surfaced as a consequence became imagined as an ideological battleground, played out through daily routines, name and position changes, tense emotional exchanges, and, most importantly, through a construction of knowing the student-migrant "other." While the logics of surveillance and the logics of the social and cultural assimilation of overseas students were framed as conflicting discourses within these tensions among the staff and leadership of the office, and ultimately a conflict over the terms of their own professionalization, both logics, indeed, positioned the bureaucracy of the office in service to the US imperialist settler-state. In this way, state power was not only deployed and routinized by the establishment of a centralized database that enabled the denial of any systematic racial profiling through the perceived objectivity of bureaucratic practice; it was also normalized through the tensions occurring in the office, which left intact the need to maintain an authoritative knowledge of student-migrants, though there were differing claims of how to appropriately do so.

These tensions effectively produced an invaluable facade in which surveillance could occur alongside the appearance of the benevolence of "missionaries," the core secular-Christian ethos of US settler-colonial and imperialist expansion, as all still worked to surveil, track, and report, however reluctantly. Student-migrants experienced these two linked faces of the office as a continuation of the seeming whims of bureaucratic power that accompanied the surveillance state as it appeared and intruded into their lives on campus. Serving as the mediating institutional tie between the public campus, the state, and the student-migrant, the office was one facet of the various kinds of ordinary exclusions through which the students made sense of their otherness at the imperial university.[25] I turn next to multiple scenes in which the obligation to remember 9/11 and its aftermath was asserted through ceremonial rituals, marking the terms by which belonging, to the nation and to the campus, can occur.

REMEMBERING TO REMEMBER: SPECTACLES OF POST-9/11 INCLUSION

It was a bright Monday afternoon in September. The campus shuttle lurched to a stop in front of Williams and the front door creaked open. Indian and Chinese students climbed on the shuttle one by one, slumping into open seats. The bus filled up quickly, and the low chatter between friends in multiple languages impregnated the air. I smiled remembering the shuttle driver I befriended over the summer who referred to it as his "international bus." The shuttle bounced past scattered building complexes surrounded by forested areas until it reached the end of its route, turning cautiously into the main campus. Hundreds of small plastic American flags set into the patches of lawn across campus flew low on the ground, indicating something out of the ordinary on an otherwise routine start to the week. The friends I had made among the Indian student-migrants told me later that they had noticed the flags but hardly registered their significance. However, I knew what it meant. The day before had officially marked the tenth anniversary of the 9/11 attacks, and that Monday, the university had elaborate plans to commemorate it. Riverside, like other public universities whose origins were entangled in the ideological and intellectual angst of Cold War politics, was reckoning with its own identity and place in the era of state withdrawal of support and neoliberal globalization. The war on terror became a crucial locus in the emergent global imaginary that, as Isaac Kamola argued, educational institutions play key roles in producing and reproducing.[26] The events Riverside had planned for that day were a telling instantiation of the ways this shift was being marked by and on the campus.

We all filed off the shuttle once it pulled to a stop. The campus was bustling with its usual activity, as students with backpacks swung on their shoulders and books in their hands scurried in different directions, some chatting with friends and classmates, some alone. To give me company, Ani had offered to meet me to attend the 9/11 commemoration and was already waiting for me near the stop. I waved hello, and in response, Ani immediately pointed to a set of white folding chairs that were placed temporarily near the entrance of the main campus buildings, indicating he thought it might have something to do with the ceremony. I followed his gesture and noticed the chairs set in rows in front of a circle of small trees that sat in the center of the driveway. The university called the circle of trees the Memorial Grove, a post-9/11 dedication where each tree had a plaque in front of it with the names of the twenty-one alumni who had lost their lives during the attacks. The establishment of the Memorial Grove was not the campus's only tribute. Riverside's alumni association also donated a tribute named "The Arch." With some time to pass before the ceremony was supposed to begin and without having any real information on its details, Ani and I decided to go visit The Arch. We made our way down the pathway behind the large modern-styled student activities center and found the sculpture set among the trees in one of the campus's wooded areas. There were some people already gathered by it. Two twelve-foot bronze pillars vaguely resembling the World Trade Center stood a few feet apart from one another. The names of the twenty-one alumni were listed along the sides, with vines carved along each pillar reaching above until they entangled in an arch between the two.

Unimpressed, Ani scoffed, "Oh, that's it? I thought it would be a lot bigger." Ani had not known the sculpture existed or that the university was commemorating 9/11 that week. Neither did any of his friends from Williams. This was not especially surprising. The Indian student-migrants I had befriended often seemed estranged from the social and cultural life of the university. The ceremony's organizers signaled the program was about to begin. Whispers passed among some of the younger students present, but most of the crowd performed an appropriately solemn silence. The gathering grew gradually as students trickled in. Ani and I looked across the faces, neither of us recognizing anyone. It seemed none of the South Asian student-migrants were present. Indicating he was unmoved by all of it, Ani leaned in after a few moments and whispered, "This is boring. I'm going to the lab." I remained behind as the program continued with the US national anthem, speeches emphasizing the value of diversity and peace, and a procession led by bagpipe players, family members of the honored alumni, and military guards. The procession ended at the Memorial Grove, where the university community was asked to temporarily cease its activities and observe a moment of silence.

Memorializing events of mass death and loss that involved members of a university's community has become a ritualistic feature of campuses' memorial culture. Following the contemporary shift to public performances of collective mourning and remembrance, which was especially evident in the aftermath of 9/11, the memorializing of 9/11 at Riverside was meant to convey that there was a direct, authentic link between the campus and those events, and that grieving over that loss was occurring; it was also a participation in *remembering* to remember the loss.[27] As Esther Peeren contends, in this lies the element of compulsion, the obligation to "never forget" that accompanies the post-9/11 nationalist discourse.[28] Performing acts of remembering to grieve 9/11 has been necessary to participate in the collective, public memory of US nationhood and reflects one's allegiances and belongingness to the nation. Through such acts of memorialization, the public university institutionalizes remembering 9/11 as an act of patriotism integral to a collective campus spirit. In doing so, it reinforces the exceptionality of American grief, which in turn, is connected to the ways the institution draws its own boundaries of community participation and belonging as it works to assert its relevance in the transition from Cold War politics to the war on terror. At the same time, within that connection, the contradictions of 9/11 remembrance, fundamentally tied to a racial logic, are also disclosed. On the one hand, the compulsion to memorialize the United States' 9/11 encounter with mass death and violence is partly the anxiety of imperialistic decline, the discursive and ritualistic attempt to reassert US power and its importance through sanctioned affective responses. For public institutions like Riverside, the fear of decline and the reassertion of imperialistic power are interlocked with the shifts in the role of traditional sites of public good and the ways they are imagined. Yet, on the other hand, it is in such sites that there is a reluctant reckoning with the kinds of violences that are produced by US empire itself. The programming of the ceremony that afternoon captured this very tension.

To underscore the importance of "diversity and harmony" to the university, individuals representing different faith communities were invited to offer their respective prayers for the families of the alumni, for the university community, and for "world leaders." The last of the prayers came from Nadia, the spiritual chaplain for the university's Muslim Students Association (MSA). Nadia was known to be protective of the students in MSA, playing both a spiritual and maternal figure in their lives.[29] While she also called for peace as the others had, her prayer momentarily reoriented how the campus's collective post-9/11 remembering could occur. Using the institutional platform that sought a multicultural performance of prayer meant to be in service to the sanctioned narrative of US victimhood at the hands of the racialized 9/11 terrorist enemy, Nadia defiantly recalled the Muslim, Arab, and South Asian communities who suffered from the racial violence in the aftermath of 9/11. Her prayer was an indirect call to remember the FBI national tip line that allowed ordinary American citizens to racially profile, surveil, and report on their neighbors,[30] the secret detentions and deportations of thousands of men configured as "terrorist threats,"[31] and the rampant local harassment, physical attacks, public humiliation, vandalization, property damage, and even killings these racialized communities faced.[32] The legacies of post-9/11 policies and the violence that ensued have been formative to the collective national psyche, the effects of which continue to reverberate. It was in this context that Nadia's prayer hung in the air, an uncomfortable insistence that the obligation to "never forget" inherent in the ceremony that morning would have to recall these memories as well. In doing so, it laid bare the angst of the university as a conflicted, contradictory space whose attempts to hold together the (neo)liberal ideology of multicultural harmony with the state-mediated compulsions of 9/11 remembrance were fragile. This unstable and contradictory tethering that renders remembrance as part of the inclusion politics of the campus points to Jasbir Puar's contention that liberal multiculturalism operates fundamentally as a mode of governmentality.[33]

As part of the ten-year anniversary, Riverside was also hosting a national 9/11 exhibit that September. One evening, I was hanging out in the engineering lounge with Ani and Aarti, another friend in Ani's department, when I mentioned the exhibit and my interest in seeing it. Aarti rolled her eyes. "It's a little too much," she complained. "What is?" I asked. With a look of disgust, Aarti continued, "Why does the US make a big deal about it? In India, terrorist attacks happen all the time. Why are they still having such strong reactions about it? Yeah, they lost people but that's three thousand compared to people we lose all the time in situations like this in India." Aarti was an upper-caste Hindu student from Mumbai, a city that has been a site of significant acts of aggression due to long-standing intractable conflict involving India's troubled histories with Pakistan, Kashmir, and anti-Muslim violence within India. The attacks in Mumbai in November 2008 that occurred across multiple days and locations received the most international attention, partly because India's wealthier classes were also targeted this time. The events became known as "India's 9/11," a rhetorical gesture that drew on and imbued India with the urgency of the post-9/11 discourse, effectively reinforcing the geopolitical alignments between India and the United States.[34] While the attacks were framed as the event that revealed India's shared experience with terrorist activities, Aarti suggested that if the struggle around national identity in the modern era included a claim to victimization by Islamist terrorism, then India was the more authentic victim. Echoing a crucial premise of Hindutva's civilizational purity narrative, which constructs the Indian Hindu as the long-suffering victim under constant threat of violence by Muslims both within and surrounding India,[35] Aarti took the position that the claims to victimhood by the US and India were not even comparable.

As Aarti dismissed the United States' assertions to memorialize its own victimhood, Ani, who was always ready to play devil's advocate to provoke his friends, argued with Aarti over the appropriateness of both the American and Indian reactions to "terrorist attacks." The impromptu debate seemed to spark enough curiosity in them that they decided to accompany me to the exhibit. It was being displayed in a relatively new building, the Asian Center, donated by a wealthy Chinese American businessperson. We made our way across campus until we arrived at a large, modern building with elaborate red entranceways. Inside, we were met with high ceilings, winding staircases, elaborate gardens, and indoor fountains. It was the university's largest single donation, which according to the university's own description, was meant for the purposes of promoting "understanding of Asian and Asian American cultures, and their relationship to other cultures."

At the bottom of the black metal staircase was a spacious lobby with black floor tiles and a reflection pool in the center. Hanging above was a large tattered American flag, its image reflected back in the pool below. Present at the site of the attacks on the World Trade Center, the flag was one of the artifacts. The rest of the artifacts were displayed behind glass cases placed along the walls. We were apparently alone on the floor as we slowly walked from artifact to artifact. Building fragments, parts of a gun, rusted keys. The signs indicated that each item had significance because of its presence at "ground zero" the day of the attacks. The exhibit was meant to recall memories and reinvoke the sentimentality tied to 9/11, but Ani and Aarti were unmoved. Both students commented on how trivial and unimpressive the items were. When we came across what may have been more direct features attempting to evoke emotional responses—the panel from a fire truck that responded to the attacks, the "victims board" with notes from family members for loved ones that went missing, the large board with the image of the city and the statue of liberty that was used to prevent commuters from approaching the rubble at one of the train stations—Ani and Aarti remained skeptical. In fact, Aarti found the entire display to be evidence of the point she had made earlier; America was self-absorbed and it overreacts.

The three of us arrived at a large mural hanging on one wall titled *New York Remembers* with bright prints depicting a detailed timeline and various related scenes of 9/11. Aarti looked closer at an image of the destroyed towers in the mural for a few moments, then turned to us and confided matter-of-factly, "Actually, I think it was an inside job." An apparently avid viewer of political documentaries, she had seen several regarding 9/11 and shared some theories from them, including that the US government itself had caused the attacks. Drawing from arguments she heard in the documentaries, she and Ani scrutinized the photo of the World Trade Center and putting their engineering training to work, debated the probability of planes leading to the collapse of the buildings from an engineering perspective. Engaging casually in this theorizing exercise in front of an exhibit dedicated to the commemoration of the attacks, Ani and Aarti reflected how 9/11 hardly registered in their own immediate lives and memories.

Displays of multicultural tolerance, including those seen in commemorative rituals and acts of memorialization performed on 9/11's anniversaries, have become part of the modern, neoliberal landscape of US institutions of higher education. As a public university that has traditionally served as a commuter campus, Riverside's turn to draw in larger numbers of overseas students into fields most pertinent to the United States' position as a global power must be considered in relation to these iterative acts of building national identity and national memory. Though these students and their migratory paths were entangled in the racial geographies and practices of US imperialism tied to the post-9/11 moment, they refused the performances of obligatory remembrance that have become exercises in linking belonging on a modern American campus to the reassertion of American power. Perhaps, such practices were never meant to include these students, but the institutional scenes described here highlight how they figure into the fraught nature of inclusion politics that unfold on liberal American campuses. September 11 worked into these young people's desire to become modern selves through educational migration in conflicted ways. Becoming compliant, racialized subjects obligated to consent to the US surveillance state in exchange for an American education failed to translate to an affective obligation to the US nation, to "remembering to remember" the exceptionality of American suffering and the United States as modern-day terrorism's (read: Islamist) primary victim. That detachment from US nationalist narratives points to how the insistence on partly marking a campus's inclusion practices through acts of 9/11 memorialization contributes to leaving one of its most important student-migrant populations—the desiring migrant subject that is also purportedly desired by the US nation-state—on the margins of the public university.[36] The ideological work of the surveillance state, cultivated through bureaucratic routine, acts of spectacle, and multicultural performativity contributed to creating ambivalent spaces of (un)belonging for Indian student-migrants at Riverside. The next chapter points to housing, work, and policing as three such spaces, the practices of which configure these young people's racial and class location within the political economy of the public university campus.

4 · Inclusion's Exclusions

The sun had set and it was already dark as I hopped off the campus bus in front of Williams Apartments. The Indian and Chinese students who disembarked with me scattered quietly and quickly. I followed the darkened pathway around the buildings to Ani's place. There was more chatter and traffic at Williams late in the evening as students went to visit friends or exercise at the recently established gym in the commons area. I recognized a couple of the Indian women that crossed my path, giggling and speaking Hindi. One carried a cooking pot, the other carried small ziplock bags of spices. They smiled sheepishly at me, explaining quickly that they were on their way to a neighboring friend's apartment to cook and eat together. I nodded and smiled back as they headed in the other direction, their chuppals[1] shuffling against the concrete. It was a common sight; surrounded mostly by other Indian and Asian youth at Williams, students often spent evenings gathering to cook and share Indian meals together. That night, Ani and Arjun decided to do so in Ani's apartment. When I reached the apartment, a couple of young men I had not met yet were at the door, arriving with their own pots and ingredients to cook in Ani's kitchen. The apartment got crowded quickly, and the tiny kitchen was no match for the elaborate South Indian dishes they were planning on making together that night. The young men restrategized, agreeing their preparations would be more efficient if they used separate kitchens instead. The two students who had just arrived picked up their pots again and walked across the outside corridor and knocked on the neighbor's apartment door. The students there were also from the same South Indian state, Tamil Nadu. After a few brief exchanges in Tamil, they disappeared into the apartment with their supplies.

In Ani's apartment, I took a seat on an uncomfortable couch with rigid red cushions. Ani and Arjun were in the kitchen, taking turns tending to a vegetable masala and preparing some white rice they had bought at a local "Indian" grocery store. The store was actually owned by a Pakistani man the Indian youth referred to as "Uncle." Though the store was not too far from the campus, none of the students had access to a car. The Pakistani owner made an arrangement with them. If a student hoping to do "Indian shopping" could coordinate a number of others at Williams, Uncle would come pick them up at Williams, bring them to the store to shop, and drive them back. The system was helpful to both: the Indian migrant youth got food and spices familiar to them, and the Pakistani owner found a steady supply of customers for his business. The arrangement and the reference to the owner as "Uncle" created a unique fictive kinship attachment between them that was unusual in the context of anti-Pakistan sentiment, which would otherwise surface among the Indian students.

Jason's girlfriend, Priyanka, was there that evening too, though Jason was still at work. Wire-rimmed glasses resting on her round face and her straight, long, black hair tied in a low ponytail, she was dramatically pacing the short distance between the kitchen and the sitting area. Not really concerned whether any of us were actually listening, Priyanka was lecturing about organized religion. She impatiently scolded us for not embracing atheism as she had, a noteworthy stance for a Brahmin woman. It was a topic she had gotten especially interested in bringing up with us lately, and the men, both of whom kept their different religious practices private, would mostly respond with indifference or exasperated silence. Tiring herself out from her unheeded warnings about religion, Priyanka collapsed in defeat beside me. Before long, she and I started giggling and teasing the men about the reversal of gender roles unfolding in the room. The men smiled quietly, unwilling to humor us beyond this gesture. Priyanka and I were often the only two women who were part of the gatherings of this otherwise homosocial friend group, and it was usually the men cooking while we chatted and waited to eat. When it was nearing midnight, the other men finally returned to the apartment carrying plates full of fried fish and chicken biryani, the aroma of Indian spices wafting through and soon filling the small apartment. We hungrily filled our plates, found seats on the couch and floor, and devoured the late-night dinner with our hands. Priyanka attempted to take up her cause once again, hoping to find a more interested audience for her stance on atheism, but she was overpowered by the men's preferences to banter about celebrities, crushes, and romance (always presumed to be heterosexual in nature in these spaces), exchanges we enjoyed late into the night as we ate and hung out.

Most of the Indian men had never cooked before arriving at Riverside. Their need to save money and their preference for Indian dishes meant frequent messages and phone calls home to their mothers, who would walk their sons, step by step, through the process of preparing Indian meals. While the act of cooking meals regularly is often gendered as the domain of women and their role in constructing home life, the transitory nature of their position as young, unmarried men living overseas seemed to allow for a suspension of such normative gender ideals.[2] The men became considerably skilled at cooking elaborate Indian meals, which they regularly shared with one another. The longing for the familiarity of home fulfilled by these shared meals[3] allowed for a re-gendering of cooking and preparing meals, even if only tentatively, as a meaningful, collective social practice for the men.

The overwhelming presence of Indian students at the housing complex contributed to these kinds of arrangements among the youth. Many took comfort in being neighbors and roommates with other Indian student-migrants, permitting them to share in expenses and engage collectively in familiar domestic and social practices. Such practices point to the more hidden economic activities that formed part of their social interdependencies built on sharing, reciprocity, and cooperation. Williams's lower rent costs were the main reason Indian migrant youth lived in the housing complex; however, the mutuality enabled by collective living practices among the large numbers of Indian students at Williams also offered some financial and social ease. In the context of regularly holding social gatherings, sharing groceries, cooking and eating together, celebrating Indian festivities on the common grounds, and studying with one another in each other's apartments, Indian migrant youth conveyed a sense of familiarity at the housing complex that helped manage the strangeness of American campus life. As one of the young men said, "It felt like home." This kind of sentiment as part of the migratory experience is not uncommon; searches for belonging in the places migrants land are often formed through nostalgic ideas of a familiar home left behind. Living together at Williams fostered intimate social ties among these youth that helped nurture a sense of a coherent, familiar home grounded in a shared difference.

While the formation of social networks was an important facet of the moral economy of the students' lives as transnational migrant subjects, this chapter attends to how these communal networks emerged in the context of campus encounters that involved segregated dwelling, exploitative labor practices, and racial profiling. As has been noted, the growing presence of overseas students, an effect of the internationalization strategy, has become part of the US higher education marketing campaigns purporting global, multicultural, and inclusive campuses. Yet, this chapter offers a different kind of picture of these students' inclusion, revealing how the class-inflected, racialized stratification of the public university marking their everyday lives worked to contain and regulate their place as Indian middle-class student-migrants on an American campus. As such, these young people had to reckon with and make sense of how these encounters figured into their desire to become modern selves by pursuing an education in the United States.

LIVING APART: INHABITING
THE NEOLIBERAL CAMPUS

Similar to those following other migratory routes, student-migrants formed social networks before they even arrived in the United States. Using social-networking forums, such as Facebook, Indian youth were able to connect with other incoming students and those who had arrived at Riverside previously, who would then help them organize and prepare themselves for their move overseas. Using these networks, some students were able to arrange their flights together and get informal advising on visa procedures, housing, courses, and even instructions on everyday needs like what kind of kitchenware and clothing to carry with them. This advising was mainly offered by Indian student-migrants who were already attending the university, or the newer cohort's "seniors."[4] The seniors would maintain pages online for the incoming classes, fielding questions or making any necessary arrangements. At Riverside, this network of "seniors" and "juniors" mainly occurred under the auspices of the Indian Graduate Student Association (IGSA), which would not only manage the online sites for advising but had also agreed to provide other services. For instance, through IGSA, seniors created and maintained a "library," which was essentially a collection of books located in a specific IGSA officer's home where students could borrow course books that seniors had donated. Further, they organized shuttles to pick up incoming students at the airport, a service that, notably, was previously provided by the international student office (now called the Visa and Immigration Office) but was eliminated more recently with budget cuts. Also, as noted in the previous chapter, the orientations held by the Visa and Immigration Office were now almost entirely focused on tracking and legal procedures; for this reason, IGSA organized their own, alternative orientation for new Indian students to help them adjust to the new country and an American campus. Such practices, both through IGSA and otherwise, exemplified how migrant networks extended into and were activated on campus. Student-migrant networks were critical to navigating and managing everyday living and studying in the United States, and students seemed to especially turn to these relationships in their moments of uncertainty. The acts of sociality, care, and reciprocity that developed organically through these networks illuminated the subversive conditions of obligation and responsibility that formed a moral economy among these migrant youth.

Padma was one of Ani's undergraduate juniors from back home; she was now a first-year graduate student in Ani's department at Riverside. One evening, she had shown up to his apartment to work on an assignment with Ani's suitemate, Roshan. Still, Ani felt responsible for her while she visited and decided to cook for both of us. Prateek, Ani's fourth suitemate, was sitting at the round dining table set outside of the kitchenette. A large steel bowl of raw carrots was on the table in front of him. Not being able to afford food spoiling, Prateek was determined to peel, cut, and cook all of them that night. In the kitchen, bulk packs of cereals and Maggi noodles crowded and wobbled on top of the fridge as Ani pulled out frozen vegetables and other produce. Shutting the fridge door, he opened and closed the cupboards, searching for lentils and spices. Ani made it known to everyone he was craving sambhar[5] but specifically, as he put it, the Kerala-style he recalled from his childhood visits to his father's family home in Tamil Nadu's neighboring state of Kerala. He remembered sambhar being much sweeter in Kerala, and he was determined to find his way to the taste he remembered and longed for that evening. Knowing my family was from Kerala, Ani hoped I could help him recreate the dish from his childhood memories of back home. I called my mother, who was no stranger to my own urgent calls throughout my adulthood for instructions and recipes on Indian dishes. As I relayed to Ani her directions for the sambhar she made regularly throughout her life, both in India and after immigration to the United States, Ani remained unsatisfied. He insisted we were both wrong. Confidently dismissing my mother for her apparent lack of insight into authentic sambhar-making, Ani stopped listening to me and started dumping sugar into the large steam cooker.

Jason walked through the front door, returning from his job at the campus deli. After dropping his bag off in his room, he joined Ani in the kitchen to make another vegetarian dish. Neither of them was vegetarian but meat was expensive, so they limited the meat dishes they prepared. Pots and pans clattered in the kitchen. As the familiar aroma of sambhar spices wafted into the sitting area, Padma shared how nervous she was about an assignment that was due the next day. Though she had come to work with Roshan, who was in the same year, she was hoping to check her answers with Ani, her senior. She was worried about being in an American classroom for the first time. Wanting to make certain she had done the assignment the right way, Padma had already checked her answers with Aarti but wanted to confirm with Ani as well. The seniors laughed and teased her from the kitchen for checking her assignment with everyone. Embarrassed, Padma defended herself, "I can do it on my own. I just don't know if it's what the professor wants exactly." The uncertainty Padma felt was common among the incoming students, and the presence of senior classmates became an important support as the youth adjusted to American classrooms and the expectations that came with them. While classmates in the same batch, or cohort, worked on assignments together, seniors would regularly take time in their schedules to provide informal tutoring to them, and often even directly providing answers to assignments. It was a common and acceptable practice among these students, an expected act of reciprocity and care passed on from one batch to the next.

Yet, this shared practice was quite different from the norms among American students; that difference occasionally led to problems for Indian migrant youth. This was revealed when Arjun, who was a senior to the new Indian students in computer engineering, started regularly giving answers on assignments to a friend group of his juniors. He had a very specific motivation for doing so—he was attempting to win the heart of one of the students in that group, Sweta. Arjun was perpetually falling in love with different Indian women at Williams, and Sweta was his latest unrequited love interest. Though she never expressed any romantic feelings for him, Arjun believed persistence was key, an apparent truth he confided he picked up from Bollywood. It was with this belief that Arjun went especially out of his way to aid Sweta and her entire group of friends as they adjusted to academic life in the United States. This included frequently writing Sweta's assignments for her and staying up all night with her and her classmates to tutor them. Unfortunately, they came to rely on Arjun's assistance to such an extent that for one of their class projects, they submitted identical answers, which Arjun had provided them. The professor of the class immediately realized what they had done, considered it a violation of academic ethical standards, and failed the group of friends. He then posted on their shared online site a warning that if any of the offending students, all of whom were Indian student-migrants, approached him to discuss the matter, he would report them to the disciplinary board. It was an instantiation of how the networks formed among Indian migrant youth that were premised on tacit alliances of mutual assistance confronted American academic expectations, including that most assignments should be produced through individual effort and that doing so was part of assessments of appropriate ethical behavior.

In spite of such instances, the networks formed among the Indian migrant youth at Riverside were crucial to rooting their lives as student-migrants. There is often a distinction drawn between kinship ties and friendships, mainly because the latter is considered more ill-defined and reliant on individual dispositions. Yet, grounding both is a complex blend of affective motivations and the obligation to reciprocate care and favors.[6] The networks that formed among Indian student-migrants slipped between obligations of friend and conational kin, built on gestures of intimacy, deference, and duty. The existence of these networks created a sense of debt that was expected to be repaid from one batch to the next, thus, cohering webs of obligation across spatial and temporal boundaries.

While the moral economy produced through these networks relied partly on existing notions of social duty that circulated transnationally, it must also be situated in the context of institutional practice. The social networks formed among these youth also occurred in the face of collective social estrangement on campus. At the same time that their collective migratory lives on campus generated meanings of home, belonging, and obligation, there also existed a deep sense of exclusion by the institution. Williams Apartments, one of Riverside's two main graduate housing complexes, was set apart at a considerable distance from the campus center, but as mentioned earlier, the rent costs at Williams made it the most affordable option in campus residence available to graduate students. With financial resources that consisted almost entirely of student loans they had received back in India, most of the Indian middle-class migrant youth lived and socialized here. Indeed, Williams was known for its largely Indian and Chinese student-migrant demographic.[7] The apartments had basic amenities. Provided furniture included beds, student desks, living room seating, and a dining table. The kitchen had a refrigerator and stove. Yet, the complex was poorly maintained. There was often flooding, mold, and basic repairs that went unaddressed for long periods of time. Further, though they were apartment units, the arrangements mirrored common American dorm living. Most of the Indian youth lived in two-bedroom, dorm-style apartments, with two students sharing each room, a shared living space and kitchen, and one and a half bathrooms.

Many of the students would complain about or laugh off the conditions of the complex, including the confined space and prolonged lack of privacy. Jason shared how, as an adult, having to share his bedroom with another man was difficult for him. Reflecting on how the arrangement of sharing a bedroom at Williams felt like an extension of his undergraduate experience as a teenager, he said he believed there should be a qualitative difference in what provisions were available to him as an adult in a graduate program. As he explained, "First of all, you're in graduate school, you have a lot of stuff to do. Second of all, the more you grow up I feel like you have more private life. So for all that, I think at least a single room would have been better. Yeah, but unfortunately no." For Jason, the allusion to his "private life" included the difficulties of pursuing sexual interests. Jason was in a romantic and sexual relationship with Priyanka, so he and Ani had to make additional efforts to negotiate the use of the room. Neither would communicate about it explicitly; rather, they would check in with each other regularly regarding their respective whereabouts and schedules. Often, it would be a matter of simply paying attention to and respecting a closed door. While they tried to maintain such efforts, at times things could get strained for the two friends as they negotiated their needs for privacy when their living quarters hardly provided for personal space.

Williams Apartments had a terrible reputation across the university. It was widely accepted on campus that living conditions at the apartment complex were, undoubtedly, substandard. One staff member at the Visa and Immigration Office commented, "You've seen Williams Apartments, right? It's nasty, I wouldn't want to live there." Echoing the sentiment, another of the staff shared, "There are complaints about housing. And, as you can tell—well, I've been over there a couple of times. It's a hellhole." Poor housing conditions and the economic factors that lead to a predominantly Asian student-migrant population at the complex meant that its tenants were effectively segregated. This was an important form of exclusion that was formative to these young people's relationship to the university. Such racialized and classed spatialities not only impacted the possibilities of social interaction but also figured into how Indian migrant youth made sense of the ways they could inhabit the campus.[8]

While students expressed comfort in the social relationships and networks that were fostered at Williams, some students found the segregation palpable. As was discussed in chapter 2, the longing to consume and participate in American youth culture was a significant aspect of how they imagined American campus life and becoming modern migrant figures. Yet not only were the academic departments they entered at Riverside populated predominantly with Asian overseas students—so was their housing. Some of the students were indignant that they were denied the American cultural and social life they believed should have been part of their migratory experience. No one was more vocal about this perceived injustice than Karthik, a second-year engineering master's student who frequently shared commentary on his deferred longings tied to a specific vision of American youth culture. He laid this out clearly one evening.

As we often did in the evenings, a few of us were gathered in Jason and Ani's bedroom. As usual, we perched ourselves on the edges of each of the beds, which were placed up against the walls, set only a few feet across from each other. The white walls were bare, except for a single cal-

endar hanging by Jason's bed, a mild defiance of management rules for-
bidding wall hangings. Two matching faux wood dressers were pressed
up against the walls near the door, with deodorants, aftershave, and other
sundries laying cluttered on top. A small television sat on the dresser on
Jason's side, a hand-me-down given to him by an uncle who had settled
in New York. The two student desks placed at different angles in the back
of the room were mostly neglected except for Ani's backpack sitting on
the accompanying chair. Our conversation meandered from one topic to
the next when Karthik, who had let himself into the friends' unlocked
apartment, walked through the door of the small, confined bedroom.
Both amusement and disdain for our choice of social activity flashed
across his face. Karthik, clean-shaven with a dark complexion and hair
kept short, was a twenty-three-year-old student-migrant from Calcutta,
one of the few students in this friend group who was not Tamilian.

Snickering, Karthik helped himself to a seat on a corner of Jason's
bed and chided us for sitting around doing nothing but talking to each
other. We knew where this mockery was headed. Karthik often alternated between telling exaggerated, entertaining stories about his romantic pursuits and expressing his disappointment with his experience
in the United States. This visit, his focus was on the latter. "You know, I
was offered a very good job after my undergrad," Karthik started. The
other men groaned and shifted in their seats, seemingly readying themselves for Karthik's self-aggrandizing accounts. Ani muttered a mocking, dramatic "ohhh" under his breath that made the other students
smirk. Karthik continued, "Really! It was a good job right after graduation. But I said no because I wanted to see *America*. I wanted to experience *American* culture." The heavy, exaggerated inflection every time
he invoked "America" would be tinted with a shift in his accent, presumably an attempt to mimic an American one. I nodded along while the
other students sat there quietly staring at the walls they were facing, not
clearly indicating if they were listening or not. Encouraged by my un-
divided attention, Karthik vented anyway.

Making a direct connection between this deep disappointment and
living at Williams, Karthik complained, "There's nothing to like about
Williams. Here, it's just Chinese and Indians who stay here. I know a few
of the Americans who stay here. I talk to them. They only stay because
they can't afford it. If they could, they would stay somewhere else. But
you know, they don't want to be around Asians." Karthik did not stop

there. He started listing each of the other housing complexes where he would have been able to live near and with Americans. I interjected, "So why aren't you living in one of those?" Karthik retorted with a grin, "Will you pay for it? Those apartments are too expensive—I can't afford them. I mean, I already pay four hundred dollars for this place. That should be enough." Manu, another friend who was visiting and had mainly stayed quiet through the evening, feigned indignation and joked, "Yeah! You should be able to get the American experience for the four hundred dollars you already pay." We all laughed, amused at what Karthik was suggesting, and what Manu made explicit in his wisecrack. Their commentary on campus housing as a conduit to the "American experience" may seem crude, but it was emblematic of the kinds of calculations of exchange these youth often made about their migratory lives. Proximity to and consumption of American youth sociality were precisely what many of these students believed they were owed by the university in return for the financial costs they had incurred to study and live on an American campus. Their realization that their financial limitations as student-migrants were what prevented them from acquiring a crucial aspect of the desiring that drew them into the transnational educational sphere was reconciled through racial and class terms.

The women I befriended also felt this sense that their housing situation excluded them from American social and cultural life, a consequence of their racial and class positioning. Aarti, the young woman who accompanied me to the 9/11 exhibit, had made this clear one night over chai. Needing a break from a study group at her friends' apartment, Aarti invited me over to her place at Williams. After laboring in the kitchenette for a few minutes, she returned with two cups of steaming chai that faintly smelled of cardamom and ginger. Aarti took a seat next to me on the shabby, stiff living room seating that was identical to the ones in other students' apartments. She shared the dwelling with three other Indian women, and familiar Indian foods, drinks, and practices were part of their space. Yet, echoing Karthik's frustrations, Aarti believed this homogeneity exacerbated a sense of segregation and distancing from Americans. For her, this was directly due to racial and economic linkages and the kinds of difference those linkages produce globally:

> I had a friend who had to live in Jefferson Apartments since there was no place in Williams. I stayed with her for a couple of days

over there just to see how it is. Because the rooms are much bigger, brighter. And there are a lot of facilities included. So, they're
really nice apartments. So, I would have liked to have stayed there
if I could afford it. But I couldn't. And, it was very obvious that there
are people, like, say from European countries. Obviously the euro,
or the pound, they cost more than the dollar. So they can afford
those apartments easily. And there are a lot of Americans because
obviously they can afford the apartments. But when you come to
Williams, it's only Asians.

Though Aarti offered an explanation about their housing realities based
on the supposedly neutral point that there is an obvious difference in
the value of currencies, it translates into an uncomplicated conflation
of class privilege, national origin, and racial difference. What especially
bothered her is her sense that this exclusion of Asian student-migrants
is in direct contradiction to the diversity talk of the university:

That's a little bad because if they really want cultures to merge, they
should have an accommodation for all the graduate students in one
single place. So they can all interact. Why keep Asians separately?
Because these are cheaper apartments, so obviously they know that
we can afford these and not those. So, why? This is the kind of discrimination that I don't like. So, if they really want cultures to come
together, the way they say. Oh, like, "we want everyone to come together and interact." I mean, basically it's the motto of the offices,
and everyone. Why do you keep them separately this way? I don't
know if it's deliberate, but then it's there. It's kind of—maybe not
deliberate but obvious [*Aarti laughs*].

Aarti's uncertainty on whether the university intentionally used housing costs and practices to discriminate against Asian student-migrants
echoed the kinds of sensemaking students conveyed around the uncertainty they experienced with other bureaucratic practices by the state
and the institution, as explored in previous chapters. This understanding was pervasive among the students who immediately connected the
exclusion of housing practices they experienced due to classed differences as part of their racialization, which they often saw as an exclusion
from whiteness in particular. While Aarti alludes to this racial dimen-

sion in her reflection on the European and American presence at Jefferson Apartments, Karthik had made the desire for and exclusion from whiteness even more explicit. He did so by evoking the idea of "real" Americans, a notion I heard other student-migrants use at times as well. For Karthik and others, this realness was not equated with legal citizenship or even an upbringing in the United States. Karthik and some of the other men had made this clear to me when they would, at times, refer to my own inadequacies as an American. Teasing me, Karthik once broke my identity down into percentages: "You are like 30 percent American only. And 70 percent Indian. You are not a real American." At the time, he refused to make it clear what markers he was using for these calculations, dismissing me with a laugh. However, when he was venting about the exclusionary nature of Williams Apartments, this issue of authenticity, of the "real," surfaced again, making it evident that both legal and cultural citizenship were insufficient. Rather, it was whiteness. At one point in that conversation, Karthik had switched from emphasizing his desire to know Americans to *either* Americans or Europeans. I interrupted, "Wait, why Europeans? You said you wanted the American experience." Karthik retorted matter-of-factly, "Yeah, you know, whites. Chinese and Indians are basically the same culture. People who aren't Asian. You know what I mean."

To understand what Karthik meant, these accounts have to be situated within the broader discourse of US raciality and the particular place that the American multicultural campus has in relation to it. In *Immigrant Acts*, Lisa Lowe explains that while the discourse of multiculturalism has provided the foundation for contemporary US nationalism, it also serves to obscure the histories of racial inequality, exploitation, and exclusion that characterize US political and economic processes, both historically and in the present.[9] As Indian migrant youth at Riverside essentially testify to their experience of campus segregation, they also point to the referent of "Asian" difference as part of the racialized spatialities of university life. In naming the absence of whiteness from the physical living spaces that were part of these young people's everyday life, they perceived how the economics of housing functioned to maintain the centrality of whiteness to the authentic American campus experience. In noting this conflation of whiteness and the campus as an institutional space,[10] these students were unsettled when they recognized the ways in which they, the Asian "foreign" students, were held at a distance from it. Some of the men admitted that this exclusion not only prevented access to authentic American living arrangements and leisure activities but also to sexual and romantic encounters with white women, all of which embodied a proximity to the youthful freedoms they imagined were attached to American whiteness. Williams Apartments may have been a dwelling space that enabled the familiarity offered by the social bonds fostered in ethnic enclaves. However, these students were also longing for a different kind of familiarity; they were seeking the familiar imagery of the American good life attached to whiteness that is part of the ideological churnings of US settler colonialism and empire, captured and promised by the global circuits of media, film, the professional elite, and college brochures. For some of the migrant men, it was a lesson offered up by the institution that the channels to US modernity they imagined and desired for themselves were mediated by racial and class lines.

While some of these youth may have justified encounters with state surveillance as an effect of their own migrant status as guests or strangers, they were not as quick to rationalize how the university housing practices placed them on the literal and figurative margins of campus. It is through their discontent around Williams that they recognized and named the contradictory ways in which they were considered by the university. Though they felt they were offered promises of inclusion and engagement in the sociality of the American campus, the university did not meet these obligations to Indian student-migrants. Instead, the subpar living conditions at their place of dwelling and the isolation from the rest of the campus functioned as a ghettoization that racialized the Asian student-migrants who lived there as the university's global "other." Williams, in this way, was a site of institutional practice that illustrated how the experience and meanings of racial and class inequities are inscribed onto the physical and social geography of the campus. The notions of home and selfhood that were produced by Indian student-migrant networks were shaped by such othering practices as well. Next, I explore how these networks were also tied to part-time work, another domain of institutional life students had to navigate. Indian student-migrants were crucial forms of temporary labor for the university, and thus, labor served as an important site of negotiation of their place as student-migrants on a campus that, otherwise, kept them at a distance.

LABORING AS INCLUSION

Arjun sat on Ani's bed, leaning against the wall, shoulders slumped over. I asked what was wrong. It was Sweta again. Arjun and Ani had become especially close over the last few months, their friendship mainly centered on helping Arjun win over Sweta's affections. Arjun had diligently spent all the time he possibly could with her, using the guise that he was helping her, as well as her friends, with their academic work. Still, Arjun confessed that there seemed to be no progress. He looked up at me desperately and said, "You're a girl. What should I do?" I smiled nervously; knowing I was one of the only women who spent time with them, I wanted to offer something. Arjun seemed unwilling to accept Sweta's many subtle hints that she was not, in fact, interested. He was certain that all the time she was allowing him to spend with her and her friends must be a sign she could like him too. I tried to mask my skepticism but failed. Ani leaned forward in his seat, declaring with a mischievous smile, "You have to keep trying. You see in all the romcoms that the girl may not show interest at first, but you have to be persistent." I found the advice troubling, but Arjun nodded along. Both the young men were now determined to ward off my doubts. Arjun noted another possibility for their scheming—preparing Sweta for the coveted part-time job at Riverside's affiliated IT Center that Arjun would soon be leaving.

Securing part-time work on campus was, perhaps, one of the most important aspects of these students' presence on campus. Burdened by significant student loans, borrowing from kinship networks, or having wiped out family savings all added pressure for many of the students to limit, as well as have some autonomy from, the debts they had incurred. The type of part-time work, the supervision, and how much the job paid were some of the key considerations for the youth. The position at the IT Center held a much higher pay than most of the jobs on campus and directly involved work that students in computer engineering were studying. As Sweta's senior and as someone who knew how to navigate the competition for landing the position, Arjun understood how significant it would be if he could secure the position for her and hoped to use it to secure her romantic interest in return.

Though Arjun's agenda was personal and manipulative, seniors regularly provided advice and connections for part-time work to their juniors. This meant that Indian student-migrants often moved through the same circuits of labor on campus, including providing clerical work in the university's administrative offices and facilities, offering assistance in the labs and offices of academic departments and programs, and working in food service with the various vendors in Riverside's food courts, where they were usually receiving minimum wage. Some students would work in more than one place, attempting to supplement their living expenses and, whenever possible, save some money. I spoke with Fred, an administrator at the university staffing office. He began the conversation with more official rhetoric about what the university was offering students. As he put it, they were providing students with "the experience and the income to be able to fulfill what their ambitions are, which is to complete a degree and then move on from there onto their lives." However, Fred soon admitted the absolute necessity of student labor to the campus. Without students working in the various sectors of campus life, the university would have to make hires from outside, which would mean significantly higher labor costs. Fred explained this economic importance: "When students work, they're usually temporary employees who do not have the kinds of perks—fringe benefits is another term that is often used—which can run anywhere between 20 and 50 percent. If you're a government employee, it can run over 50 percent depending on the state. So that's an additional expense, which the taxpayers, if it's a state institution such as this, would have to pay. So it is a cost savings."

Students as temporary workers, then, are a crucial means to keeping labor costs and overall expenses down for the university. Indian student-migrants, in particular, are an important source of cheaper labor for the campus. Not only were these youth strapped with debt and struggling with the high living costs of studying in the New York metropolitan area but, as migrants on F-1 visas, they were subject to restrictive visa regulations. Student-migrants are allowed to work up to twenty hours per week, but they are prohibited from working jobs off campus. Violating these restrictions can have severe consequences, particularly due to the close surveillance required of universities by post-9/11 national security measures. For these reasons, Indian migrant youth were working in a range of part-time jobs throughout the campus. They were cooking, preparing, and serving food, and cleaning up counters and floors in the food courts, deli, and cafés. In offices that were increasingly understaffed, these students were running the errands, filing, entering data, processing paperwork, or aiding other students. And in academic departments, students were conducting lab experiments and research for faculty. In this way, Indian student-migrants were essential to the internal operations and economy of the university campus, both through their tuition and living costs and through their labor. In turn, these students' relationship with work played an integral role in how they made sense of their everyday lives at Riverside.

Students often expressed that earning a pay through part-time work was a valuable experience because it offered some financial independence. It not only allowed them to manage necessary living expenses but also gave them some autonomy to pursue youthful longings for leisure activities. Alleviating some of the guilt of borrowing and relying on their debt, campus jobs allowed these young men to have some money to shop, go dancing, buy alcohol, and give gifts to romantic partners. The students loved traveling to and adventuring in American cities as well. The men would use the savings they had from their jobs to share the cost of renting cars and visit neighboring cities and states, sometimes sleeping in their vehicles to avoid the additional cost of hotel rooms.

Still, some forms of work were more desirable than others, mostly determined by financial considerations. This was usually tied to which jobs had higher pay, though it was not always that straightforward. Ani, for instance, had held numerous jobs before ultimately securing one at the Visa and Immigration Office. One of these was working at the deli in the Student Union, where Jason continued to work. The Visa and Immigration Office position offered the total twenty hours he was permitted to work while classes were in session (going over would jeopardize his visa), and it paid him several dollars an hour more than the deli did. However, Ani was considering cutting down on his hours at the office and working the remaining time allowed at the deli because he could bring leftover food home after closing, saving him money on food expenses.

Many of these youth would attempt to make these kinds of calculations, balancing adhering to visa restrictions, cutting down on living costs, and maintaining their academic responsibilities. The student-migrant networks that formed among them, again, were important here. Youth regularly discussed their respective jobs with each other, sharing their experiences with different places of employment on campus, warning each other of unscrupulous employers, commiserating about their strained financial situations, and recommending their juniors to the positions they held previously, as Arjun wanted to do for Sweta. Guidance from within these networks also figured into the kinds of risks student-migrants would take in relation to the work restrictions on their visa status. If university personnel learn that a student-migrant had violated these restrictions, they could be reported to the Social Security Administration, risking falling out of legal immigration status. Most students understood clearly these limitations, but decisions around taking such risks were determined by their financial circumstances and the advice of other students. Warnings and suggestions regarding work, exploitative practices, and legal considerations circulated freely and informally through word of mouth among the youth, a particularly important collective moral responsibility expected of seniors. I first learned of the exploitative practices occurring at Orchid, an Asian fusion restaurant, in this context of advising.

Ani and I had just climbed off the shuttle in front of Williams Apartments, along with the other Asian students heading home from classes and work. Noticing Ani, one of the other Indian students smiled and waved, and fell into step with us. Vivek, a junior in Ani's department, was preoccupied, sharing with Ani that he needed to find some part-time work. Vivek confided that he was considering working at Orchid because he had heard from others that the owner would allow him to work more than twenty hours. We had reached Ani's apartment building, but Ani stopped, not comfortable leaving Vivek. "Yeah, they do," Ani replied confidently. He then continued with a caution, "But I had a couple of friends who worked there. They told me he cheated them. He'll let you work over the twenty hours by paying you the extra hours in cash. But my friends said that after they worked, when it came time to pay them, he would pay less for those extra hours than what he owed. It happened a few times." Hoping for the extra hours to make the money he needed, disappointment flashed across Vivek's face. After we separated from Vivek, Ani shared with me that his other friends left the job but never asked the owner about the underpayment.

Though the Indian student-migrant networks made the owner's exploitation common knowledge, incoming students still gravitated toward working there. The owner was an Indian man who gave many of the Indian student-migrants jobs almost immediately, which they needed in order to receive their social security numbers. Securing a social security number is critical to navigating the various official aspects of residence in the United States more easily. Arriving on F-1 visas, these migrant youth had to be offered a paid job in order to receive a social security number, and many of the places of work on campus would not give work to F-1 students if they did not already have one. Some of the Indian students concluded that while they may have, at times, been cheated in payment for their labor by the owner, they were certain it was their shared ethnic identity with him that helped them secure the work and vital legal documentation that make life in the United States more tenable.

In this way, the owner had a steady supply of desperate Indian student-migrants to replace anyone who left the restaurant. Holding out the promise of maneuvering around the twenty-hour restriction by not documenting those hours and paying under the table allowed the owner to keep the student-workers in line. Whenever the owner decided not to pay what he promised, students like Ani's friends realized they had no recourse because of the illegal activity and their visa status. Even standing on a sidewalk, Ani felt responsible to caution his junior, Vivek, of these circumstances. Sharing stories, warnings, and strategies regarding work was understood as a vital and immediate obligation within these student-migrant networks, particularly because of the legal ramifications.

Troubling accounts of student-migrants being cheated or exploited for their labor were not uncommon and also occurred within academic departments. This issue surfaced during one of the "drinking parties" held in Williams Apartments, a weekly ritual among the migrant youth. At the start of a weekend, the young men would take turns buying a few bottles of liquor and invite others over to share in an evening of drinking. In their apartment, Jason and Ani moved the bottles finished off from the previous weekend and placed them on a rack sitting in the corner, already burdened by the empty liquor bottles that had accumulated over the months. They smiled proudly at each other, amused at how the rack indicated the large amounts of alcohol they had been consuming. Lights were turned off except for the bright fluorescent overhead lights in the kitchen. Friends trickled in, taking a seat where they could in the living area. Rum or whiskey was poured into disposable cups, passed over to each of the youth chatting mostly in English, while a laptop made its way around the group of friends. As mentioned earlier, unlike many of the other cliques that formed among the migrant youth, this particular friend group was more regionally diverse. Those regional differences would surface as each student demanded a chance at selecting the music playing on the laptop. Throughout the night, a range of music would be played, from Punjabi and Hindi love songs to the latest Tamil film hits interspersed with different genres of American pop music. Each selection would be followed by a berating from the others, teasing about the selection made by the offending youth, and demands for "something better" before the computer would be passed to someone else.

Priyanka and I were usually the only women present, but lately she was not coming over as much. Priyanka had told me that she was starting to believe they only allowed her to be part of their circle because she was in a relationship with Jason. She felt the men neither enjoyed her company nor regarded her feelings and opinions. On many occasions, I had seen how aggressively they would ridicule her. Priyanka managed it well, her sharp wit allowing her to negotiate her difficult position as the only woman present in their social gatherings. She was not one to take teasing passively and would reciprocate in kind, sometimes even instigating the exchanges. Still, at times, the men would gang up on her, mocking her relentlessly, and occasionally cruelly. There may have been myriad reasons for this treatment, including that it was common knowledge that Priyanka was in an ongoing sexual relationship with Jason. While the men may have perceived the US campus as a site of sexual adventuring where sexualized behaviors are not policed or shamed, they were much more ambivalent about Indian women who were sexually active and not necessarily concealing it. Priyanka's presence in the group of men was a regular reminder of the ways she transgressed their double standards.

I was the only woman at this evening's drinking party, and sights turned on me for teasing in Priyanka's absence. The consumption of alcohol served as a badge of masculinity. The more the men drank that night, the more aggressive they acted around me—their teasing becoming unusually abrasive and rude. I became quieter, sorting out how to handle the drunken aggression of their mean-spirited attention, and feeling increasingly self-conscious that I was the sole woman hanging out with a group of men drinking late at night. Perhaps it was partly because of their own ambivalence toward the moral propriety of my solitary presence as an unmarried woman in that space that they deemed it appropriate to treat me to their vitriol. Regardless, such behavior was a reassertion of gendered dynamics that coded these social spaces as masculine by rendering them hostile to non-men.

One of the friends, Dileep, seemed to take special amusement in insulting and combatively questioning me in front of the others. He was a doctoral student in the same department as Ani and Jason. I had only met him a handful of times. He looked tired, helping himself to shot after shot of whiskey, drinking and getting intoxicated quickly. Several of the students asked Dileep whether his situation had improved. He sighed with a faint smile. Playing with the edge of his cup, he looked up and noticed that my attention had turned to him. Breaking with his more aggressive demeanor from just a moment before, Dileep softened his tone with me and explained, "I've been having some trouble with my advisor."

As a doctoral student, Dileep's department offered him funding his first year in the program; his advisor was required to pay him for his work. According to Dileep, however, she neglected to pay him for months. When the advisor finally did pay him retroactively what he was owed, she informed him she no longer had funds to continue to do so but asked him to keep working in her lab. Feeling he had no choice in the matter, Dileep continued to provide her with his unpaid labor while searching for work in another lab that would offer him funding. After several months, he finally landed a funded position in another lab on campus. Though the position in the new lab would require some training and other adjustments since the work was entirely unrelated to his own doctoral research, he was relieved to have secured some pay for his labor. Dileep believed it was a worthwhile compromise since his own advisor disregarded her students' research interests, insisting they work on "the ideas she was curious about only." Some of these tensions between graduate students and faculty advisors can be common within university culture, but the practice of withholding pay while still pressuring a student to provide labor was troubling because it was exploitative. Dileep was uncomfortable approaching the department chair to intervene in the situation. The new lab had asked for a recommendation letter from his advisor; Dileep still needed her support and did not want to make his financial or academic situations worse. He shared in a resigned tone, "I'm trying to get the pay she owes me, but I don't think it'll happen. Anyway, I can't really do anything about it." In reading the

shift Dileep made from displays of masculine aggression to a gentler exchange with me in tandem with his retelling of this exploitative situation
with his advisor, I point to how everyday performances of masculinity
are part of an uneven, fragile project. In moving between an assertion of
masculine dominance over me, the sole woman at the social gathering
that night, and revealing his powerlessness in relation to his location as
a student-migrant and student-worker on campus, I suggest that Dileep
was negotiating his own contested sense of a masculine self.

The other men were listening to our exchange, the details of which
they had heard before. When Dileep described his new lab to me, they
rowdily cheered and shouted "Treat! Treat!" It was the playful demand
that the person who has something to celebrate treat their friends to a
reward. Though it was usually expressed in a lighthearted tone, there
was always an underlying expectation that it was only right to treat one's
friends in light of celebratory news, a duty to reinforce friendship bonds,
share in success, and stave off envy.[11] The men were inebriated and
unrelenting, their loud insistence that Dileep treat them with his first
paycheck at the new lab yet to die down. As treating his friends would
signify a small act of reclaiming his own masculine status, a hint of guilt
flashed across his face, but Dileep finally retorted, "Hey, I haven't been
paid for three months. Let me first take care of my debts." The men collapsed into laughter and boos in response.

Nikhil, the engineering student from Punjab introduced briefly in
chapter 2, shared similar difficulties navigating his life as both a student
and a worker at Riverside. I first met Nikhil in the engineering lounge
one afternoon while Ani and I were passing time waiting for Jason to
finish class and come meet us. The lounge was a strictly student space,
and Indian migrant youth used it regularly to meet up, chat, take breaks
between classes, and, often, watch movies on the flat-screen television
placed near the front of the lounge. Ani flipped through websites online
to a pirated version of a 2001 Mira Nair film named *Monsoon Wedding*,
thinking it was the kind of film that would keep me, his US-raised Indian
friend, entertained while we waited. Focused on the life of a wealthy,
New Delhi–based, Punjabi family and their negotiations of love and obligation, the film was an international hit that became part of a new wave
of cinematic depictions of the Indian transnational elite.

Ani and I settled in as the images flickered on the screen and dramatic dialogue in Hindi filled the empty lounge. We were engrossed in

the film when a young Indian man brusquely opened the front door. It was Nikhil, one of Ani's engineering classmates. Noticing Ani, Nikhil walked in closer, raised his voice over the sounds of the film, and without any real greeting, curtly told Ani that their mutual advisor was looking for him and wanted to speak to him right away. Barely looking at Nikhil, Ani slowly moved forward in his chair, muttered a quiet "okay" under his breath and rushed out to meet her. There seemed to be no love lost between the two men, a tension I will return to shortly. Nikhil stayed behind; he turned and looked at me with some curiosity, smiling as if he was trying to place me. He casually made his way behind the sofa where I was seated, placing his things down on a table. He slid out a stool, its legs scraping against the floor, as he stared at the television screen, attempting to sort out which film I was watching. "Is it too loud? Do you want me to turn it down?" I asked. Nikhil shook his head no but furrowed his brows at me. Having most likely noticed my American accent, he replied, "Do you understand Hindi? Or are you reading along with the subtitles?" I responded with a smile, "No, I definitely need the subtitles!"

We watched the film together for a few minutes, but Nikhil seemed only partly interested. "Where are you from?" he asked. I told him I grew up in New York and that I came to Riverside for my fieldwork. "What about you? Where are you from?" I returned. As we eased into a conversation about our respective backgrounds, Nikhil eagerly and openly shared about himself. Even in that early exchange between us, he expressed a deep angst about his prospects for the future. Gazing at the television as he spoke, where scenes of the easy, lavish Indian transnational life flittered across the screen, Nikhil alluded to his difficulties securing a promising future back in India. As mentioned in chapter 2, he believed attending a university in the United States offered choices he did not have at home. It was in this context that Nikhil diligently negotiated a life on campus as both a student and a worker.

When he and I decided to get some dinner the following week, he shared exactly how much negotiating that balance figured into his time as a student-migrant. Nikhil had been working all day before I met him that evening. In the morning, he worked for his advisor at the lab in his department. In the late afternoon, he started his shift at the library circulation desk. When I saw him in the evening, he was visibly tired. His advisor had offered him ten hours a week to work on a project with her, which he deemed incredibly valuable considering his academic struggles in India. Still, it was a lot. When I asked how he balanced his schedule as a full-time student and holding two jobs, Nikhil flashed me a tired smile. "Actually, I work two other places also," he replied. Apparently, Nikhil also worked shifts at a bakery on campus, as well as at the nearby off-campus Indian restaurant, *Aroma*. I shot him a puzzled look, knowing students on F-1 visas were prohibited from working off campus. Nikhil noticed and quickly clarified, "But it's fine. They pay me in cash and nothing has happened since I've been there." Similar to how Orchid's Indian owner managed student-migrants' legal status, this restaurant also paid Nikhil surreptitiously. Yet, this situation was a lot riskier because the restaurant was not on campus. Nikhil and the staff would negotiate this risk by monitoring which customers walked through the doors. Occasionally, when faculty from the department came into the restaurant, Nikhil would make certain not to go out on the floor: "I'd stay in the kitchen and help there until they leave." It was not the first time Nikhil had worked off campus while on an F-1 visa. He did so when he had first arrived in New York, working in his uncle's small vendor shop in one of the office buildings in Manhattan. And so, Nikhil felt more comfortable with the risk-taking involved than other students. He referred to himself as his family's "most expensive kid." His wish to alleviate the burden of that role was what led him to work several jobs simultaneously, including ones that violated the terms of his visa.

Still, while he spoke of these off-campus jobs casually, he was well aware that it was, in fact, a serious risk he was taking. Nikhil did not get along with the other Indian student-migrants in his department, and he was never invited to the men's drinking parties. In this way, Nikhil navigated campus life without the student-migrant networks described earlier, hoping to build strategic relationships in other ways with potential employers and faculty in order to secure work and academic opportunities. This put him at odds with his peers, who were aware of his extralegal work activities. During one of their drinking parties, some of the men, including Ani, decided to prank Nikhil. Starting an online chat on Facebook, Ani and his friends feigned interest in Nikhil's work experiences, gradually asking him specific, detailed questions that documented the illegal nature of his choice to work off campus. I was at the party, and the students knew I had befriended Nikhil. They showed off the chat exchange, laughing at Nikhil's naivete as he answered their questions honestly. Eventually becoming suspicious and worried as the men started to prompt him to make more explicit confessions, Nikhil attempted to deny ever working at Aroma or engaging in off-campus work.

The possibility of having their visa status revoked, facing deportation and even criminal charges, makes violations of work restrictions on student visas especially serious, as was seen in the Tri-Valley University case. Working off campus was a particularly risky act; while this deterred some students from doing so, others like Nikhil were willing to take the risk. The financial need underlying that willingness, as well as Nikhil's kinship connections involving working-class jobs, such as with his uncle in the city, may also explain the other students' own classed distancing mechanisms. Regardless, Nikhil's choices placed him outside of the moral economy formed among the other Indian migrant youth; not navigating the campus in the same way made Nikhil the target of their ridicule and threats of exposure, and it often positioned him as their competition. His naivete, as well as his desperation to make calculations that proved his autonomy as a man, placed him in vulnerable situations and left him to sort out how to manage legal, academic, and financial issues on his own.

One of those issues included a challenging relationship with his advisor. Nikhil's academic failures back home created anxiety for him. When his advisor offered him paid work in her lab—which is less common for master's students—as well as the promise of a place in the PhD program in the future, Nikhil was grateful. As he explained, "It's like how I do here determines my value there. I've done all right, even though I didn't do well back in India. Here, I am about to start a PhD program next year. I don't want to mess that up. I'm working really hard for my advisor now." His advisor's promises offered him some security in an otherwise precarious professional trajectory. Nikhil owed his advisor. This was why he was immensely cautious when confronted with his advisor's delays in compensating him for his work, which was, apparently, a recurring issue with this particular faculty member. Nikhil reminded her a number of times about the missing pay but worried about the delicate situation. As he put it, "You know, you have to be careful about what you say. I don't want to make her upset or anything. That'll mess things up. But yeah, if she doesn't pay, I probably wouldn't be working as hard as I have been in the lab." Nikhil was surprised and frustrated that the delays were occurring since he believed he had been putting in additional effort, and his

advisor had assured him his work was going well. To guilt her into ending the delays, Nikhil reminded her that the cost of his university health
insurance was tied to his paid work. As he explained to her, "If I have a
gap, then the health insurance goes away." Nikhil also reflected on the
considerable difference in their financial situations, finding it incompre-
hensible that she would repeatedly put him in this position.

Indian migrant youth clearly recognized how exploitative labor practices were part of their relationship to the campus. Still, facing financial
constraints, visa restrictions, and anxieties over their education and professional futures, the students also believed they had to tread carefully.
This is not to suggest that they did not advocate for themselves. While
it may have been delivered in cautious, subtle appeals to supervisors to
consider their financial necessities or by leaving a job entirely, the youth
did make some effort at rectifying such situations. One afternoon, when
I had agreed to meet Ani in his lab, he revealed to me how he attempted
to push the boundaries of this delicate balance.

I walked down the corridors of the second floor of the engineering
building, poorly lit by yellow-hued overhead fluorescent lamps. The
faintest smell of ammonia seemed to hang in the stale air. I turned my
head left and right searching for the small lab among the rooms lining
the old hallways where Ani said he would be waiting. When I finally
reached the room, I found Ani pacing around the counters of the small
space, which was scattered with various instruments and tools. He called
me over to the experiment he was monitoring, attempting to explain its
premise. In his usual self-deprecating manner, he quickly dismissed its
importance and led me to the small adjacent office the students shared
since he still had to wait and observe whether the experiment would
work. As was his playful tendency, Ani made jokes while we waited; one
after another, he made fun of me, his friends, the experiment, and the
state of his education and future job prospects. After some time, however, Ani became uncharacteristically serious as he looked at the keys
he was absentmindedly playing with in his hands. "Jason and I went to
the FSA office again today. They still haven't paid us our raise," Ani admitted, frustration surfacing in his voice.

The Faculty Student Association (FSA) was Riverside's designated
fiscal agent responsible for administering funds for the campus. Jason
and Ani had worked at the university deli for some time but had not received the raise workers are entitled to after working a certain number

of hours each semester. They had both worked at the deli for over a year, and this was the third time they visited the office to ask about the raise they were promised. Ani was getting visibly agitated as he recounted their exchange with the staff in the office that day. "It's that same blond American girl every time we go. Every time, she forgets us until she looks us up in the database and says she remembers our *long names*," Ani said, scoffing as he emphasized those last words. And each time, the woman would tell them the same thing; the missing raise would come in a separate check as a back payment. Yet, Jason and Ani had still not received anything.

The frustration over not being paid what they were owed was compounded by his indignation at the way they were treated at the FSA office. "At least, that's how she handled it the first two times. But today, she was really rude," Ani continued. Forgetting their multiple prior visits to the office, the staff member combatively asked them why they did not come sooner. When they reminded her that they did, she dismissed the point, contending that it was their responsibility to keep returning to the office until they received their checks since it was their pay at stake. In that moment, sensing the woman's disrespect and disregard, Ani lost his temper. Raising his voice, he snapped back at her, "We came three times! How many times do you suggest I come? Why should I keep coming for *your* pay, since it's *your* job?" Overhearing the exchange, another employee tried to intervene and look up their accounts, but the first woman was so incensed by Ani's unexpected reaction she instructed her coworker to not bother in order to put the two Indian migrant men in their place. In response, Ani asked for the employee's name, demanding to speak to the manager to hold her accountable; they were told the manager was not in the office at the time. As Ani narrated this exchange, he relived his anger and his sense of powerlessness. I asked him if he would return later to find the manager. Ani rolled his eyes at me and retorted, "Do you really think I'm going to report her?! No. I just wanted to threaten her. They do have to give us our backpay though." Ani had asked around about the FSA office, gathering from the other student-migrants, as well as the manager responsible for a number of the on-campus vendors, that the FSA had a reputation for poor management of student pay. He worried reporting the employee would only mire him more deeply in the office's bureaucracy, further delaying the raises he and his roommate were owed.

Yet, for these youth, the experiences of work were not a straight-forward matter of negotiating pay owed or other abusive, exploitative labor practices. Students gleaned racialized understandings from their encounters as workers, drawing from colonial and postcolonial constructions of Global South populations. Anxieties around their racial subjectivities often drew from a sense of how they were being classed in Western contexts. This angst surfaced from time to time, ponderings that only appeared in the privacy of student-migrants' relationships with one another. Ani, Jason, and Priyanka shared these reflections one evening at Williams.

I had arrived at the building at the same time Ani returned from the small gym in the commons area. Jason was leaning against the balcony railing of their apartment, quietly smoking a cigarette in the warm autumn air. I waved hello up to him as the two men exchanged some words in Tamil. As we made our way up to their apartment floor, murmurings of Tamil could be heard from one of the young men speaking on the phone behind a door left ajar across the hallway. Jason had already left the balcony and Ani went to wash up. Priyanka arrived shortly afterward, and we waited in the living room, catching up on news from the day. Hearing Priyanka's voice, Jason came out into the living room holding a paper bag. Jason and Priyanka were never a couple to express affection through public displays. Without any other greeting, Jason quietly handed her the paper bag and walked back to his room. Priyanka pulled out a wrapped vegetarian sandwich Jason had made for her at the deli where he worked. It was a small, quiet act of care between the two lovers, one of their subtle indices of affection that could be caught occasionally.

Jason and Ani came and joined us in the sitting room afterward. I asked the two men if there were any updates from the FSA office. Ani smiled and responded to my question with "No, nothing. We are just poor cheap labor to them." The three youth laughed. As student-workers, these youth had to reckon with their racial and class positioning as exploitable, cheap labor for the campus, making sense of how that fit with their own self-fashioning as part of the aspiring, globally mobile, Indian middle class destined for successful, professional futures. How did they reconcile this double location? The three friends shared a sentiment that I heard many others raise. These part-time jobs were their only real engagement with American life and the university community. As Ani noted, "Yeah, everything's not perfect but I still like working. You get to interact with Americans." With a laugh, Jason chimed in: "Yeah, even if they can't always understand you." Like most of the other Indian student-migrants, Jason spoke English fluently. However, when he was serving food at the deli, the customers would regularly ask him to repeat himself because they apparently could not understand him. Jason felt embarrassed by this because it simultaneously highlighted his differ-ence and made him feel incompetent. To make the transactions easier, he felt pressured to alter his accent. As Jason put it, "It was pretty surpris-ing for me, because all you had to change was the way you pronounced the letter *R*. Just polish it a little bit. Fake an accent, they're okay with it."

Sharing an incident of her own, Priyanka echoed the sentiment that such issues were still worth the engagement and inclusion within the university the students were able to experience by serving as workers for the campus. Priyanka had been working part time at the university library, but recently her manager confronted her because she had ex-ceeded the twenty-hour work restriction on her F-1 visa. It was an ac-cident. She exceeded the limit only by a few hours because she covered for some of the other student-workers. Her manager caught the viola-tion and raised the threat of deportation in order to reprimand her for it. He warned Priyanka that if the Department of Homeland Security ques-tioned him, he would not lie. Bothered by the exchange, Priyanka said to us, "Why does it matter if I want to work and need to work? Anyway, like these guys were saying, it's the only time we get to meet real Americans. What does any of that have to do with Homeland Security?" In spite of incidents that would mark their racial difference, or tensions around their legal status as migrants, these youth believed that it was only by providing their labor to the campus that they could be included in the university community and the "America" they had come to experience, a conclusion they reached partly due to segregated housing conditions and studying in departments that lacked significant numbers of domes-tic students.

Still, this was not the only way they reconciled their experiences with work that often involved forms of exploitation. As student-migrants, a sense of the temporariness of their experiences was important to the way they negotiated their own raced and classed positioning. Though these youth worked a range of part-time jobs on the campus, they de-ployed particular ideas about what kinds of work were appropriate for them. For instance, when Sweta had first started at Riverside, she worked a minimum-wage job at the food court on campus. I ran into her on the shuttle one night as she was heading to work the night shift there. We chatted on the way about how she was navigating part-time work on the campus. Sweta did not enjoy the work she was doing serving food—it paid little, and night shifts were especially exhausting with a full-time academic load. Similar to many of the other students, Sweta had not told her parents she was working in food service. While they may have been concerned it would affect her studies, Sweta knew their main source of disapproval would have been because their daughter was engaging in low-wage, service labor; further, as a young, unmarried woman taking on night shifts in this kind of work, Sweta was concerned it would have been perceived by her family as particularly morally unbecoming. The latter issue was not one that Indian men had to consider, pointing to how Indian women's negotiations of work life as student-migrants included a preoccupation with enacting respectable femininity. For this reason, she kept this information from them, hoping it was temporary while she actively searched for, as she put it, a "white-collar" or "office" part-time job, which would have been more acceptable to her parents. Arjun's willingness to work closely with her to secure this more acceptable form of work at the IT center was exactly the opportunity she had hoped for.

While there is a gendered element to Sweta's concerns that led her to keep her work in food service a secret from her family back home, the classed notion of more appropriate campus work was common among the Indian men as well. Ani had not only worked at the deli; he also had served food at the food court. There, he befriended a coworker, a Mexican woman who was not a student and had been hired externally. Throughout their friendship, she would often complain to Ani about Indian students taking jobs. Ani dismissed the idea because, according to him, "These aren't the jobs Indians do." While Ani's coworker regurgitated the reactionary trope of "stealing jobs" often used against migrant labor, Ani was quick to take up existing linkages of racial difference and laboring subjects in response. In doing so, he reasserted the notion that low-wage jobs are associated with *other* racially minoritized populations, not with Indian men like him. Even as he recognized that the institution understands Indian student-migrants as a source of cheap and readily available labor for the operations of the campus, Ani's comment was indicative of the real and perceived middle-class distinctions these students represented, even while working low-wage jobs.

This kind of classed and racial narrative strategy is important to how they made sense of the vulnerabilities they sometimes faced working in these positions. Ani's classist and racial presumptions that Indians are above this form of labor, which they were in fact providing the university, were presumptions widely shared among the Indian overseas students.[12] While such jobs allowed them to manage their financial costs, it was not what they believed they were meant to do. Rather, accepting the conditions of low-wage work was the sacrificing they necessarily had to endure in a temporary, transient present—an offering that would be, in return, rewarded with the successful professional futures they believed they rightfully deserved. In this way, the notion of temporariness that was essential to their aspirational narrative contributed to how these youth organized their lives and carved out neoliberal belongingness on the campus. Importantly, this liminal temporality of educational migration also served as a disciplinary function, marshaling consent that helped perpetuate the dynamics of labor on campus.

As noted previously, the ambiguity that has marked the racialization of South Asians situated them uneasily within existing US racial classification schemes, but always in ways that have been mediated by class. That ambiguity figured into how Indian student-migrants experienced housing and part-time work, as the youth recognized that their shared racial location was shaped by class backgrounds, positioning them as the campus's segregated Asian foreigner or as the migrant "other" providing working-class labor. This racial sensemaking, however, was premised on the notion of being mistaken or misunderstood as something they were not, as was seen by Ani's comments suggesting that Indian middle-class men like him deserved and were destined for a different kind of future. In the next discussion, I consider how the logic of a mistaken identity was especially prevalent in these young people's accounts of security and policing on and near campus, an aspect of university life that tracks the threat of racialized state violence more explicitly into their encounters.

A CASE OF MISTAKEN IDENTITY: POLICING, PROFILING, AND DIFFERENCE

"This place is no good. This India-China. It's no good." Karthik and I had run into each other in the Williams parking lot as he headed to the apartment complex's administration office where he worked part-time. Karthik always seemed to pick up the conversation in the same place, bitterly commenting on Williams Apartments' isolation. As we both leaned against my old borrowed car, a Sikh man in a suit with a turban wrapped neatly on his head walked by us. Karthik lowered his voice, "He's a sardar. He's the only guy I've seen here who still wears the turban. I know so many of these guys who have come here and they stop wearing their turbans. They wore it back home but then they come, they stop wearing it just to fit in. A lot of guys, not just them. They come here and because the hairstyle is different here, they cut their hair. They wear their hair short." Karthik smiled, pointing to his own close-cropped hair as if he stood in for the more proper assimilative presence, a more appropriate Indian masculinity than the racialized Indian masculine difference represented by the turbaned Sikh man who passed us. In Jasbir Puar's reading of the post-9/11 profiling of and racist attacks on Sikh men, which she considers through Sara Ahmed's conceptualization of an affective economy of fear, the contested turbaned body became imbued with a terrorist masculinity in its racially and sexually orientalized resemblances to the figure of the "Muslim terrorist."[13] It is not surprising, then, why Karthik turned his own angst and internalization of the white gaze onto the turbaned man, the embodiment of a failed modern masculinity, particularly as the post-9/11 racial landscape became inscribed on and through the American campus.

"It's just to fit in," Karthik continued matter-of-factly. Though they were kept at a distance from the rest of the university community, and perhaps because of it, assimilation was important to these men, a necessity borne of the longing to perform their proximity to the cultures of whiteness and appropriate hetero-masculinity integral to American campus life. There was another related consideration here: not fitting in always held out the possibility of racial violence or profiling. That possibility as part of their racial sensemaking figured into their paths long before they arrived on an American campus, even as part of the context of sorting out ideal destinations for their education globally. Indian student-migrants' decision-making was informed by how they understood themselves as racialized subjects of Western societies. Their migration served as a channel for a configuration of modern youth subjectivities, and accounting for the stories, media events, and warnings of racial violence against Indian students was part of this configuration. The United Kingdom, Australia, and the United States were the three locations that were most referenced—situated malleably, comparatively, and hierarchically in a global racial imaginary—as the students attempted to make calculations about work opportunities, and the potential for hardship and threat to their own lives. Many of the Indian youth at Riverside expressed that the experiences of racial exclusion and targeted violence that had been reported through transnational networks of relatives, friends, and classmates deemed both the United Kingdom and Australia unwelcoming, hostile places for South Asian student-migrant youth. For this reason, many of the Indian student-migrants indicated they did not seriously consider studying in those countries. In this way, the global competition for student markets generated through internationalization efforts works through a global racial landscape. In light of these kinds of comparisons of the racialized risks of different global sites of Western education, long-existing ideas of US exceptionalism, formed through the imperialist and settler-colonial project of the United States, shaped these young people's educational migratory routes. Similar to earlier periods, the United States is now positioned as the more benevolent, more welcoming, and less racist destination for these youth. However, through their migration, these young people were forced to reckon with the realities of post-9/11 US racialization and how it positioned them on an American campus. Their encounters with the bureaucratic apparatus of the surveillance state helped set the stage for Indian student-migrants' everyday negotiations of their racial otherness in the United States. In addition to housing and part-time labor serving as two key spaces of these negotiations, youth shared that encounters with profiling and policing were also important. As Indian student-migrants described their experiences, they attempted to work out their own responsibility in why they occurred. Moving between ideas of assimilation and questioning why they were exposed to "states of exception," these encounters were crucial moments shaping their racial sensemaking.

Rationalizing racially motivated acts against Indian men by placing responsibility on their own behavior and practices was common among the Indian migrant youth at Riverside. This rationalizing was part of their reflections on their own difference and in what ways choices

around altering racial markers or managing how they comported themselves contributed to their encounters. Such reflections among Indian
student-migrants surfaced when a racially motivated attack against Indians took place in the United States on August 5, 2012. That day, Wade
Michael Page, a US Army veteran and white supremacist, entered a
Sikh gurdwara in Oak Creek, Wisconsin, and started a deadly shooting
rampage, stalking and killing six members and wounding many others.
The national discourse involved all the usual talking points, including questions around gun control, the relevance of mental illness, and
the continued significance of racially motivated hate crimes linked to
a post-9/11 racialization that conflated Muslim, Arab, and South Asian
communities. In fact, the Oak Creek events occurred during a period of
several attacks on mosques throughout the country. Yet, encouraged by
the media, many from the Sikh community sought to define and defend
their otherness as a means to distance themselves from Muslims.

In response to the events, Riverside held a candlelight vigil, once
again bringing together an interfaith coalition to refresh the message
that the institution was dedicated to multicultural unity. Led by the Sikh
Student Association, the event included elders from the local Sikh community. The program began in the Asian Center, the campus's symbolic
site of multiculturalism. In the large open space on the upper floor, older
women dressed in saris and salwar kameezes and men in button-down
shirts and slacks, with long beards and hair wrapped in turbans, were
serving guests plates of warm, home-cooked rice and beans. Young
students stood around chatting in low voices, many of them US-raised
South Asians. Nearby, a young woman was standing behind a table with
brochures, one of which asked, "Who are the Sikhs?" Guests were invited
to share messages on a large white banner, which was already covered
with scrawled notes expressing condolences: "Always in our prayers."
"We all are one." "Love is the answer." And so on. These liberal multicultural framings couched in messages of unity served to camouflage
the intersecting relations of power that underlie the heinous acts of violence they addressed. Reminiscent of the rituals of the 9/11 anniversary
commemoration, young representatives of various faith-based student
organizations were invited to speak, some offering respective prayers.
Following them, the official staff of the university's diversity-mandated
offices condemned the "hate" this most recent spate of racial violence
represented. The speakers' solutions were diversity, tolerance, and ac-

ceptance, faithfully staying close to the administration's core messaging of the "inclusive" campus.

While I came across one undergraduate Indian student-migrant I had befriended, none of the Williams's Indian graduate students I knew were present for the event. A few days later, when I spoke with Ravi about the Oak Creek incident, he conveyed hard and fast lines about who deserved that kind of violent attention. "They had it coming to them. Why wear the turban?" he said to me with disapproval in his voice. Ravi proudly committed himself to what he considered to be "integration." It was for this reason that he intentionally attempted to speak English with an artificial British or American accent. Though the other Indian youth relentlessly ridiculed him for doing so, Ravi felt that to truly navigate the Western world, he had to demonstrate that he was appropriately Western. He extended this conviction in his judgment of the violence perpetrated against Sikhs in Oak Creek.

> You should try to project yourself as harmless and useful as possible to society. I mean, I'm not saying you shouldn't follow your culture or anything, but try to show that we are like you too. The difference is not huge, we have the same aspirations, the same feelings as you. We have to show them that. And you don't show them that by being rigid with your religious system or the clothes that you wear, or anything like that. What I'm saying is don't overtly show off your faith, don't overtly show off that "we are different." Don't give such an impression.

In our exchange, Ravi offered specific integration strategies for Sikhs, insisting that minimizing their difference and meeting their assimilative potential were their responsibility. According to him, it would help prevent others from profiling and enacting violence against them. In this way, though the long-existing assimilation model has been extensively challenged, some of the Indian migrant youth still saw themselves negotiating how to adjust in ways that were acceptable to the white American gaze. Students, such as Ravi, then, returned to the notion of their own obligations to the American nation and its (white) citizens to perform as the "good" migrant subject who can somehow regulate or neutralize their own racial difference through pertinent alterations involving their accents, bodies, hair, and religious markers. Such considerations were an essential dimension of their situated negotiations of that obligation and figured into their ideas of belonging and racialized exclusion as student-migrants from South Asia.

Beyond such exercises in regulating one's difference, Indian students also believed being understood as a racialized threat was simply a matter of a mistaken identity. This was true for students from other South Asian countries as well. For instance, Tariq was a Bangladeshi Muslim doctoral student who was stalked and questioned by the FBI and the Department of Homeland Security on campus. According to the state agents, Tariq was a person of interest in an investigation concerning an attempted bombing. He felt he was targeted both because of the student visa delays he was subjected to and also because his full name included "Mohammed," a signifier that he believed mistakenly connected him to Arab men and, therefore, to a more authentic terrorist threat.

Still, the explanatory logic of being mistaken was especially prevalent in the ways Indian migrant men reconciled their encounters with racial profiling, which for them meant the inseparability of race and religion. While Tariq distanced himself from the terrorist identity by claiming the mistake of being linked to Arabs through his name, the non-Muslim Indian men at Riverside always believed it was because they were mistaken for being Muslim. In the post-9/11 context, non-Muslim populations rushed to offer "accurate" descriptions of their cultural difference that would distinguish them from the more threatening otherness of Muslims.

In her analysis of the "mistaken identity" narrative, Jasbir Puar argues that the being "mistaken for," the translation of resemblance into misrecognition enabled by an affective economy of fear, is not, in fact, an actual mistake; it is the very function and point of racial logic.[14] Even as these youth repeatedly reasserted mistaken identity as their explanatory defense and attempt to distance, they understood the ways they were being racially located through it. As mentioned in the previous chapter, they consistently pointed to facial hair as the most noteworthy attribute that would lead to this confusion. The men would share how their fathers would often implore them to shave their facial hair specifically because it would mark them as Muslim men in the United States and, therefore, as a threat. As described earlier, the assumption that it was only because they were being mistaken as Muslim that they were racially profiled is, in part, tied to the considerable subordination of and collective violence targeting Muslim communities within India, which has always been a feature of the postcolonial landscape of the South Asian region but especially exacerbated in the context of Hindu nationalism's rise in India. As the post-9/11 moment sanctioned a global alignment around the notion of the Muslim terrorist "other," which linked with the existing structural Islamophobia within India, scapegoating Muslims and anti-Muslim stereotypes and bigotry traveled easily with non-Muslim Indian student-migrants. Occasionally, I would hear students referring to Indian Muslims as poor and uneducated, Pakistanis as dangerous and violent, and a conflation of religious practices of different Islamic interpretations with religious fundamentalism. As Saba, an Indian Muslim student-migrant, said to me, "If you're in India and you're an Indian Muslim, you already hear and see things." At the same time, this notion of being misunderstood as Muslim-looking fits into the long-standing resistance to racial categorization within the US-based South Asian diaspora. As Susan Koshy has contended, South Asian immigrant leadership confronting racial violence in earlier periods in the United States initially preferred to frame the incidents as a misunderstanding than to claim South Asians were victims of racism.[15] Both of these considerations are important to understanding the racial sensemaking of Indian non-Muslim migrant men studying abroad, particularly as they faced racial profiling or its potential. Ultimately, they did not necessarily take issue with the conditions of the "state of exception"; rather, they conveyed that they should be an exception to the exception because they were not, in fact, Muslim.

This was true in the accounts given by Rishi, one of my undergraduate friends who shared his multiple experiences with racial profiling, from traveling through airports to being searched and questioned by the campus police. Each time, he believed it was because his facial hair denoted him, mistakenly, as a Muslim. One of those incidents had occurred during final exam period on campus. Long, late nights in the library studying meant little time for anything else. Not having shaved for weeks, Rishi had grown a thick beard, which he believed instantaneously marked him as Muslim and, therefore, as suspicious and a potential terrorist threat. One night, the university police pulled up next to him as he reached the library, stopped him, and demanded to search him and his bag before even asking for his university identification. Profiling is a crucial strategy of surveillance, and as Puar explains, "What is being preempted is not the danger of the known subject but the danger of not-knowing."[16] Policing on public university campuses—the purported bastions of multicultural, liberal inclusion—mobilizes the mechanism of the racial profile, composed visually, affectively, and informationally to surveil, render vulnerable, and control, in the Deleuzian sense, those who embody the difference whose presence was enabled by that inclusion.[17] Deeming it unfair, Rishi was mortified by the incident: "It was really embarrassing. It happened right in front of the library, and everyone could see me because it was finals week. I could see hundred people right there." The spectacle that implicitly invited the public to participate along with the police turned Rishi into a humiliated, racialized object for public consumption. Acts of humiliation meant to emasculate and render the "Muslim-looking" man powerless have been an important mode of sanctioned war-on-terror violence, constructing and normalizing a racialized masculine subject as the perpetual terrorist threat.[18]

On another occasion, Rishi had rented a car and was driving home from the main campus late at night when the campus police stopped him once again. Rishi was surrounded this time: "Two more cop cars come. And I'm in a cage kind of a thing, with three cop cars around me at 2 a.m." Detaining Rishi without giving any cause, the police checked his Indian license and asked him personal questions regarding his plans after graduation and his intentions to leave the United States. Rishi recognized that the questioning was strange and inappropriate, and the situation terrified him. Yet, like so many of the other young Indian men, he still believed there was a personal responsibility that had to be acknowledged: "They're doing their duty. I should have shaved or something if I would have wanted to avoid such a situation, you know?" These kinds of encounters served as moments in which students worked out their own racialization in relation to the national security state through contradictory framings, ways of reconciling that racialization while simultaneously attempting to distance themselves from it through the idea that individual behavioral choices, such as not shaving facial hair, lead to being mistaken for a more authentic racial threat, the Muslim man.

Interestingly, Rishi linked being mistaken for being Muslim because of facial hair to the racial profiling of Black men to suggest that assessing the possibility of violence in a person had to be tied to physical attributes: "There's no other way for him to judge a person without racial profiling.

Like without seeing the color, without doubting the person. Say they may doubt me because I might have a beard. They may doubt a Black guy who is, you know, in bad clothes or something. You'd doubt him. Why? Because, you know, they think that there's something wrong. In this person, in this point of time." Rishi insightfully drew a connection between the profiling and policing of South Asian men and of Black men, whose respective bodies are racialized and gendered as marked by, though in different but interrelated registers, their potentiality for violence. They are both figures circulating in the affective economy of fear.[19] However, rather than evoke the possibilities for alliance with other targeted subjects that can come from shared racial/racist experiences with state violence, a matter that became especially significant with the ushering in of the Black Lives Matter movement, Rishi used the connection to justify the incident. It was indicative of the anti-Black logic of (un)belonging that was reproduced by some of the Indian migrant youth. Distancing himself from the racialization that his own reflections suggested, Rishi contended that it was ultimately a matter of the greater good of security: "They have to maintain security. If they have that doubt, they obviously have to make sure that they're trying to maintain the campus safe."

Though Rishi recognized that bodily markers could lead to other incidents with racial profiling, he defiantly refused to alter choices around his facial hair. As he put it, "I still like to keep facial hair, so I still keep it. I don't really care. If they want to stop me again, then stop me. Ask questions, it's fine with me. I won't change the way I live just because it's a comfort for them." While this stance was partly an exercise in asserting his masculine agency, he also rationalized it with the common trope used to justify the intrusive practices of policing, surveillance, and interrogations: if you had nothing to hide, then ultimately there was no need to worry. In other words, by suggesting that it was really a matter of being *mistaken* as a threat, Indian migrant youth like Rishi could assert they were, in fact, safe when the truth was revealed.

Encountering policing practices was not an uncommon experience for many of the Indian men. Jason and Ani shared one such incident that had occurred the previous night when a friend with a car invited them to accompany him to the local supermarket. After arriving, the three friends had briefly split up and later returned to the car separately. While Jason and Ani waited for their friend to make it back, a police vehicle pulled up behind them and flashed its lights; the officers

approached the students sitting in the parked car to question them. Narrating the story with laughter and jokes, as they did with most things,
the two friends attempted to consider the perspective of the police officers. Jason and Ani were convinced that each minute action and decision they had made had complicated the situation with the officers even
further. For instance, Ani had been wandering the parking lot for a few
minutes in search of the car before he had located it. And, as they waited
for their friend in the parked vehicle, neither of the men was sitting in
the driver's seat. They also had decided to turn on the interior light.
Even Ani's decision to borrow a friend's university identification earlier
in the day to buy something from a campus vending machine became
significant when the police officer ordered to see some form of identification and Ani mistakenly offered his friend's card instead. The young
men also pointed to the ways that differences in cultural conventions
in engaging with police, such as whether to exit a car when an officer
approaches your vehicle, figured into the encounter. Thus, what would
otherwise be innocuous details, they insisted, served to shed more suspicion on them.

Jason noted, "Yeah, they didn't seem happy. They didn't believe what
we were saying. It didn't seem like a normal questioning, more like an
interrogation." Still, the two friends concluded that, to some extent, it
was justified. Drawing on readily available Islamophobic cultural con-
tent, they rationalized that their own personal behavior and appearance
had everything to do with it. Ani explained:

> I had, like, a full-grown beard. He might have thought I was Mus-
> lim. He may have been suspicious because of that. I knew about the
> beard even before that. I knew I was taking a risk at some point. . . .
> Everyone kept saying that. It's not advisable for a brown person to
> have a beard. There's nothing wrong with [what the police did].
> You know, I was kind of acting suspicious. With my beard and flip-
> flops. It's typical, that's how they show in movies. You know, like, a
> person who's planting bombs, he has a big beard and he's walking
> around in flip-flops.

I was confused about the relevance of wearing flip-flops. "It is, you
know, like a *cheap* terrorist," Jason clarified. Ani added, "Yeah, I was acting like a *poor* terrorist." Laughter passed between the two men. Jokes

and laughter intermingled with expressions of distress. Jason reflected, "We were confused, first of all. Like why would they just walk over and do this. And then, I was shocked. And laughing also, but still in a kind of panic. Kind of wrapped up together." I found myself also defaulting to questioning how their own behavior contributed to the situation. "Wait, you weren't laughing while they were there, were you?" I asked incredulously. "No, no!" Jason exclaimed. "Then, my half-eaten donut was in my hand," Jason held up his hand to act out the gesture, mocking the banality of their intentions juxtaposed with the gravity of the encounter with the police. Their exchange of jokes became more absurd. Ani continued, "Yeah, I was giving them a nervous smile too. I mean, I just wanted to prove that I wasn't what he was thinking. I was giving him a smile to be, you know, polite. I just wanted to prove—" Jason finished Ani's sentence, "Prove that he wasn't a terrorist!" Ani responded facetiously, "Yeah, how could this be the face of a criminal? Like, trying to be cocky. So yeah, I think that helped." The men could not stop laughing. Continuing their exercise in considering the police officers' perspective, the men intuited that when the state already presumes someone is a terrorist, all his actions can be read as terrorist activities.

ANI: The entire scenario was like . . . I mean, if you look at it from his point of view, when you think about someone as a terrorist and look at him . . .

JASON: I think it looked like someone is sitting inside a car, planning a blast or something.

ANI: Yeah. [Jason] was showing his hand, waving at me. And, then, I immediately ran to that side. Then, I sat in the back seat and he wasn't sitting in the driver's seat.

JASON: Yeah, then [Ani] turned on the light inside of the car. Because we wanted to take my gun inside it. [*Jason and Ani laugh.*]

ANI: Right, he was taking some bomb out. Thinking about him as a terrorist and me as a terrorist, it's funny for us. That bomb would also not properly go off. [*More laughter from the men.*]

Of course, the jokes and laughter served to ease the anxiety the incident had created for them. At the same time, it also functioned to capture their sentiment that it was absurd to racialize them as terrorist others. Echoing the contentions of some of the other non-Muslim Indian youth, Jason and Ani were convinced it was because they were mistaken for Muslim. According to them, then, it made sense that their own behavior that night unintentionally marked their bodies as both Muslim and "terrorist," both poor and dangerous—different raced and classed tropes they linked together through the portrayals in Indian film they had watched, the insidious influence of Hindu nativist constructions of Muslims that were reinforced by the global discourse of the war on terror. Together, such tropes lent themselves easily to these students' understanding of being constructed as the racialized terrorist subject in the United States as a case of mistaken identity, of being Muslim-looking.

Both Ani and Jason had previously experienced being stopped by the police on the street, but according to them, this situation felt different, creating a realization about their own shifting racialized realities within the US context. As Ani noted, "Now they were looking at you like you were a terrorist. I was in the masses that was being protected earlier [in India]. And, now I feel like I'm on the other side where they're protecting people from me." Jason expounded on Ani's insight, "There is one thing for sure. You will be stopped in the future. This is going to happen, right? You'll be stopped quite more often than an American. Like if he's white, he won't get stopped that much. So that's one thing. I kind of knew that but after this, it's kind of like, this is real. This is how it is." In troubling the framing of Indians in the US diaspora as aligning with whiteness and avoiding Blackness, Koshy has argued that it was more so that Indian migrants arriving from more privileged backgrounds sought "to move unconsciously and unobstructed through the public sphere, as they do in India."[20] Jason's and Ani's comments captured her point. Though these students were not upper-caste, Ani's explicit allusion to how freedom of movement and practices of public safety and protection were intended for him in India reflects how his own relatively privileged location there allowed him to avoid the kinds of targeted state violence to which India's Dalit, Muslim, tribal, and other dispossessed communities are often subjected. Yet, now, in the United States, he perceived how he embodied the potential threat from which others needed protection. While this realization was rationalized by these students on the premise of a mistake, a misrecognition as Muslim men, Jason's comments also revealed their discernment that this was part of their racialization as one of whiteness's "other." To be a part of the US racial landscape would mean accepting the possibility of future and recurring encounters with state surveillance and profiling. As Jason explained, "This is how it is." Students like Rishi, Ani, and Jason adjusted to such lived encounters of being monitored and policed by situating it within the broader discourse of the perpetual risk that the "terrorist" is seen as posing. The image of the Muslim as terrorist circulated both within India and globally, lending itself easily to the construction of racialized masculinities among these men in the post-9/11 era. The experiences were a source of stress and confusion for these young people, but students also framed them as a necessary and justifiable condition, one that they had to accept as student-migrants in the age of terrorism.

CONFRONTING INSTITUTIONAL EXCLUSIONS?

Across their experiences with housing, part-time work, and policing, Indian student-migrants made different kinds of market-type calculations about what they believed the university owed them in return for their financial costs, what kinds of promises were broken, and what their own personal duty was in performing as the desirable, assimilable migrant subject. In this way, the logic of indebtedness, of owing and being owed, that was attached to their desiring for modern selfhood figured into the ways they made sense of campus encounters. At the same time, reconciling those encounters meant reckoning with how the interrelated racial archetypes of Asian foreign other, poor cheap labor, and the terrorist threat configured raced and classed meanings about their place at the university. Mediating the fraught relationship of belonging between these students and the university was the formation of Indian student-migrant networks transnationally and locally, which served as a meaningful co-ethnic web of obligations, care, and reciprocity. The obligation to share was the premise of these networks, signifying an alternative logic of social cohesion to the logics of market exchange; reciprocity among one another was a moral duty that drew Indian student-migrants into a mutual sociality. Still, when students recognized the exclusions involved in their relationship to the university, these networks did not translate into a means of organizing to improve their collective conditions as student-migrants.

While the Visa and Immigration Office made it clear that their role in the students' lives was now almost entirely focused on security compliance, the Association of Graduate Students (AGS), Riverside's graduate

student government, did acknowledge their responsibility to the large
student-migrant populations from India and China, an important part of
Riverside's graduate student body. Beyond offering direct funds for the
Indian Graduate Student Association's social events and providing legal
and tax clinic services, both complex matters for student-migrants, AGS
also had advocacy responsibilities. Though AGS attempted to address
a number of issues that affected student-migrants' lives, such as rent
hikes, insufficient graduate student pay, excessive fees and eliminated
services at the Visa and Immigration Office, and poor maintenance of
Williams Apartments, the representatives indicated that mobilizing
overseas students to improve their living conditions was incredibly challenging. The following exchange was with Mark and Bobby, two of the
executive members:

BOBBY: I think part of the reason there are issues with quality of life
    is because international students would be less vocal to vent those
    changes.
MARK: Yeah, it goes back to what I mentioned about having a really
    hard time mobilizing them. Maybe it's even something that people
    are not necessarily used to doing, you know. Going out and protesting
    and saying that "I'm paying $750 a month. My roof shouldn't have
    mold."

When Ravi shared his thoughts on why Indian students remained less
vocal, his explanation rested on racial difference. As he contended,
"Probably because this place is inhabited by these Indians and Chinese,
they tolerate the pretty poor conditions they have here. They just tolerate it and [the university] gets away with all this. I don't think American
students would just let them do all this and walk on top of them. They
will start suing or doing something." This contention is strange considering that within India, student culture is known to be highly politicized,
and students are often on the frontlines of major political events both
nationally and on their campuses. Ravi's construction of Asian students
as docile, submissive subjects in comparison to the assertive American
student points to how such racialized commonsense framings become
part of how these youth, among the campus's largest student-migrant
populations, reconcile their subpar living conditions.

Without collective mobilizing around issues affecting their lives on campus, these young people were thrown upon their own resources while sorting out their personal responsibility in the exclusions they faced. This reticence must also partly be understood as an effect of middle-class moral sensibilities of sacrifice that were a facet of their migratory paths. Logics of sacrifice hinge on the idea that something must be surrendered or destroyed now for something better to be gained afterward.[21] The relinquishing of wealth, resources, security, comfort, or a meaningful sense of belonging is reworked as a suffering endured in the present with the conviction that better, successful futures awaited these young students in return. This experience of temporary sacrifice or suffering as the campus's global "other" was an extension of the narrative of sacrifice that accompanied their pursuit of an education in the United States. In the context of the flexibility stressed by global capitalism, the notion of temporary sacrifices and suffering serves as a part of the moral calculus of their migration. In the process, such logics help obscure the structures of exclusion and subjugation embedded in institutional practices, a self-disciplining that effectively served the project of neoliberalizing the campus. However, as Hugo Reinert has explained, another key premise of sacrificing is uncertainty, the question whether the sacrifice will yield what was imagined to be its return.[22] The last chapter begins with these students' final days on campus as they approached graduation and faced the possibility of a precarious future on the other side. It is in this moment they must name and confront what it means for their transformation as modern, global subjects when the future they were owed does not arrive as imagined.

5 · The Precarious Path

"Why did they take us then?" Amita asked. The question reflected her frustrations with the lack of job prospects in the United States—jobs that Indian student-migrants assumed would be available with an American education. Before I could reply, Amita nodded and answered her own question, "Because they wanted the money." Graduation had arrived for my group of friends at Riverside. Amita was more fortunate than most of the other Indian student-migrants; her family was wealthy, and she had no student loans. Though she was disappointed to do so, she had given up on her job search in the United States and intended on returning to India to open a business that her parents would financially support. Amita not only had the security of returning to her family's wealth but also, because she was a woman, considerations about her marriage were a more pressing concern for her family—a pertinent issue I return to later in this chapter. The situation was different for Indian men, most of whom not only had accrued financial debt through their migration but also felt burdened by a notion of masculine success that was specifically tied to whether they could remain to work in the United States and return what they owed. Further, how these young men experienced this debt and their relationship to their families back home was intimately tied to the heteropatriarchal norm that men are meant to be providers. However, an endless submission of résumés to various US-based companies yielded endless rejections, mostly due to the students' legal status. The young students were concerned and resentful, wondering why the university would accept them into their graduate programs if the US job market would only reject them afterward. They shared in Amita's realization, recognizing more clearly their significance as purely economic subjects drawn in by the university's internationalization agenda.

As has been noted, most of these students were in departments that had large and growing numbers of overseas students, particularly from Asian countries. The vast majority of Indian overseas students were pursuing their master's degrees, which was a significant development at the university. Since most students in the master's programs were expected to pay their own expenses, Riverside was encouraging departments to raise their master's student enrollments as a means to increase revenue. The university had also begun a tuition sharing policy as incentive for academic departments to grow these enrollments. As the chair of one of the engineering divisions explained, "There's been an explosion in the number of master's students that have come. And that was a conscious decision by the department. In the past, master's students were sort of a burden. You never got anything out of it because in terms of research or anything else—the students did their courses and got out. But the university started this tuition sharing policy, where the fraction of the tuition that you get for the master's students now comes back. And that helps us."

A faculty member in the computer science department elaborated on the economic significance of increasing enrollments of overseas students in master's programs: "Because you know, master's students pay tuition. So they make money. And especially if they keep cutting state funds. They have to compensate it somewhere, some other means. So they found a good avenue. And international tuition is very high, so the university makes a lot of money." In other words, raising overseas-student enrollments in master's programs was a calculated strategy by the institution to generate revenue, particularly in the face of cuts in public funding and financial crisis. Faculty members shared how the economic dimension of this development transformed the composition of their student body, as students were now overwhelmingly arriving from the Asian region and, in particular, India. Faculty across departments expressed conflicted sentiments about the growing presence of Indian student-migrants; while decrying the academic quality of these students, it was also evident to them that the rise in their enrollments had become a necessity for these departments. That need was directly tied to the limited availability of domestic students with the same qualifications in technical professional fields—there are now nationwide efforts to rectify this problem. Mirroring students' own realization of the effects of a market-oriented education, one faculty member in the Mathematics Department shared, "Americans providing education is just basically totally exchange. Education becomes a business."

Though some Indian student-migrants hoped the US educational system would allow them to thrive in ways they felt they could not back home, others struggled to adjust to an academic system that vastly differed from their own. Their main frustrations involved the sense that much of the course instruction and advising in their departments at Riverside did not prepare them adequately for the work they were expected to do. Indian student-migrants also sensed partial treatment by faculty, creating conditions that heightened competition between them and making some feel they were unsupported in their academic ambitions. These youth were especially frustrated with what they felt were faculty advisors' callous disregard for their financial circumstances. As Aarti shared, "This is like the general feeling about all the professors. Like they don't really care about you. Or about you or your family. Or what pain you're going through. They just want their work to be done."

Still, many of the students believed the large numbers of enrollments in their departments from the Asian region were actually a testament to their greater skill, interest, and hard work compared to their American counterparts. When faced with the racialized moral anxieties about stolen jobs by foreigners, these youth often mobilized race and nationality themselves to explain difference in deservingness within these professional industries. As Mital commented, "I think Asians are more analytical than Americans. And I think they're more smart with certain kinds of skills. Maybe that's why the technology sector, it's filled with Asians. People from different cultures have different skills, and if you have the skill, you can really have a payoff attached to it. But if you have really high payoff, in one sense, that could be people feeling that 'oh this guy is really having a very high payoff and I'm not getting it.' Well, maybe that's because he's good at something." Dressed as meritocratic hierarchies and formed through a neoliberal market ethos, these young people's culturalist explanations, which resonate with the prevailing upper-caste constructions of merit discussed earlier, suggested they were naturally owed a place in professional fields in the United States. While such moral calculations underlying their migration shaped their sense of themselves as good migrant subjects, Indian student-migrants were unsettled when the university did not reward it. When graduation neared and most of the students struggled to secure work, this sentiment was amplified.

GRADUATION DAY

It was graduation day. Graduates' family members and loved ones dressed in semiformal attire were scattered throughout the parking lot when Karthik and I arrived. We rushed to the stadium to meet the others as they waited to walk inside for the ceremony. Wanting to defer facing the dismal job market, Karthik had transitioned into the PhD program and would not be graduating that day with his friends. Since most of them did not have any family nearby to attend the ceremony, we went to show the other students support. After finding the group of friends and taking some photos, Karthik and I went inside and watched the ceremony from the balcony. Camera flashes and excited murmurings emerged from the proud family members sitting along the benches on either side of the graduating students dressed in red caps and gowns. As each department was announced, followed by individual student names, the graduates moved down the aisles and up to the stage to receive their degrees. When the computer science students were called, Karthik and I both laughed. Nearly every name announced seemed to be of South Asian origin. Becoming contemplative, Karthik quietly commented, "And every one of them has got a job." He returned to the point several times throughout the program that afternoon, not only reflecting on how computer science students secured work easily, often in high-salaried positions, but also on how it was a starkly different situation for the Indian student-migrants in other fields who faced poor job prospects after graduation. As he shared, "There is no work to show for it. We didn't know that it was like that here. That dot-com was the only booming industry. Who knew it would be like that . . . who knew the sorry state of America?" Karthik insisted that if he had known, he would have made the same choices as his peers pursuing careers in the IT industry.

It had become common knowledge among Indian student-migrants on campus that graduates from fields involving computer software and hardware skills, namely computer science and computer engineering, were essentially guaranteed jobs. Often, these positions offered starting salaries nearing six figures. Navin, who was a first-year student in computer science, secured an internship for the summer like most computer science students. When he shared that the internship position in California was high paying, Navin recounted how his mother teasingly commented on the unfairness that in one month he would be making ten times her monthly salary. The high-paying internship meant that Navin would not have to borrow from his loan to pay for his tuition fees the following semester. He could even cover his younger sister's fees as she started college the following year. Yet, for students in the other departments, including the other branches of engineering, applied mathematics, and business, it had become nearly impossible to find work in one's own field even after graduation, a situation that was exacerbated by the effects of the 2008 economic recession in the United States.

The pressures accompanying Indian student-migrants' graduation were also compounded by the restrictions of their visa status. Students on F-1 visas are given permission to apply for optional practical training (OPT) after graduation, a status that allows them to stay and search for work in their fields in the United States for a period of almost three months. However, employers in most of these fields were often not willing to manage the additional challenges and costs of hiring individuals who were without work (H-1B) visas. New graduates were required to leave the country within ten days if they did not attain employment in their fields once the OPT timer expired. Faculty in these departments recognized these worrying trends, yet the numbers of overseas-student enrollments continued to grow.

Struggling to secure work under these circumstances, students were concerned about the immense uncertainty surrounding their futures. For students who had no wealth or financial support and who were using student loans to finance their educational migration, this was a particularly startling realization. Many of the youth complained that the obstacles of their legal status were discriminatory and unfair. For instance, Ravi, gesturing to the narratives of merit inherent to both the logics of US exceptionalism and to upper-caste Indian claims of castelessness, praised the US government for using the "talent" Indian student-migrants brought from abroad. He believed it was a strategic and reasonable decision since American citizens did not have the skills necessary for those industries; therefore, it should not have been seen as a loss for the United States at all. Extending Ani's raced and classed logic of what kinds of jobs are meant for Indians, Ravi also contended that Indian students had a moral obligation to only accept jobs meant for them: "Indians, we ourselves should have certain morals. We shouldn't be taking the low-skill jobs. Leave the rest of the jobs for American citizens. You are hiring Indian students because you do not find many skilled workers for the jobs we will take. They should have morals for themselves and try not to somehow overcome the restrictions put by immigration and try to work a low-skill job." According to Ravi, then, Indian student-migrants had a duty to fulfill a need for professional labor for the US nation-building project. Yet, that moral obligation also entailed not working so-called lower-skill jobs that Americans could fill themselves. In one breath, Ravi accommodates the anti-immigrant narrative of stolen jobs while rationalizing his own desire to stay and secure work in the United States. Distinguishing the position of the Indian educated class in the global racial-capitalist economy in this way distanced these youth from the implications of anti-immigrant labor policies. This conviction compounded Indian student-migrants' resentment when faced with their struggle to find work after graduation.

COMPETITIVE FRICTIONS AND THE QUESTION OF MARRIAGE

At the same time that the everyday production of masculine becoming was rooted in the friendship bonds between these migrant youth, the months leading to graduation also raised to the surface particular kinds of frictions often grounded in a deeper sense of competitiveness between the men. Who secured a well-paying job during this period served as indicative of who was truly the one to have made the savvy, strategic choices, signifying claims to masculine success. This was, at times, reflected through references to women and the allusion to desirability on the marriage market. In Arjun's case, his ability to secure a well-paying job before he even graduated gave him the confidence that it would raise his profile among Sweta and her friends and could possibly change Sweta's mind about his desirability as a partner. Professional success, he hoped, could secure the romantic success he had been aggressively pursuing.

The place of women in shaping this competitiveness was briefly captured during a cultural event held by the Indian Graduate Student Association (IGSA). It was a celebration welcoming incoming students, or "freshers," at the beginning of the academic year. The party was being held in one of the large ballrooms in the activities center. In the entrance hall, a few Indian students were excitedly preparing for their performances. Young women crowded the bathroom, laughing and talking as they fixed their makeup and rushed to change from street clothes into their formal evening dresses. The ballroom with high ceilings, cream-colored tiled walls, and deep red, gold, and blue panels was decorated with balloons strewn around the room. Trays of Indian dishes were sitting on long tables set along one side, and round tables covered with white tablecloths were laid out across the rest of the floor. Groups of ten to twelve students sat at each while IGSA representatives gathered near the stage to begin introducing the program.

The room was full of hundreds of Indian overseas students mostly dressed formally, the young women wearing extravagant evening dresses and the young men dressed in button-down shirts and jeans or slacks. The freshers, arranged in pairs of men and women, began the event by catwalking through the aisles; some took the activity seriously while others were visibly embarrassed and awkwardly rushed down the aisle arm in arm. The students in the audience mocked and teased them, whistling and clapping. The men at my table were especially rowdy throughout the program, shouting mocking comments to entertain themselves, and laughing loudly at each other's jokes. Several students claimed they only attended the event because IGSA provided dinner, but they were clearly enjoying each other's company, as well as gossiping about which women in the new batch were attractive.

During the event, a few of the students performed a skit, which was almost entirely done in Hindi. In between bouts of laughter, Karthik translated the dialogue for us at the table since the rest of the group of friends did not speak Hindi. In the skit, two men, one studying computer science and the other studying business, were fighting with one another to secure the hand of the same woman. She needed to choose between the two. The two men went back and forth, each trading insults and offering up reasons why he would be the better suitor than the other while the young woman, and the audience, considered each argument. The final blow came from the young man in the computer science field, who argued that while he was guaranteed a profitable job in the software industry, the other suitor, because of his poor choice to study business, would struggle to even find employment after graduation. How could he possibly take care of the woman? The audience of Indian migrant youth erupted into laughter. The skit not only highlighted their shared understanding of the unevenness in opportunity between student-migrants in the IT field and those in other fields, it also mocked the implications it had for their notions of masculinity. It returned to the idea that a testament of their masculine success was about making smart, calculated choices, such as which field would offer high-paying work after graduating with a US-based degree. Further, for these young men, the responsibility in building households was directly tied to their ability to demonstrate their success in securing work overseas in their fields. Not being able to do so suggested they would not be able to take care of their family, or a woman for that matter, and therefore, they would have failed in becoming successful men abroad. The skit displayed how the middle-class narratives of masculine roles in heteropatriarchal family-making, as linked to men's relationship with work, were formative to Indian youth's gendered subjectivities.[1]

Desirability on the marriage market was framed differently for Indian men than it was for the young women at Riverside, indicating the gendered and classed differences in how students and their families negotiated the challenges of finding work after graduation. This is not to say that women did not also feel pressured to find work, especially if they had the burden of loans. Aarti, for instance, had relatives who could not afford to travel or study in the United States, so it was perceived as a significant achievement when she was able to do so. Still, this was only possible because she had used student loans to finance her study overseas. As it was for other students, it was a source of anxiety for Aarti. As she put it, "I was very desperate about this. I wanted to cover the loan that my parents had taken for my education." However, failing to even receive a job interview, which was a common occurrence for student-migrants in the materials science engineering specialization, Aarti was asked by her family to return to India rather than waste any more time or money in the United States. Aarti may have wished to repay the loans to ease the burden on her family, but her family insisted that this should not be the priority for their daughter, pointing to the gendered differences in the moralization of indebtedness and how it articulates with migratory decision-making. Feeling that being a dutiful daughter meant returning back home, Aarti agreed and decided to leave shortly after graduation, which she managed to accomplish one semester earlier than her batchmates.

One winter evening before her departure, I ran into Aarti in the lobby of the student activities center where a small shopping fair was being held for the holidays. Wearing a light jacket over her petite frame, her straight hair laying across her back, she was slowly picking up beauty care items, searching for gifts for her girlfriends and family back home. She asked me to help her since she always had a difficult time finding the right color in makeup. As I walked around the tables visiting the different vendors and helping her choose, we chatted about the dilemmas of internalized inferiority complexes and the obsession with skin color and colorism that plagued both the United States and India, particularly as it manifested in beauty industries, including through the marketing of skin bleaching creams. It was an exchange reflecting a detail that was always relevant in Indian student-migrants' commentary on beauty standards, and which reminded me how an ascendancy to whiteness colonizes even casual consumerist routines and reflections on what constitutes the desirable.

Our conversation eventually shifted to Aarti's feelings around leaving the United States and finally returning home. Aarti indicated that while she would miss the sense of independence she was able to nurture as a single woman studying overseas, she knew that as the only child and daughter, she had obligations to return to be with her family. This was especially important considering she would be expected to marry within a few years. Aarti shared that her mother had discovered her relationship to her boyfriend back home. Since he was not of the same ethnic and caste background, her parents demanded she end the relationship immediately. An appropriate marriage for Aarti was a more urgent preoccupation for them than her career ambitions. Unlike for the men, who were expected to secure a stable and well-paying career within the United States, receiving an American education was seen as sufficient in enhancing a woman's profile for marriage. This was true for many of the young Indian women whose decisions around staying to work in the United States were contingent on these kinds of considerations. Saba, who was graduating from computer science, was excited at the promising job prospects available to her. Her desire to stay and work in the United States was not only to pay off her debts but also because she wanted to advance in her career. Though her parents were supportive of her, Saba explained that relatives and others in her community perceived her career ambitions as selfish and excessive, criticizing her for not planning her future around the more important obligation to marry and have children. In this sense, the role that marriage played in Indian student-migrants' anxieties about their transnational obligations was gendered differently. There existed an expectation that once educated abroad, and even with the accrual of financial debt, unmarried Indian women's primary obligation was ultimately to prioritize family and their own future domestic roles as wives and mothers, creating more ambivalence among Indian women about their decision-making on prolonging their search for professional work after graduation. For students such as Aarti, not being able to secure work immediately in the United States while having financial debt meant her dependency on and obedience to her family. There are resonances here with Radhakrishnan's description of how an idealized Indian womanhood centering women's place in the domestic sphere continued to inform the gendered ambitions among women of the transnational professional class.[2] Indian migrant men at Riverside did not face the same kind of imminent pressure to consider marriage that the women described. Still, the presumed gender norms of the heteropatriarchal family structure also situate educated middle-class masculinities as necessarily tied to men as the natural breadwinners. The expectation of Indian men to demonstrate they could be the primary source of financial support for a household after investing so significantly in an education in the United States by going into financial debt drove their apprehensions about their futures.

FROM CAMPUS TO PRECARIOUS FUTURES: "BODY SHOPPING" STUDENT-MIGRANTS

As graduation approached and passed, students became noticeably more anxious, frustrated, and despondent. In the summer months following graduation, many of the Indian men would sleep late into the afternoon. As one of the students joked, "What's there to stay awake for?" Socializing would often include commiserating about the job search. Even Rohit, who had displayed confidence early on about the job search in the United States, admitted he was feeling discouraged. He had not received any interviews and the search was going poorly. Rohit reminded me, "I need to stay in US and find a job here. If I go back, it could take me ten, fifteen years to pay off my loans. But it doesn't look good." When Ashok, the Riverside student-migrant who had graduated the previous year, shared his continuing struggle for job security, he highlighted the added strain their visa restrictions created. After the end of a drinking party, a few of us drove Ashok home to his off-campus house, which he shared with several other Indian men who were also Riverside graduates from the previous year. Ashok showed us the place before we joined him in his room to chat some more. As was the case for the past several months, the issue of work after graduation was the consuming topic for the young men.

Ashok explained to us that when he had graduated from the biomedical engineering department at Riverside, he had submitted job applications to companies throughout the United States, but he was not offered anything. Ashok's lab advisor allowed him to keep his job in the lab; as a student, it was considered a well-paying position but as a graduate, it was significantly lower than what Ashok expected for his training and education. To make matters worse, the advisor, knowing Ashok was desperate for work after graduating, reduced the already low salary without informing him he would do so. Ashok had started his job search again the following year but still had not heard anything. Connecting his angst about the failed job search with his earlier reflections on young Indian middle-class men's longings for the good life promised by an American education, Ashok commented, "I don't know, we'll see. Going back and doing nothing, that's the worst. When you are not doing it on purpose. Being in America, it's that dream. To go to America, to come study here, live here. Coming here to study, it's the easiest way to come here. Coming after you study and have work experience, it's much harder to do that." When I attempted to commiserate with him about the anxieties around securing work after graduation, Ashok gently chided me, "Yeah, but you don't have to worry about getting deported, right? You don't have to think about that." His worries about job security were not only compounded by the burden of paying off his accumulated student debt but also by his need to find a position that would offer H1-B visas before his OPT status ended; otherwise, Ashok would be forced to leave the country. The other young men listened intently, nodding along in agreement as Ashok shared concerns that had become imminent for all of them.

Similar to Ashok, other Indian student-migrants reported submitting large numbers of applications but not even receiving preliminary interviews for most of them. When they did, they were dismissed as candidates as soon as the employer realized they would have to secure an H-1B visa for them. Ani confided that he lied on some applications, suggesting that he did not require an H-1B visa; those companies called him immediately only to lose interest when Ani clarified his visa situation. Ravi shared that many of the jobs he wished to pursue required security clearances, but because of his F-1 visa status, he was not being considered. He was perplexed by this restriction. Extending his previous comments about the importance of minimizing racial difference through appropriate practices of belonging, Ravi emphasized the value of judging job applicants based on their moral behavior not their legal status. To make this point, he made a direct connection to the compliance with national security regulations demanded of student-migrants. The state, which had been monitoring him for two years, should have seen that he paid his bills on time, had good credit, and never committed any crimes. As Ravi contended, "I projected myself as trustworthy, you know. They have me documented, all right. So even if they give me such sensitive jobs, they can still keep track of me. They have hold over me, so they can always catch me anytime they want." Certain it would deem him a worthy, morally good, migrant figure—Ravi welcomed being *seen* and *known* through state surveillance. However, that sacrifice of personal freedoms always hinged on Ravi's assumption that he would attain his aspirations for professional success and upward mobility. It was a debt he believed he was now owed by the US state in return for fulfilling his obligations to US national interests.

Burdened with financial debt, visa restrictions, and the desperation to secure work in the United States, a route these graduates could consider was entering the IT field through consultancies. Consultancies are mediating agencies that have also been known as "body shopping."[3] Several of the young men struggling to find work were considering this option, which they had learned about from their seniors. Located in the United States, consultancies function as recruiting agencies seeking out recent graduates in STEM fields from American academic institutions. These agencies, then, train them in specific software programs and place them to work on projects for companies with which the agencies have contracts. As the intermediary party, the consultancies take a significant portion of any income their workers receive. In his work, Xiang Biao has detailed the significance and exploitative nature of body-shopping practices.[4] Biao argues that these practices thrive on the narrative of skilled-labor shortages in the IT industry, a narrative that encourages an inundation of a readily available and temporary labor supply. The increased efforts to internationalize higher education are facilitating this necessary condition by generating a large source of indebted STEM graduates desperate to stay in the United States and work. Exploiting and profiting from these circumstances, body-shopping agencies are becoming a burgeoning business. Riverside student-migrants explained that they would not even need to contact consultancies; through online professional networking sites, the consultancies, typically operated by other Indian nationals, would know when students would be finished with their academic program and approached them as they neared graduation. Conditions for consultancies were known to vary, but among Indian student-migrants, these agencies had a reputation for being exploitative. The initial living conditions were often difficult. The consultancies had to train the graduates since many of the students did not have a background in software, and during the training periods, which could last a few months or until the graduates were placed on a project, they would house three or four graduates in one apartment and give them a per diem for food, which could be around ten to fifteen dollars. Students reported that often consultancies would rework graduates' résumés in order to reflect experience using the required software, which they did not actually have. Of course, this had the potential of putting these migrants on temporary visas in vulnerable positions, illuminating how logics of indebtedness, gendered aspirations, and migration policy regimes worked in tandem to discipline these youth for conditions of precarity.

In recent years, scholarship analyzing neoliberal capitalism has pointed to the concept of precarity to describe the growing collective experience of uncertainty defining political, social, and economic life.[5] As part of the economic restructuring of late-stage capitalism, the experience and sensibilities of precarity are specifically tied to the conditions of labor in a period characterized by flexible accumulation and casual and temporary forms of work. As the commitments of the Fordist era are disappearing, there are growing pressures to enter unguaranteed, "flexible" labor arrangements, leaving larger segments of the world's populations vulnerable to a life marked by uncertain and unsupported futures,

including for the relatively privileged middle classes. While some scholars have argued that this shift is producing a new class category of its
own, others have contended that such hasty formulations disregard the
ways that instability and uncertainty have always marked the working
lives of poorer populations, particularly in Global South contexts.[6] However, as Brett Nielsen and Ned Rossiter have argued, acknowledging this
unevenness in the material experience of precarity should include attention to the articulations across those differences.[7]

As large numbers of the Indian middle-class youth that arrived on
American campuses and paid for a professional education were prevented from staying and securing stable work in their fields, they were
being redirected to enter a pool of casual and exploitable labor for the
global knowledge economy with the promise to remain in the country
to repay their debts. In other words, entangled precariously in the linkages between a global education that indebted them and labor markets,
these middle-class migrant youth served as an invaluable source of indentured, lower-skilled labor for the IT industry. Placed on the margins
of the knowledge professional class, then, the students who felt pressured to take the option of consultancies faced a direct reckoning with a
different kind of life offered by an American education than the one they
imagined they deserved. This was particularly unsettling, as any suffering or sacrifices they felt they had already endured as student-migrants
were bearable precisely because of the better, secure, upwardly mobile
futures promised by entry into the transnational professional class after graduation. Instead, limited options and legally imposed timelines
threatened to short-circuit their aspirations. Being positioned as indebted migrant subjects meant confronting the realization that what
awaited them beyond graduation was more likely the precarious bar-
gains required of neoliberal modernity.

Some students were willing to take the route of body shopping if
necessary, but most did not want to do so. This reluctance was not only
because of the difficult working conditions of these consultancies but
also because students who were in other fields had no interest in doing
software work. As Jason explained:

> There are these consultancies. You've heard about them, right? It
> doesn't matter what you did for the last twenty-four, twenty-five
> years. They take you, and they train you in some computer lan-

guage. And then they push you in some computer industry and then you earn. I feel like it's not fair. If I'm in materials science right now, there's a reason I didn't take computer science, right? I feel like it's losing your purpose. I spent six to seven years studying something else, and then you get trained in totally different area for three months. I don't know if I can do that for the rest of my life.

This discontent about turning to software work was tied to many of the young men's sense of a loss of freedom of choice, a freedom they believed would be provided by their educational migration. The students were unhappy about being funneled into basic software work, something they had no interest in and would mean unstable and exploitative working conditions. However, it also deepened the resentment among some of the youth that, as Indian men, their racialized location in the global economy was forcing them into the IT industry, despite their educational choices and training at an American educational institution.

Student-migrants' financial debts were not their only consideration here. Ani noted that friends and family back home were pressuring him to learn software programming and consider working through a consultancy in case he could not find a job in his own field. He would often joke "yeah, yeah, computers, computers" as his characteristically understated commentary on that pressure. Echoing Jason's sentiments, Ani had no interest or substantial skill in computer-related fields; more importantly, he believed that taking a job with a consultancy was perceived as a last resort and therefore would be shameful to do. On the other hand, returning to India with debts unpaid would have been even more mortifying for him. In exploring the affective imaginaries that have emerged with neoliberal restructuring, Lauren Berlant contends, "Shame is the trace of disavowed class anxiety, the darker side of aspiration's optimism."[8] During one of our late-night group walks across campus to grab snacks, Ani and I were trailing behind the others when he shared that he had a difficult conversation with his mother in a phone call earlier that day. Upset about an exchange she had with her wealthy sister, Ani's mother pleaded with him to remain in the United States to work, regardless of the nature of the job, including if it was managed by a consultancy. The financial hopes his mother had pinned to his migration and the gendered expectation that sons should become providers loomed over Ani as he reached the final days of his American education.

Having her only son return from the States as an educated, indebted, and unemployed man, especially when facing her wealthier relatives, was unbearable for Ani's mother. Parents' sacrifices are often imagined as a nurturing part of their affective bonds with their children, a type of relationship that exists outside of the logic of market exchange. Still, the expectation of return for those sacrifices is crucial to these students' migration narratives and their sense of themselves as successful men. As Moshe Halbertal argues, "Like all such attempts it is in constant danger of collapsing into a market exchange, especially when it is constituted, as an offering, as part of a hierarchical order of dependency."[9] Ani's mother's request invoked the debt Ani felt he owed in exchange for his parents' sacrifices, sacrifices that helped ensure his migration in the first place and were meant to enable the transformative process of modern becoming for Ani and his family. In a sense, his mother had called that afternoon to suggest Ani, as a son, had sacrifices to make in return; not doing so would mean his migration, and their collective class story, would be marked as a failure in masculinity. While Ani and his friends may have felt shame in not realizing a sense of successful modern manhood on their own, individual terms, the material and affective debts structuring their migratory paths determined how these students' futures would be bound to both home and the United States.

One afternoon, a few of us went on an outing to a town in the neighboring county where there was a growing Indian community; with an increasing number of Indian businesses and restaurants emerging, the town was becoming known as a "Little India." In the midst of their despondency, the young Indian men wanted to go to the area and have some traditional south Indian food. We headed to one of the many dosa[10] houses that had emerged there and that the youth had heard had good South Indian cuisine. At the restaurant, the group excitedly ate from the elaborate buffet of South Indian dishes, such as vada, sambhar, and masala dosas—foods they had not eaten in a while and for which they were feeling especially nostalgic those days. Bellies full, we drove to a nearby beach to walk on the boardwalk in the warm weather. The contentment of the afternoon lunch gradually wore off, and the young men returned to exchanging worries about their search for work and the lack of responses from employers. The issue of the time restrictions placed on OPT was a primary concern. As noted, if students did not find work in a relevant field within the first three months after graduation, they had exactly ten days to leave the country. The group of friends started questioning and debating whether and under what circumstances authorities would discover that they had not complied. It was a risky question that started hypothetically but had an undercurrent of serious consideration, playing with the legality of their movements, optimistic that more time would save them. Dileep, the PhD student who had difficulties with his advisor, cautioned the juniors, reminding them of another senior student who overstayed her visa after graduation, got deported, and was prohibited from returning to the United States.

During our conversation at the beach, Mital asked me about my own university's business school, the Wharton School of Business. Mital had heard that all the Indian student-migrants who attended Wharton were from wealthy families, the children of big businessmen and government officials. He asked if everyone I knew at my university was wealthy, especially compared to our group of friends at Riverside. That summer, the young men had become especially reflective about class differences and how they contributed to constructing life chances. I asked Mital about his job search. He was worried but attempting to stay optimistic. Seemingly reassuring both of us, Mital said, "Back in India, we guys are used to that kind of a culture. If we have a problem, we just go and face it." As Berlant has argued, the desperate attachments to the fantasy of a good life that is becoming increasingly unattainable, including for previously privileged classes, are precisely what makes it a *cruel* optimism.[11] Mital rewrites these affective shifts accompanying the growing precarity of middle-classness they were encountering as Indian migrants by specifically tying his optimism as inherent to the masculine sensibilities of young, Indian middle-class men who not only are resilient in the face of obstacles but are also destined to overcome them. Still, Mital appeared to want to work out how he ended up with expectations that were not met: "I always had the feeling that guys out there, they're doing something awesome. But the expectation, it was imaginary. I thought it had something to do with America, one of the nations that really make money out of education. I thought it was something even better. But it wasn't clearly so. It's like, flying in the sky. Even if you go to the moon, the sky will be higher than the moon. From here, you don't know which one is higher. But that's the thing with imagination, right?" Mital's choice of wording, "make money out of education," unwittingly captured a double meaning—both the idea of the United States profiting

from young migrants' educational consumption, as well as Mital imagining that one can make money by receiving an American education.
Echoing Ani's metaphoric use of the moon as "America" shared in the
beginning of this book, Mital expressed the disillusionment that accompanies this fantasy. It was only after his time in the United States that he
realized arriving on the moon was not enough; the kinds of desires for
becoming successful, globally mobile, modern men that they held were
perhaps more than what was possible.

Fundamentally about their hopes for upward mobility, the young
men's disappointing job search that summer often brought to the surface these sorts of reflections. When some of the men gathered to watch
a New York Knicks basketball game on television in Ani and Jason's room
one evening, the allure of wealth and mobility surfaced as a topic again.
As they watched the game, they commented in Tamil about the various
players and strategies. Attention soon turned to a basketball player who
was in a highly publicized relationship with the wealthy celebutante and
reality television star Kim Kardashian. When Jason admitted that he
enjoyed watching *Keeping Up with the Kardashians*, Arjun berated him.
"How do people like that stuff?" he asked in disgust. Wearing a lungi[12]
and resting his back against the wall, Jason sat up and defended himself,
"They're glamorous, it's fun to see. I like seeing all the places they go.
The best hotels, restaurants, places. I wouldn't see those places otherwise." I asked Jason if he thought he could eventually attain that kind
of upward mobility and wealth after studying in the United States. Mo-
tioning with his hand and drawing a circle in the air, Jason responded
matter-of-factly, "It's circular. You just go back around to where you
were before. Maybe slightly higher. Unless you're in computer science.
Then, you can stay and get a job." His own comments making him reflective, Jason continued after a moment, "Do Americans think all Indians are poor? You know this movie, *Slumdog Millionaire*? I think now
Americans think all Indians live in slums." Jason explained he started
feeling this was the case when a white American classmate asked him
if India had microwaves, cell phones, or the internet. Jason's transition
from contemplating his own class stagnation as a middle-class student
who migrated to the United States for an education to a film that portrayed urban poverty in contemporary India was significant. The contentious reception of the film among Indians, a film directed by a white
British filmmaker and showcased to Western audiences, illustrated how

struggles over representation of the authentic India are worked out on the lives, experiences, and images of the economically dispossessed. Situated in this context, Jason's comments are reflective of the collective Indian middle-class anxieties about Indian modernity that are produced at the nexus of a colonial past, a neoliberal present, and a racial-capitalist United States. Despite these young people's reticence to assert explicitly any sense of obligation to the Indian nation, Jason's reflections were indicative of how these men's notions of masculine success, or failure, were entangled in a preoccupation with India's own success as a modern nation. His resentment of the film for reinforcing an imagery of India as an impoverished country, which he perceived as implicating his life as an educated migrant in the United States, was enmeshed in his own raced and classed insecurities that the promises of Indian modern selfhood imagined to be attached to an American degree would not materialize.

I end with young Indian men's open-ended ruminations and angst about failure as it is precisely what characterized the finals days of their encounters with the internationalizing university as student-migrants. After all, graduation marks the official moment the university is no longer expected to hold any responsibility in its exchange with its overseas students, despite the ways in which the institutional project to internationalize contributes to the conditions of precarity many of the youth faced. Educational migration may have proffered the unobstructed success and security of entering the Indian transnational professional class for some, but most of the Indian middle-class migrant youth at Riverside had to reckon with more uncertain, indebted, and precarious futures, including by becoming flexible, compliant workers for the global knowledge economy.

Epilogue · The American Dream and Its Others

In a moment when "going global," the mantra accompanying the turn to internationalize campuses, is ubiquitously accepted as an essential, universally beneficial, and modern facet of university life, this book is an attempt to consider the particular material conditions and affective imaginaries shaping the lifeworlds of Indian middle-class migrants, central figures of the internationalizing university. As the desire to become modern "men of the world" drew these student-migrants into the transnational educational sphere, the collusion of the state, the neoliberal market, and the educational institution located these young people ambivalently across national borders and onto the American campus. If universities have been important sites in producing the imaginary of the "global," as Isaac Kamola argues, then this book points to the ways that the transnational lives of Indian student-migrants serve as dynamic nodes in this production.[1] Even as the rhetoric of crisis pervades the discourse of the future of US higher education, the narrative of US exceptionalism persists in the global educational imaginaries of Indian migrant youth. Undoubtedly, the US university is a setting that continues to be important to peddling the American Dream as a compelling one. Still, as the exorbitant rise in tuition costs, trillions of dollars in student debt in the United States, and a growing dependence on precarious, contingent labor on American campuses become mainstreamed issues in US political discourse, debate, and protest, the notion that an American degree will offer a better, upwardly mobile, secure future is coming undone for many in the US citizenry.

It is precisely in this moment, then, that marketing the US degree to middle-class youth from the postcolonial nations of the Global South serves as not only an effective strategy in generating revenue for educational institutions and the US economy—it is also meaningful because it draws in student populations whose strivings still hinge on the ideological premises of US global hegemony. For Indian student migration, such strivings have a longer history; as chapter 1 contended, educational migratory circuitries linked the desire for Indian modernity that has been a part of the postcolonial project of India to the development of US higher education, which was a crucial feature of US settler-colonial and imperialist expansion. With the emergence of the internationalizing university in the context of neoliberal globalization, the United States continued to be positioned as an idealized site of possibility for modern selfhood among the Indian middle-class migrant men I befriended at Riverside. This desiring for a modern becoming was a productive force animating the migratory lives of these youth, but I have argued that such desiring works in tandem with a logic of indebtedness. While earlier periods may have centered the nation-state and national development in that logic, I have pointed to how the sense of owing and being owed among Indian student-migrants in the contemporary moment was forged through material, moral, and affective obligations produced by the global education market and kinship ties.

This was not to suggest that nation-state interests are irrelevant to the educational migratory routes of these youth today. Though these young people may have wished to detach themselves and their futures from any real obligation to the Indian nation, such self-fashioning is filtered through a framing of modern Indian masculinities that is still in service to a liberalized Indian state. Further, I have illustrated how the consolidation of the post-9/11 surveillance state played a role in the sensemaking of student-migrants arriving through the racial geographies of the war on terror. Their gendered and racialized interpellation as potential terrorist threats by the surveillance state occurred both through their travels across national borders and during their time on campus. The shifts in practices occurring in the campus's international student office were especially noteworthy here. While the office's deeper entrenchment in the surveillance and neoliberal "management" of the university's student-migrants indicated the discursive evolutions accompanying the transition from the Cold War to the war on terror, it also highlighted another university site in which the ideological work of the "military-industrial-academic" complex persists.[2] The Indian youth discussed in this book felt conflicted about the ways they were positioned ambivalently as the (good) student-migrant and the (bad) potential terrorist migrant figure, but being compliant subjects of the surveillance state was often interpreted by these young people as part of their obligations in the exchange for an American education.

The interlinked logics of desiring and indebtedness that structured the migratory circulations of Indian student-migrants came to bear on how they negotiated the (un)belongings underlying their encounters with the campus. As these Indian migrant youth were set apart through segregated housing practices from the culture of whiteness embedded in the core of American university life, incorporated into the campus economy as part-time casual labor, and subjected to policing and profiling as racialized subjects on and near campus, notions of owing and being owed—which were productive of their classed, gendered, and racial sensibilities as migrant men—worked to reconcile for these young people the fraught inclusion politics of the internationalizing university. Throughout this book, I have attended to how the neoliberal reorganizing of the public university as a global campus is mediated through the imbrications of racial capitalism, US imperialism, and higher education. I have argued that Indian student-migrants, situated in these imbrications, are ultimately being produced as indebted migrant subjects primed for the precarities of the global knowledge economy.

Part of the intention of this book has been to bring Indian student-migrants' encounters with the internationalizing university into focus as part of the terrain of inquiry of critical university studies. A closer exploration of how their migratory lives are enabled by and productive of the internationalizing campus and its "going global" imaginary allows for another crucial lens through which to recognize the exclusionary violences that have always been and continue to be inherent to the bedrock of US university life, tied as it has been to the production and sustenance of US global hegemony. In a sense, then, I hope this book has served what Sara Ahmed described as being "insistent to go against," to exist as an account of and obstruction to oppressive institutional flows.[3] Still, I am not convinced that such accounting is nearly enough. The vacillations of the US two-party electoral system may have effects on the internationalizing university, particularly in relation to the terms by which migration policies are framed. However, as the global pandemic exposes the political, social, economic, and environmental havoc wrought by the violences of racial capitalism, there seems to be a palpable need for us to set our collective educational imagination to something that transcends the illusions cast by the institutional and electoral horizons of American liberalism—horizons that never really offered solace to those subjugated or dispossessed by those violences.

This means moving beyond Aihwa Ong's call to recuperate American universities as spaces of "ethical exception for the production of cosmopolitan citizens" fostered by a higher education that involves both "lessons on democracy and human rights" and professional degrees.[4] Rather, there must be a more intentional, assertive, and collective refusal to forget the political and libidinal forces of racial capitalism that have been at play all along. For Indian student-migrants, such refusal also includes remembering that as figures channeled by and through US empire, a culture of resistance has been a part of the history of their migratory circulations. Nonetheless, as the desire for Indian modernity that compelled these young people across US national borders inextricably linked the postcolonial imagination to US exceptionalism, I suggest that the terms of that resistance were its own undoing. Today, as reflected in the accounts shared in this book, there seems to exist a palpable absence of collective protest among Indian student-migrants, despite the kinds of exclusions they face as financially indebted students, exploited and underpaid campus workers, and segregated, surveilled, and profiled racialized figures placed on the margins of the campus.

Beyond the temporal and aspirational narratives encouraged by neoliberalized educational spaces that feed this absence, perhaps, we can borrow again from Berlant's notion of cruel optimism to deepen our insight. As Berlant contends, "For everyone, regardless of their ethnic and racial origin, all sorts of normative emotions about how the fantasy and actuality of the good life might be tethered together stand in for affective urges for a better social world beyond what the conventional forms deliver."[5] Yet, what if the large numbers of Indian student-migrants arriving on American campuses (students who happen to fill the seats of academic departments marked as vital to US global power) recognized that their living conditions—which are characterized by massive student debt; restrictive migration policies; work as exploited, casual labor under conditions of austerity; racial-religious-gendered exclusion and violence; and precarious, unprotected futures—are interconnected with the political and economic conditions of others who are also subjected to the violences of the neoliberalized university?

It is noteworthy that, in their accounts, Indian student-migrants hardly acknowledged the realities of Black, Indigenous, and other students of color on the campus or in their lives. The problematic inclusion politics of the campus that kept the migrant youth segregated and surveilled is partly to blame for that disregard, but it also attests to the anti-Black and anti-Indigenous racist logics that necessarily configure Indian migrant fantasies of attaining the American Dream. Any consideration of the exclusions of student-migrants on campus must be articulated with those logics. Rather than fantasizing that a proximity to whiteness will draw them closer to the successful (individualist) futures they each think they are owed, what if every moment of exclusion they faced as Indian student-migrants opened up possibilities for political solidarity and collective dissent alongside BIPOC (Black, Indigenous, and people of color) students on campus?

By dreaming beyond the anemic, entrapping, frayed horizons of the American Dream, alternative educative publics and possibilities for the promise of more just, collective futures can be envisioned. Radical scholars who have taken seriously the structural conditions linking the expansion of US higher education with the continuing effects of US settler colonialism, the transatlantic slave trade, and US militarization have sought to offer ways to repurpose educational spaces by moving past the recuperative aims of critical university studies. Theoretical conceptualizations of the undercommons, the third university, land education grounded in rematriation, and even the abolition of the university altogether have all offered invaluable material with which to decolonize the dreams we attach to knowledge seeking and knowledge production.[6] Student-migrants must join these efforts, as it is migrant desiring that perpetuates the delusional faith in the viability of the project of "America."[7] To do so, I suggest returning to the idea of indebtedness. What kinds of claims can be made on the American university by Indian student-migrants—a matter of what the university, in fact, owes to these young people—is an important question. However, rather than mobilizing a market logic here, which reproduces the very same conditions that indebt them as student-migrants and leave them on the margins of campus life, I insist on pushing past the limitations dictated by institutions. It is in that reframing of notions of indebtedness that a different set of expectations and responsibilities regarding owing and being owed emerges. Certainly, as a migrant population pursuing educational opportunities at institutions that exist as a result of continuous Indigenous dispossession, there are debts to Indigenous communities that even migrants of color experiencing marginalization, exclusion, or violence themselves must confront.[8] Facing such complicities enables asking more broadly: What is owed to one another in this world? What is owed the land, the earth? What is owed to our collective futures? By asking questions that recognize such debts and responsibilities, and by enacting political solidarities through that recognition, a genuinely inclusive, global, liberatory university is, indeed, possible.

Acknowledgments

Despite all the moments that writing a book may feel like a solitary journey, it is impossible to do without the love, patience, and support of others. There are so many who have offered this kindness to me so that I could complete this work. First, I want to express my deepest gratitude to my fieldwork interlocutors who allowed me to show up at their door to watch, listen, spend time, build friendships, ask questions, and write about their lives. I am certainly aware that they did not need to do so, yet they graciously accommodated me. I hope they find that this book has done justice to the story.

This project took shape under the generous guidance of Ritty Lukose, Deborah Thomas, and Kathleen Hall. It is because of their labor and support—intellectually, professionally, and emotionally—that I was able to turn my questions and preoccupations into this book. I'm so grateful for their early readings, as well as their deep intellectual insights and encouragement, which continue to shape me and my work. I especially want to thank Ritty for being there from the beginning of my academic trajectory. Her mentorship has always involved closely attending to my intellectual and political commitments, guiding me in ways that pushed me to be a better scholar without losing sight of those commitments. I'm thankful for that gift and for our friendship.

Carol Fadda read an early and very rough draft of my manuscript, offering invaluable feedback and insight that helped make the next iteration of the writing and analysis so much better. Despite her own incredibly busy schedule, she generously gave her time to read in such meaningful ways, and for that I am immensely grateful. A number of other scholars have read parts of the manuscript or contributed in other ways to the work of this book. I especially want to thank Nishaant Choksi, Dan LoPreto, David Pérez, Tony Tiongson, Chris Eng, Dana Olwan, Danika Medak-Saltzman, Ameena Ghaffar-Kucher, Moh A., Neha Vora, and Anooradha Siddiqi. I am so thankful for the loving friendships that I had the chance to build and enjoy with Chris Eng, Biko Gray, and Terrell Winder as we joined the faculty at Syracuse University. Organizing and struggling, sharing meals and outings, and laughing at everything with them made the time I have spent in Syracuse so special. I have also been fortunate enough to have the support and friendship of my SU colleagues Azra Hromadžić, Mona Bhan, Natalie Koch, and Sabina Schnell. I want to thank Dean Kelly Chandler-Olcott and my colleagues in the Department of Cultural Foundations of Education for their supportive spirit as I wrote and completed this book. Barbara Applebaum, in particular, has been a constant source of patient counsel, care, and friendship during my time in the department; without it, I'm certain many moments would have been more difficult for me. I will always be grateful for the ways she shows up for me. I have also had the privilege of working with some incredible students over the years. Let me extend a special thank-you to Shiilā Au Yong, Atiya McGhee, Chivonne Munroe, Treasa Praino, Chelsea Bouldin, Ana Borja, Easten Davis, Cassie Guzman, and Ahlam Islam. The sincerity and insight they have brought to the classroom, to the politics of justice, and to the work have been inspiring.

I could not have asked for a better editor for this book than Elizabeth Branch Dyson. Elizabeth always made it clear to me that she saw the importance and potential of this project and shepherded it to publication with enthusiasm, intelligence, and wisdom. It has been an honor to work with her on this book. I also want to thank the anonymous reviewers, freelance copyeditor Carrie Love, Mollie McFee, and the rest of the team at the University of Chicago Press for all their assistance and labor in ensuring the book came together.

This book was written across a number of years, cities, and coffeeshops. The Salt City Market in Syracuse was my most recent refuge as I reached the final stages of writing. I am so thankful for the kind staff and fellow regulars that befriended me during this time. A special thanks to my favorites, Al Cutri, Anthony DeMario, Daniel Russell, Steve Rogers, Marcus Abner, and Liam Kirst. I also want to give thanks for that healing night by the water delivered to me by Jay Spaker, the sorcerer of beautiful nights. Jay, I'm grateful for everything our connection has given us. There are so many dear, deep, and core friendships that have sustained me across space and time as I journeyed to and through this book. I especially want to thank Shauna-Kay Steer, Arif Ullah, Nargiza Yusupova, Sushma Seth, Saurabh Patwa, Sean Anthony, Gonza Kaijage, Brian Lozenski, Celine Thompson, Nishaant Choksi, Anurag Bhaskar, Ranjit Mathew, Sannaki Munna, Lali Khalid, and Eduardo Lara. Thank you for keeping me grounded with your love, generosity, humor, and encouragement.

A special thank-you to my family, immediate and extended—I'm grateful for the love and the lessons. My younger brother and my older sister are two of the most driven people I know. It is always with admiration that I speak of their work ethic, which I constantly strive to emulate. It is to my mother and father, whose loving support has meant so much to me, that I owe my greatest debt. My father passed away as I was completing this book. Losing him the way we did has been the biggest heartbreak I have known. I hope he recognized how much his own story of migration came to inspire my intellectual preoccupations. I pray that my work honors him. I love you and I miss you.

Notes

INTRODUCTION

1. All names and some identifying markers have been altered to protect anonymity.
2. Geertz, "Deep Hanging Out."
3. Institute of International Education, *Open Doors 2020*.
4. Ong, *Neoliberalism as Exception*.
5. Readings, *University in Ruins*; Slaughter and Leslie, *Academic Capitalism*; Tuchman, *Wannabe U*.
6. Ahmed, *On Being Included*; Giroux, *Neoliberalism's War on Higher Education*; Gutiérrez y Muhs et al., *Presumed Incompetent*; Hamilton and Nielson, *Broke*; Warikoo, *The Diversity Bargain*.
7. See Boggs and Mitchell, "Critical University Studies and the Crisis Consensus"; Vora, *Teach for Arabia*.
8. Baldwin, *In the Shadow of the Ivory Tower*; Chatterjee and Maira, *Imperial University*; Lee and Ahtone, "Land-Grab Universities"; Wilder, *Ebony and Ivy*.
9. Ong, *Neoliberalism as Exception*, 144.
10. Kamola, *Making the World Global*.
11. De Wit, *Internationalization of Higher Education*; Hutcheson, "In the National Interest." Both de Wit and Hutcheson offer a comprehensive history of the broader development of higher education policy and international education programming.
12. Fernandes, *India's New Middle Class*; Lukose, *Liberalization's Children*; Chowdhury, *New India*.
13. See Turner, *The Ritual Process*. My use of "liminal" draws on Turner's conceptualization of a transitory encountering, a "betwixt and between" phase crucial to the production and transformation of social life.
14. Biao, *Global "Body Shopping"*; Radhakrishnan, *Appropriately Indian*; Bhatt, *High-Tech Housewives*.
15. See Connell, *Masculinities*. Raewyn Connell's pioneering work on hegemonic

masculinities, though highly debated, has played an especially influential role in the field. See also Whitehead, *Men and Masculinities*.

16. Jeffrey, Jeffery, and Jeffery, *Degrees without Freedom*. See also Morrell and Swart's "Men in the Third World" and Judith Butler's seminal work, *Gender Trouble*, which theorizes the production of gender as performative, relational, embodied, and discursive.

17. See Osella and Osella, "Migration, Money and Masculinity in Kerala"; Choi and Peng, *Masculine Compromise*; Pande, "Mobile Masculinities."

18. Lazzarato, *Making of the Indebted Man*.

19. Cavallero and Gago, *Feminist Reading of Debt*. See also Harker, Sayyad, and Shebeitah, "The Gender of Debt and Space" and Kar, *Financializing Poverty*.

20. Dorn, *For the Common Good*.

21. Dorn, *For the Common Good*.

22. Kymlicka, *Multicultural Odysseys*. My use of liberal multiculturalism references Kymlicka's position that recognizing cultural difference and accommodating minority group rights enable a more inclusive and effective state model for integration in liberal democracies.

23. Ahmed, *On Being Included*; Urciuoli, "Compromised Pragmatics of Diversity"; Warikoo, *The Diversity Bargain*.

24. Tsing, "The Global Situation." I draw on Anna Tsing's usage of placemaking here to trace the global circulations of these migrant youth through the particularities of places.

25. Ministry of Education, *All India Survey of Higher Education 2019–20*.

26. Aslany, *Contested Capital*.

27. Some Dalit and other lower-caste youth may also be invested in denying caste identity, though often tied to mitigating the kinds of discrimination they can face in various settings. See Dutt, *Coming Out as Dalit*, as an example attending to the significance of denying caste among lower-caste communities.

28. See Connell, *Masculinities*; Chakraborty, *Mapping South Asian Masculinities*.

29. Sachar Committee, *Social, Economic and Educational Status of the Muslim Community in India*.

30. See Smith, *Institutional Ethnography*.

31. Gusterson, "Homework." This scrutiny is what Gusterson calls doing "the homework"—studying the institutional conditions we, as academics, are situated in as productive of the material and discursive forces wrought by neoliberalism.

32. Fong, *Paradise Redefined*.

33. A version of chapter 1 was published previously. See Thomas, "Student-Migrants and the Diasporic Imagination."

34. Deleuze and Guattari, *Anti-Oedipus: Capitalism and Schizophrenia*. Also see Collins, *Global Asian City*. Focused on the relationship between migration and the urban landscape of Seoul, Collins specifically calls for the centering of a theory of desiring in analyses of migratory processes.

35. Mauss, *The Gift*; Gregory, *Savage Money*; Graeber, *Debt: The First 5,000 Years*; Hours and Ahmed, *Anthropological Economy of Debt*.

36. Deleuze, "Postscript on the Societies of Control."

37. Chatterjee and Maira, *The Imperial University*.

38. Grewal, *Transnational America*. I draw on Grewal here as she argues against the dismissal of the nation-state in Michael Hardt and Antonio Negri's conceptualization of imperial power as articulated in their controversial work, *Empire*. As Grewal contends, the global networks being produced are not only characterized by deterritorialization but they also simultaneously produce and recreate power centers, a reterritorialization that allows "the United States to remain a hegemon" (21).

39. Koshy, "Category Crisis"; Dhingra, *Life Behind the Lobby*; Koshy and Radhakrishnan, *Transnational South Asians*; Rana, *Terrifying Muslims*.

40. Parts of this chapter were published previously. See Thomas, "Precarious Path of Student Migrants."

41. Berlant, *Cruel Optimism*.

CHAPTER ONE

1. Krieger, "Universities or Visa Mills?"

2. Hopper, "Immigration Officials."

3. A. Alexander and Jdsahr, comments on Bartlett, Fischer, and Keller, "Little-Known Colleges" [comments no longer available]; Krieger, "Universities or Visa Mills?"

4. Bartlett, Fischer, and Keller, "Little-Known Colleges."

5. Lee and Ahtone, "Land-Grab Universities."

6. La Paperson, *A Third University Is Possible*.

7. Sood, *Expatriate Nationalism*.

8. See Macaulay, "Minute on Education"; Pietsch, "Many Rhodes."

9. Fischer-Tiné, "Indian Nationalism," 328.

10. Mukherjee, *Nationalism, Education, and Migrant Identities*.

11. Gould, *Sikhs, Swamis*; Ramnath, *Haj to Utopia*.

12. Ramnath, *Haj to Utopia*.

13. Leonard, *Making Ethnic Choices*; Bhatt and Iyer, *Roots and Reflections*; Bald, *Bengali Harlem*.

14. Hindusthan Association of America, "Ourselves," 1.

15. Sarkar, "Hindu Sociology."

16. Hindusthan Association of America, "Course of Reading," 7.

17. Considering this overlap between the nationalist cause and HAA's commitments, it is not surprising that Indians involved in foreign student leadership were also prominent leaders of the armed struggle against British rule. These included important Indian nationalist radicals such as Har Dayal, Taraknath Das,

and Surendra Bose, who was not only a student but also general secretary of the HAA. Ker, *Political Trouble in India*.

18. Bassett, *The Technological Indian*.

19. Wang, *Transpacific Articulations*. While Wang counters the privileging of labor migration in Asian American histories of racialization by centering the student-migrant as a valuable political figure of Asian diasporic formations, I insist here that the articulations of educational *and* labor subjectivities among Indian migrants became uniquely productive to forging an Indian diasporic imagination.

20. Singh, "Opportunity in India and America."

21. Hindusthan Association of America, "Vacation Work"; Roy, "Self-Support in American Universities."

22. See also Oberoi, "Ghadar Movement and Its Anarchist Genealogy."

23. Dayal, "India in America," 5. Har Dayal, a radical nationalist and a prominent leader of the Ghadar Party, wrote about the predicament of Indian student-migrants, stating they had "energy and brains, but little money." Therefore, the opportunities students had to support themselves through manual labor in the United States were invaluable.

24. Das, "Why Must We Emigrate to the United States of America?"; Narayan, "Why Emigrate?"

25. Das, "Why Must We Emigrate to the United States of America?," 80.

26. See Ramnath, *Haj to Utopia*.

27. Shastri, "Inaugural Address," 3.

28. Hindusthan Association of America, "Policy of the 'Student,'" 4.

29. See Lowe, *The Intimacies of Four Continents*.

30. Scheffauer, "The Tide of Turbans," 618.

31. Immigration Commission, *Reports of the Immigration Commission*, 28.

32. Bose, "The Future of the Hindusthanee Student in America."

33. Brooks, "Apostle of Internationalism," 67. Reflecting this shift, in 1919, after the cessation of World War I, the highly influential US-based Institute of International Education (IIE) was established, serving as the key organization mobilizing and managing student mobility and exchange.

34. Hardikar, "The Immigration Bill."

35. Sood, *Expatriate Nationalism*; Sohi, "Repressing the Hindu Menace."

36. Pegues, *Space-Time Colonialism*.

37. De Wit, *Internationalization of Higher Education*; Hutcheson, "In the National Interest." See these works for discussions of the expanded involvement of the US state in higher education, related legislation, and the connections to foreign policy interests. See also Nye, *Soft Power*.

38. President's Commission on Higher Education, *Higher Education for American Democracy*, 15.

39. Ngai, *Impossible Subjects*.

40. Dudziak, *Cold War Civil Rights*.
41. Stein, Andreotti, and Susa, "Beyond 2015." Stein, Andreotti, and Susa have noted that the growing turn among newly independent Asian nations to pursue higher education in the United States was also compounded by pressure from international development actors offering aid and assistance to focus on developing primary and secondary education rather than national systems of higher education, creating a tremendous global imbalance in higher learning that was tipped in the favor of the United States.
42. Nimbark, "Some Observations."
43. Gandhi, "What Educated Women Can Do," 2.
44. Kumar, interview.
45. Helweg and Helweg, *An Immigrant Success Story*.
46. De Haas, "Migration and Development"; Massey et al., *Worlds in Motion*.
47. Mishra, "India Forum."
48. It was during this period that the Third World Liberation Front had emerged, leading to the creation of radical academic programming focused on race and ethnic studies on campuses.
49. Laly, interview.
50. Tuck and Yang, "Decolonization Is Not a Metaphor," 19.
51. Committee of Concerned Indian Students and the Committee for Human Rights, "Documents of the Committee"; South Asian Students Association, "A Running Dog"; South Asia People's Organization, "Two Years of Janata."
52. South Asian Students Association, "Political Activists Hanged," 6.
53. India Forum Staff, "Subscribe Now."
54. India Forum, "A Note to Fraternal Groups."
55. Indians for Political Freedom, *Political Crisis in India*; Committee of Concerned Indian Students, *India: Democracy or Dictatorship?*
56. India Forum Staff, "Report: Surveillance and Intimidation," 20.
57. South Asia People's Organization, "Report: Diplomatic 'Excesses.'"
58. India Forum Staff, "Report: Surveillance and Intimidation," 14.
59. As proof of the Indian government's attempts at infiltration and intimidation, a letter sent to Berkeley by the Indian government was published and circulated widely. The letter requested information about several Indian student-based organizations and its members.
60. Grimes, "Protests Rising."
61. India Forum Staff, "Report: Surveillance and Intimidation," 23.
62. Richwine, "Indian Americans: The New Model Minority."

CHAPTER TWO

1. See Dhareshwar, "Caste and the Secular Self"; Deshpande, "Caste and Castelessness"; Lukose, *Liberalization's Children*.

2. Deshpande, "Caste and Castelessness."
3. Subramanian, *The Caste of Merit.*
4. Deleuze and Guattari, *Anti-Oedipus: Capitalism and Schizophrenia.*
5. Kamat, "Neoliberalism, Urbanism and the Education Economy."
6. Biao, *Global "Body Shopping."*
7. For further discussion of this reconciliation between neoliberal reform and Hindu nationalism, see Subramanian, *Caste of Merit.*
8. Radhakrishnan, *Appropriately Indian.*
9. Ong, *Flexible Citizenship.*
10. Radhakrishnan, *Appropriately Indian.*
11. Rao, "The Globalization of Bollywood."
12. Grewal, *Transnational America,* 5.
13. See Zaloom, *Indebted.*
14. See Chua, *In Pursuit of the Good Life.* Chua discusses the tragic death by suicide of Rajani Anand, a young Dalit engineering student in India who could not afford to pay her student fees and whose father was repeatedly turned down for educational loans by banks as he had no collateral. Her death was emblematic of caste and class disparities in student lending, leading to nationwide protests that challenged both the affordability of higher education and the discriminatory practices of lending.
15. Cavallero and Gago, *A Feminist Reading of Debt..*
16. See Massey et al., *Worlds in Motion*; Schiller, Basch, and Blanc, "From Immigrant to Transmigrant."
17. Hubert and Mauss, *Sacrifice: Its Nature and Functions,* 100.
18. See Simmel, *Faithfulness and Gratitude.*
19. While no student ever directly implicated themselves in these kinds of practices, it is important to include these examples that were circulated widely among the youth. Because of their fraudulent nature, talk of such practices surfaced as rumor, but these students entirely accepted them as true, functioning as part of how they understood migration to work. Further, sharing rumors of *other* students and *others'* families reveals a moral tone-setting about the boundaries of "good" student-migrants.
20. Massey et al., *Worlds in Motion*; Gardner, *Global Migrants, Local Lives.*
21. Graeber, *Debt: The First 5,000 Years.*
22. See Saxenian, "From Brain Drain to Brain Circulation."
23. Fernandes, *India's New Middle Class*; Radhakrishnan, *Appropriately Indian.*
24. Amrute, *Encoding Race, Encoding Class.* See also Subramanian, *Caste of Merit,* for a discussion of how elite IIT graduates in Silicon Valley point to entrepreneurialism as crucial to India's position as a global power.

CHAPTER THREE

1. Chatterjee and Maira, *The Imperial University*.
2. National Commission on Terrorist Attacks upon the United States, *9/11 Commission Report*, 220.
3. Office of Inspector General, *The Immigration and Naturalization Service's Contacts with Two September 11 Terrorists*, 12.
4. Office of Inspector General, *Contacts with Two September 11 Terrorists*, 15.
5. Agamben, *State of Exception*. See also Beck, *World at Risk*.
6. Beck, *World at Risk*.
7. Office of Inspector General, *Contacts with Two September 11 Terrorists*, 129.
8. Office of Inspector General, *Contacts with Two September 11 Terrorists*, 178.
9. National Commission, *9/11 Commission Report*, 265.
10. National Commission, *9/11 Commission Report*, 47.
11. Volpp, "The Citizen and the Terrorist"; Jamal and Naber, *Race and Arab Americans*; Mamdani, *Good Muslim, Bad Muslim*; Rana, *Terrifying Muslims*.
12. National Commission, *9/11 Commission Report*, 340.
13. National Commission, *9/11 Commission Report*, 263.
14. National Commission, *9/11 Commission Report*, 344.
15. Freeman, *Time Binds*, 3.
16. Grewal, *Transnational America*; Ahmad, "A Rage Shared by Law."
17. See Jaffrelot, *Hindu Nationalism: A Reader*, for an in-depth analysis on the rise and political developments of Hindu nationalism. For insights on its global spread and how it has been propagated by conservative, upper-caste, and wealthy segments of the Indian Hindu diaspora, see Mathew and Prashad, "The Protean Forms of Yankee Hindutva."
18. These shared ideological and geopolitical objectives between the two nations have persisted as the Bharatiya Janata Party (BJP), which is intimately tied to the broader Hindu nationalist movement, has come to power under the leadership of Prime Minister Narendra Modi. For discussions on how these alignments, advanced by the seemingly endless war on terror, continue to offer a blueprint to further the Indian state's political aims to disenfranchise Indian Muslims, undermine Pakistan, curb migration from its Muslim-majority neighboring countries, and pursue settler-colonial policies in Kashmir, see Junaid, "From a Distant Shore"; Chaudhuri, "India, America, and the Nationalist Apocalyptic"; and Beydoun, "Exporting Islamophobia."
19. NSEERS was replaced with the United States Visitor and Immigrant Status Indicator Technology (US-VISIT) program, a government-wide integrated system for the automated collection and sharing of biometric data on foreign nationals.
20. Deleuze, "Postscript on the Societies of Control."
21. Hall, *The Transparent Traveler*.

22. See Nandy, *The Intimate Enemy*; Puar and Rai, "Monster, Terrorist, Fag."
23. NAFSA, *Student and Exchange Visitor Program: Training for Designated School Officials*.
24. See Brooks, "The Apostle of Internationalism." Through a focus on the Institute of International Education (IIE) and its early leadership, Brooks discusses how international education was, in fact, conceptualized as a civilizational force.
25. Chatterjee and Maira, *The Imperial University*.
26. Kamola, *Making the World Global*.
27. Peeren, "Compelling Memory."
28. Peeren, "Compelling Memory."
29. MSA's vulnerability as a student group was illuminated during my fieldwork when the Associated Press published an extensive investigative report documenting the widespread surveillance conducted by the New York Police Department that intentionally targeted Muslim communities and their institutions throughout the Northeast area. Muslim Student Associations on university campuses, including Riverside, were also subjected to this surveillance, in which undercover officers infiltrated the groups, monitored their websites and blogs daily, recorded members' names, attended group events and meetings undercover, and compiled "NYPD Secret Weekly MSA Reports."
30. Federal Bureau of Investigation (FBI), "To Track a Threat." See also Office of Inspector General (OIG), *September 11 Detainees*.
31. American Civil Liberties Union (ACLU), *Sanctioned Bias*; ACLU, *Civil Liberties after 9/11*. This also involved a US government order for mass "interviews" of men who had arrived in the country legally on nonimmigration visas, including overseas students. Lured in with false promises of help with any visa issues, many voluntarily cooperated only to be thrown into detention once in custody.
32. See Cainkar, "No Longer Invisible"; Murray, "Profiled."
33. Puar, *Terrorist Assemblages*.
34. Roy, "India's 9/11." Roy reads the lending of the 9/11 idiom to Mumbai as an interpretive framework through which Mumbai was incorporated into the narrative of a global type of terror.
35. Mehta, "Hindu Nationalism"; Chaudhuri, "India, America, and the Nationalist Apocalyptic."
36. See Somerville, "Notes toward a Queer History of Naturalization," for a reading of naturalization policies as the relationship between migration, the state, and desirability.

CHAPTER FOUR

1. Chuppals are the commonly worn, casual Indian sandals resembling the American flip-flops.
2. My contention here resonates with Choi and Peng's use of "masculine compro-

mise" as the complex and situational negotiations of masculinity men make in the process of, in relation to, and as a consequence of migration. Choi and Peng, *Masculine Compromise.*

3. Collins, "Of Kimchi and Coffee."
4. The term "seniors" is colloquially used in India to refer to classmates who are in the preceding cohorts.
5. Sambhar is a common South Indian vegetarian dish.
6. Pitt-Rivers, "The Paradox of Friendship."
7. The Pakistani and Bangladeshi students on the campus were mostly in doctoral programs where they were provided graduate funding. They could afford the higher rent of the other graduate housing complex, Jefferson Apartments, where they chose to live mainly because the conditions were better and there was more diversity in the tenant population.
8. Sibley, *Geographies of Exclusion.*
9. Lowe, *Immigrant Acts*, 30.
10. Ahmed, *On Being Included.*
11. In this sense, I read "treating" as a mode of gift-giving practice as discussed in Osella and Osella's "Migration, Money and Masculinity in Kerala."
12. Ani's assertion is particularly loaded when also considered in relation to the Indian caste system's underlying logic that different caste groups are destined to do different kinds of labor. In this sense, I want to suggest that Ani, though not upper caste, also borrows from caste logics in his own conflations of work and identity.
13. Puar, *Terrorist Assemblages.*
14. Puar, *Terrorist Assemblages*, 187.
15. Koshy, "Category Crisis."
16. Puar, *Terrorist Assemblages*, 185.
17. See Puar, *Terrorist Assemblages*, 197.
18. For an egregious instantiation of such acts, recall the scandal concerning torture, abuse, and humiliation at the Abu Ghraib prison in Iraq, publicized in 2004. See Taguba, *Article 15-6 Investigation.*
19. Puar, *Terrorist Assemblages.* Also see Ahmed, "Affective Economies."
20. Koshy, "Category Crisis," 64.
21. Hubert and Mauss, *Sacrifice: Its Nature and Functions*; Reinert, "Sacrifice"; Mayblin and Course, "The Other Side of Sacrifice"; Lambek, "Afterthoughts on Sacrifice."
22. Reinert, "Sacrifice."

CHAPTER FIVE

1. Morrell and Swart. "Men in the Third World."
2. Radhakrishnan, *Appropriately Indian.*

3.   Biao, Global *"Body Shopping."*.
4.   Biao, Global *"Body Shopping."*
5.   Ettlinger, "Precarity Unbound"; Standing, *The Precariat: The New Dangerous Class*.
6.   Standing, *The Precariat: The New Dangerous Class*; Breman, "A Bogus Concept?"; Munck: "The Precariat: A View from the South."
7.   Nielson and Rossiter, "Precarity as a Political Concept."
8.   Berlant, *Cruel Optimism*, 209.
9.   Halbertal, *On Sacrifice*, 114.
10. Dosa is a common South Indian dish.
11. Berlant, *Cruel Optimism*.
12. A lungi is a traditional South Indian wrap worn by men.

EPILOGUE

1.   Kamola, *Making the World Global*.
2.   Giroux, *The University in Chains*.
3.   Ahmed, *On Being Included*, 186.
4.   Ong, *Neoliberalism as Exception*, 156.
5.   Berlant, *Cruel Optimism*, 186.
6.   See Morten and Harney, *The Undercommons*; La Paperson, *A Third University Is Possible*; Tuck, McKenzie, and McCoy, "Land Education"; Boggs et al., "Abolitionist University Studies."
7.   See Berlant, *The Queen of America Goes to Washington City*.
8.   See Chatterjee, "Immigration, Anti-Racism, and Indigenous Self-Determination"; Dhamoon, "A Feminist Approach to Decolonizing Anti-racism."

Bibliography

Agamben, Giorgio. *State of Exception*. Chicago: University of Chicago Press, 2005.

Ahmad, Muneer. "A Rage Shared by Law: Post-September 11 Racial Violence as Crimes of Passion." *California Law Review* 92, no. 5 (2004): 1259–1330.

Ahmed, Sara. "Affective Economies." *Social Text* 22, no. 2 (2004): 117–39.

Ahmed, Sara. *On Being Included: Racism and Diversity in Institutional Life*. Durham, NC: Duke University Press, 2012.

American Civil Liberties Union (ACLU). *Civil Liberties after 9/11: The ACLU Defends Freedom*. 2002. http://www.aclu.org/national-security/civil-liberties-after-9-11 -aclu-defends-freedom.

American Civil Liberties Union (ACLU). *Sanctioned Bias: Racial Profiling since 9/11*. February 2004. http://www.aclu.org/FilesPDFs/racial%20profiling%20report .pdf.

Amrute, Sareeta. *Encoding Race, Encoding Class: Indian IT Workers in Berlin*. Durham, NC: Duke University Press, 2016.

Aslany, Maryam. *Contested Capital: Rural Middle Classes in India*. Cambridge: Cambridge University Press, 2020.

Bald, Vivek. *Bengali Harlem and the Lost Histories of South Asian America*. Cambridge, MA: Harvard University Press, 2015.

Baldwin, Davarian. *In the Shadow of the Ivory Tower: How Universities are Plundering Our Cities*. New York: Bold Type Books, 2021.

Bartlett, Tom, Karin Fischer, and Josh Keller. "Little-Known Colleges Make Millions off Foreign Students." *Chronicle of Higher Education*, March 20, 2011. https:// www.chronicle.com/article/little-known-colleges-exploit-visa-loopholes-to -make-millions-off-foreign-students/.

Bassett, Ross. *The Technological Indian*. Cambridge, MA: Harvard University Press. 2016.

Beck, Ulrich. *World at Risk*. Cambridge: Polity Press, 2009.

Berlant, Lauren. *Cruel Optimism*. Durham, NC: Duke University Press, 2011.

Berlant, Lauren. *The Queen of America Goes to Washington City: Essays on Sex and Citizenship*. Durham, NC: Duke University Press, 1997.

Beydoun, Khaled. "Exporting Islamophobia in the Global 'War on Terror.'" *NYU Law Review Online* 81, (2020): 93–96.

Bhatt, Amy. *High-Tech Housewives: Indian IT Workers, Gendered Labor, and Transmigration*. Seattle: University of Washington Press, 2018.

Bhatt, Amy, and Nalini Iyer. *Roots and Reflections: South Asians in the Pacific Northwest*. Seattle: University of Washington Press, 2013.

Biao, Xiang. *Global "Body Shopping": An Indian Labor System in the Information Technology Industry*. Princeton, NJ: Princeton University Press, 2007.

Boggs, Abigail, Eli Meyerhoff, Nick Mitchell, and Zach Schwartz-Weinstein. "Abolitionist University Studies: An Invitation." *Abolition Journal*, August 28, 2019. https://abolitionjournal.org/abolitionist-university-studies-an-invitation/.

Boggs, Abigail, and Nick Mitchell. "Critical University Studies and the Crisis Consensus." *Feminist Studies* 44, no. 2 (2018): 432–63.

Bose, Sudhindra. "The Future of the Hindusthanee Student in America." *Hindusthanee Student* 1, no. 2–3 (April and July 1914): 42–44. South Asian American Digital Archive. https://www.saada.org/item/20110818-298.

Breman, Jan. "A Bogus Concept?" *New Left Review* 84 (2013): 130–38.

Brooks, Chay. "The Apostle of Internationalism: Stephen Duggan and the Geopolitics of International Education." *Political Geography* 49 (2015): 64–73.

Butler, Judith. *Gender Trouble: Feminism and the Subversion of Identity*. New York: Routledge, 1990.

Cainkar, Louise. "No Longer Invisible: Arab and Muslim Exclusion after September 11." *Middle East Report* 224 (Fall 2002). http://www.merip.org/mer/mer224/no-longer-invisible.

Cavallero, Lucí, and Verónica Gago. *A Feminist Reading of Debt*. London: Pluto Press, 2021.

Chakraborty, Chandrima, ed. *Mapping South Asian Masculinities: Men and Political Crises*. New York: Taylor and Francis, 2015.

Chatterjee, Piya, and Sunaina Maira, eds. *The Imperial University: Academic Repression and Scholarly Dissent*. Minneapolis: University of Minnesota Press, 2014.

Chatterjee, Soma. "Immigration, Anti-Racism, and Indigenous Self-Determination: Towards a Comprehensive Analysis of the Contemporary Settler Colonial." *Social Identities: Journal for the Study of Race, Nation and Culture* 25, no. 5 (2019): 644–61.

Chaudhuri, Arun. "India, America, and the Nationalist Apocalyptic." *CrossCurrents* 68, no. 2 (2019): 216–36.

Choi, Susanne, and Yinni Peng. *Masculine Compromise: Migration, Family, and Gender in China*. Oakland: University of California Press, 2016.

Chowdhury, Kanishka. *New India: Citizenship, Subjectivity, and Economic Liberaliza-tion*. New York: Palgrave Macmillan, 2011.

Chua, Jocelyn. *In Pursuit of the Good Life: Aspiration and Suicide in Globalizing South India*. Oakland: University of California Press, 2014.

Collins, Francis. *Global Asian City: Migration, Desire and the Politics of Encounter in the 21st Century Seoul*. Oxford: Wiley Blackwell, 2018.

Collins, Francis. "Of Kimchi and Coffee: Globalisation, Transnationalism, and Familiarity in Culinary Consumption." *Social and Cultural Geography* 9, no. 2 (2008): 151–69.

Committee of Concerned Indian Students. *India: Democracy or Dictatorship?* KQED-TV, November 23, 1976.

Committee of Concerned Indian Students and the Committee for Human Rights. "Documents of the Committee of Concerned Indian Students and the Com-mittee for Human Rights [Collection of Documents]." Berkeley, CA: Com-mittee of Concerned Indian Students and the Committee for Human Rights Boards, 1976.

Connell, R. W. *Masculinities*. Oakland: University of California Press, 2005.

Das, Sarangadhar. "Why Must We Emigrate to the United States of America?" *Mod-ern Review*, July 1911, 69–80. South Asian American Digital Archive. https://www.saada.org/item/20101216-154.

Das Gupta, Monisha. *Unruly Immigrants: Rights, Activism, and Transnational South Asian Politics in the United States*. Durham, NC: Duke University Press, 2006.

Dayal, Har. "India in America." *Modern Review*, July 1911, 1–11. South Asian Ameri-can Digital Archive. https://www.saada.org/item/20101216-153.

de Haas, Hein. "Migration and Development: A Theoretical Perspective." *Inter-national Migration Review* 44, no. 1 (2010): 227–64.

Deleuze, Gilles. "Postscript on the Societies of Control." *October* 59 (1992): 3–7.

Deleuze, Gilles, and Felix Guattari. *Anti-Oedipus: Capitalism and Schizophrenia*. London: Penguin Classics, 2009.

Deshpande, Satish. "Caste and Castelessness: Towards a Biography of the 'General Category.'" *Economic and Political Weekly* 48, no. 15 (2013): 32–39.

de Wit, Hans. *Internationalization of Higher Education in the U.S.A. and Europe: A Historical, Comparative, and Conceptual Analysis*. Westport, CT: Greenwood Press, 2002.

Dhamoon, Rita K. "A Feminist Approach to Decolonizing Anti-racism: Rethinking Transnationalism, Intersectionality, and Settler Colonialism." *Feral Feminisms*, no. 4 (2015): 20–37.

Dhareshwar, Vivek. "Caste and the Secular Self." *Journal of Arts and Ideas* 25–26 (1993): 115–26.

Dhingra, Pawan. *Life Behind the Lobby: Indian American Motel Owners and the Ameri-can Dream*. Stanford, CA: Stanford University Press, 2012.

Dorn, Charles. *For the Common Good: A New History of Higher Education in America.* Ithaca, NY: Cornell University Press, 2017.

Dudziak, Mary L. *Cold War Civil Rights: Race and the Image of American Democracy.* Princeton, NJ: Princeton University Press, 2011.

Dutt, Yashica. *Coming Out as Dalit: A Memoir.* New Delhi: Aleph Book Company, 2019.

Ettlinger, Nancy. "Precarity Unbound." *Alternatives: Global, Local, Political* 32, no. 3 (2007): 319–40.

Federal Bureau of Investigation (FBI). "To Track a Threat: Inside Our Internet Tip Line," June 26, 2009. https://archives.fbi.gov/archives/news/stories/2009/june/tips_062609.

Fernandes, Leela. *India's New Middle Class: Democratic Politics in an Era of Economic Reform.* Minneapolis: University of Minnesota Press, 2006.

Fischer-Tiné, Harald. "Indian Nationalism and the 'World Forces': Transnational and Diasporic Dimensions of the Indian Freedom Movement on the Eve of the First World War." *Journal of Global History* 2, no. 3 (2007): 325–44.

Fong, Vanessa. *Paradise Redefined: Transnational Chinese Students and the Quest for Flexible Citizenship in the Developed World.* Stanford, CA: Stanford University Press, 2011.

Freeman, Elizabeth. *Time Binds: Queer Temporalities, Queer Histories.* Durham, NC: Duke University Press, 2010.

Gandhi, Indira. "What Educated Women Can Do." Golden Jubilee Celebrations of the Indraprastha College for Women, November 23, 1974. Iowa State University Archives of Women's Political Communication.

Gardner, Katy. *Global Migrants, Local Lives: Travel and Transformation in Rural Bangladesh.* Oxford: Clarendon Press, 1995.

Geertz, Clifford. "Deep Hanging Out." *New York Review of Books* 45, no. 16 (1998): 69.

Giroux, Henry. *Neoliberalism's War on Higher Education.* Chicago: Haymarket Books, 2014.

Giroux, Henry. *The University in Chains: Confronting the Military-Industrial-Academic Complex.* New York: Routledge Publishing, 2007.

Gould, Harold. *Sikhs, Swamis, Students and Spies: The India Lobby in the United States, 1900–1946.* New Delhi: Sage, 2006.

Graeber, David. *Debt: The First 5,000 Years.* Brooklyn, NY: Melville House Publishing, 2011.

Gregory, Chris. *Savage Money: The Anthropology and Politics of Commodity Exchange.* Amsterdam: Harwood Academic Publishers, 1997.

Grewal, Inderpal. *Transnational America: Feminisms, Diasporas, Neoliberalisms.* Durham, NC: Duke University Press, 2005.

Grimes, Paul. "Protests Rising on Curbs in India." *New York Times*, March 8, 1976. https://www.nytimes.com/1976/03/08/archives/protests-rising-on-curbs-in-india-gandhi-regimes-curbs-draw-more.html.

Gusterson, Hugh. "Homework: Toward a Critical Ethnography of the University." *American Ethnologist* 44, no. 3 (2017): 435–50.

Gutiérrez y Muhs, Gabriella, Yolanda F. Niemann, Carmen G. González, and Angela P. Harris, eds. *Presumed Incompetent: The Intersections of Race and Class for Women in Academia*. Logan: Utah State University Press, 2012.

Halbertal, Moshe. *On Sacrifice*. Princeton, NJ: Princeton University Press, 2012.

Hall, Rachel. *The Transparent Traveler: The Performance and Culture of Airport Security*. Durham, NC: Duke University Press, 2015.

Hamilton, Laura T., and Kelly Nielson. *Broke: The Racial Consequences of Underfunding Public Universities*. Chicago: University of Chicago Press, 2021.

Hardikar, N. S. "The Immigration Bill: Do Something Right Now." *Hindusthanee Student* 3, no. 1 (October 1916): 16–19. South Asian American Digital Archive. https://www.saada.org/item/20110903-317.

Hardt, Michael, and Antonio Negri. *Empire*. Cambridge: Harvard University Press, 2001.

Harker, Christopher, Dareen Sayyad, and Reema Shebeitah. "The Gender of Debt and Space: Notes from Ramallah-Al Bireh, Palestine." *Geoforum* 98 (2019): 277–85.

Helweg, Arthur, and Usha Helweg. *An Immigrant Success Story: East Indians in America*. Philadelphia: University of Pennsylvania Press, 1990.

Hindusthan Association of America. "A Course of Reading for the Friends of India." *Hindusthanee Student* 2, no. 3 (November 1915): 7–9. South Asian American Digital Archive. https://www.saada.org/item/20110829-305.

Hindusthan Association of America. "Ourselves." *Hindusthanee Student* 2, no. 1 (September 1915): 1. South Asian American Digital Archive. https://www.saada.org/item/20110830-311.

Hindusthan Association of America. "Policy of the 'Student.'" *Hindusthanee Student* 2, no. 5 (February 1916): 4. South Asian American Digital Archive. https://www.saada.org/item/20110830-310.

Hindusthan Association of America. "Vacation Work." *Hindusthanee Student*, January 1914, 4. South Asian American Digital Archive. https://www.saada.org/item/20110817-297.

Hopper, Jessica. "Immigration Officials: Tri-Valley U. and Students Involved in Visa Scam." ABC News, February 22, 2011. http://www.abcnews.go.com/US/immigration-officials-tri-valley-university-sham-selling-student/story?id=12974636.

Hours, Bernard, and Pepita Ahmed, eds. *An Anthropological Economy of Debt*. New York: Routledge, 2015.

"How Can We Keep Terrorists Out of America?" *Good Morning America*, October 18, 2001. https://abcnews.go.com/GMA/story?id=126658&page=1.

Hubert, Henri, and Marcel Mauss. *Sacrifice: Its Nature and Functions*. Chicago: University of Chicago Press, 1964.

Hutcheson, Philo. "In the National Interest: The College and University in the United States in the Post–World War II Era." In *Higher Education: The Handbook of Theory and Research*, edited by John Smart and Michael Paulson, 221–64. New York: Springer, 2011.

Immigration Commission. *Reports of the Immigration Commission: Immigrants in Industries 1907–1910.* Washington, DC: Government Printing Office, 1911.

India Forum Staff. "A Note to Fraternal Groups." Bulletin no. 1, March 1976. South Asian American Digital Archive. https://www.saada.org/item/20131031 -3249.

India Forum Staff. "Report: Surveillance and Intimidation Abroad by the Government of India." *India Forum*, no. 4 (April 1977): 12–29. South Asian American Digital Archive. https://www.saada.org/item/20110614-205.

India Forum Staff. "Subscribe Now." *India Forum*, no. 4 (April 1977): 55. South Asian American Digital Archive. https://www.saada.org/item/20110614-205.

Indians for Political Freedom. *Political Crisis in India: Some Pertinent Questions.* Report. Chicago: Indians for Political Freedom, 1975.

Institute of International Education. *Open Doors 2020: Report on the International Educational Exchange.* IIE Books, 2020. https://www.iie.org/en/Research-and -Insights/Publications/Open-Doors-2020.

Jaffrelot, Christophe, ed. *Hindu Nationalism: A Reader.* Princeton, NJ: Princeton University Press, 2007.

Jafri, Beenash. "Privilege vs. Complicity: People of Colour and Settler Colonialism." *Equity Matters* (blog), March 21, 2012. Federation of Humanities and Social Sciences. https://www.federationhss.ca/en/blog/privilege-vs-complicity-people -colour-and-settler-colonialism.

Jamal, Amaney, and Nadine Naber. *Race and Arab Americans before and after 9/11: From Invisible Citizens to Visible Subjects.* Syracuse, NY: Syracuse University Press, 2008.

Jeffrey, Craig, Patricia Jeffery, and Roger Jeffery. *Degrees without Freedom? Education, Masculinities, and Unemployment in North India.* Stanford, CA: Stanford University Press, 2007.

Junaid, Mohamad. "From a Distant Shore to the War at Home: 9/11 and Kashmir." *South Asian Review* 42, no. 4 (2021): 417–20.

Kamat, Sangeeta. "Neoliberalism, Urbanism and the Education Economy: Producing Hyderabad as a 'Global City.'" *Discourse: Studies in the Cultural Politics of Education* 32, no. 2 (2011): 187–202.

Kamola, Isaac. *Making the World Global: US Universities and the Production of the Global Imaginary.* Durham, NC: Duke University Press, 2019.

Kar, Sohini. *Financializing Poverty: Labor and Risk in Indian Microfinance.* Stanford, CA: Stanford University Press, 2018.

Ker, James. *Political Trouble in India 1907-1917.* Calcutta: Superintendent Government Printing, 1917.

Koshy, Susan. "Category Crisis: South Asian Americans and Questions of Race and Ethnicity." *Diaspora: A Journal of Transnational Studies* 7, no. 3 (1998): 285–320.

Koshy, Susan, and Rajagopalan Radhakrishnan, eds. *Transnational South Asians: The Making of a Neo-Diaspora*. New Delhi: Oxford University Press, 2008.

Krieger, Lisa M. "Universities or Visa Mills?" *Mercury News*, July 16, 2011. http://www.mercurynews.com/2011/07/16/universities-or-visa-mills/.

Kumar, Prem. "Interview with Prem Kumar." By Julie Kerssen. Seattle, July 24, 2007. South Asian Oral History Collection. https://digitalcollections.lib.washington.edu/digital/collection/saohc/id/70.

Kymlicka, William. *Multicultural Odysseys: Navigating the New International Politics of Diversity*. Oxford: Oxford University Press, 2007.

Laly, Amy. "Interview with Amy Laly." By Amy Bhatt. Seattle, September 20, 2007. South Asian Oral History Collection. https://digitalcollections.lib.washington.edu/digital/collection/saohc/id/214.

Lambek, Michael. "Afterthoughts on Sacrifice." *Ethnos: Journal of Anthropology* 79, no. 3 (2014): 430–37.

La Paperson. *A Third University Is Possible*. Minneapolis: University of Minnesota Press, 2017.

Lazzarato, Maurizio. *The Making of the Indebted Man: An Essay on the Neoliberal Condition*. Los Angeles: Semiotext(e), 2012.

Lee, Robert, and Tristan Ahtone. "Land-Grab Universities: Expropriated Indigenous Land Is the Foundation of the Land-Grant University System." *High Country News*, March 30, 2020. https://www.hcn.org/issues/52.4/indigenous-affairs-education-land-grab-universities.

Leonard, Karen. *Making Ethnic Choices: California's Punjabi Mexican Americans*. Philadelphia: Temple University Press, 1992.

Lowe, Lisa. *Immigrant Acts: On Asian American Cultural Politics*. Durham, NC: Duke University Press, 1996.

Lowe, Lisa. *The Intimacies of Four Continents*. Durham, NC: Duke University Press, 2015.

Lukose, Ritty. *Liberalization's Children: Gender, Youth, and Consumer Citizenship in Globalizing India*. Durham, NC: Duke University Press, 2009.

Macaulay, Thomas. "Minute on Education." In *Selections from the Educational Records, India, I 1920*, edited by H. Sharp, 107–17. Calcutta: Bureau of Education, 1835.

Mamdani, Mahmood. *Good Muslim, Bad Muslim: America, the Cold War, and the Roots of Terror*. New York: Three Leaves Press, 2004.

Massey, Douglas, Joaquin Arango, Graeme Hugo, Ali Kouaouci, Adela Pellegrino, and J. Edward Taylor. *Worlds in Motion: Understanding International Migration at the End of the Millennium*. Oxford: Clarendon Press, 2005.

Mathew, Biju, and Vijay Prashad. "The Protean Forms of Yankee Hindutva." *Ethnic and Racial Studies* 23, no. 3 (2010): 516–34.

Mauss, Marcel. *The Gift: The Form and Reason for Exchange in Archaic Societies*. London: Routledge, 1990 [1954].

Mayblin, Maya, and Magnus Course. "The Other Side of Sacrifice: Introduction." *Ethnos: Journal of Anthropology* 79, no. 3 (2014): 307–19.

Mehta, Pratap. "Hindu Nationalism: From Ethnic Identity to Authoritarian Repression." *Studies in Indian Politics* 10, no. 1 (2022): 31–47.

Ministry of Education. *All India Survey of Higher Education 2019-20*. New Delhi: Government of India, 2020. https://www.education.gov.in/sites/upload_files/mhrd/files/statistics-new/aishe_eng.pdf.

Mishra, Nirmalkumar. "India Forum." *India Forum*, March 1970, 1–3. South Asian American Digital Archive. https://www.saada.org/item/20161014-4690.

Morrell, Robert, and Sandra Swart. "Men in the Third World: Postcolonial Perspectives on Masculinity." In *Handbook of Studies on Men and Masculinities*, edited by Michael Kimmel, Jeff Hearn, and R. W. Connell, 90–113. Thousand Oaks, CA: Sage Publications, 2005.

Morten, Fred, and Stefano Harney. *The Undercommons: Fugitive Planning and Black Study*. Chico, CA: AK Press, 2013.

Mukherjee, Sumita. *Nationalism, Education, and Migrant Identities: The England-Returned*. London: Routledge, 2010.

Munck, Ronaldo. "The Precariat: A View from the South." *Third World Quarterly* 34, no. 5 (2013): 747–62.

Murray, Nancy. "Profiled: Arabs, Muslims, and the Post-9/11 Hunt of the 'Enemy Within.'" In *Civil Rights in Peril: The Targeting of Arabs and Muslims*, edited by Elaine Hagopian, 27–68. London: Pluto Press, 2004.

NAFSA: Association of International Educators. *Student and Exchange Visitor Program: Training for Designated School Officials*. Accessed March 29, 2023. https://www.nafsa.org/sites/default/files/ektron/uploadedFiles/SEVP_DSO_Training.pdf.

Nandy, Ashis. *The Intimate Enemy: Loss and Recovery of Self Under Colonialism*. Oxford: Oxford University Press, 2009.

Narayan, Shiv. "Why Emigrate?" *Modern Review* 8, no. 5 (November 1910): 530–34. South Asia Archive.

National Commission on Terrorist Attacks upon the United States. *The 9/11 Commission Report*, July 22, 2004. http://www.911commission.gov/report/911Report.pdf.

Ngai, Mae M. *Impossible Subjects: Illegal Aliens and the Making of Modern America*. Princeton, NJ: Princeton University Press, 2005.

Nielson, Brett, and Ned Rossiter. "Precarity as a Political Concept, or, Fordism as Exception." *Theory, Culture, and Society* 25, no. 7–8 (2008): 51–72.

Nimbark, Ashakant. "Some Observations on Asian Indians in an American Educational Setting." In *The New Ethnics: Asian Indians in the United States*, edited by Paramatma Saran and Edwin Eames, 247–71. New York: Praeger, 1980.

Nye, Joseph S., Jr. *Soft Power: The Means to Success in World Politics*. New York City: PublicAffairs, 2004.

Oberoi, Harjot. "Ghadar Movement and Its Anarchist Genealogy." *Economic and Political Weekly* 44, no. 50 (2009): 40–46.

Office of Inspector General (OIG). *The Immigration and Naturalization Service's Contacts with Two September 11 Terrorists: A Review of the INS's Admissions of Mohamed Atta and Marwan Alshehhi, Its Processing of Their Change of Status Applications, and Its Efforts to Track Foreign Students in the United States*. US Department of Justice, May 20, 2002. https://oig.justice.gov/sites/default/files/legacy/special/0205/fullreport.pdf.

Office of Inspector General (OIG). *The September 11 Detainees: A Review of the Treatment of Aliens Held on Immigration Charges in Connection with the Investigation of the September 11 Attacks*. US Department of Justice, April 2003. https://oig.justice.gov/sites/default/files/legacy/special/0306/full.pdf.

Ong, Aihwa. *Flexible Citizenship: The Cultural Logics of Transnationality*. Durham, NC: Duke University Press, 1999.

Ong, Aihwa. *Neoliberalism as Exception: Mutations in Citizenship and Sovereignty*. Durham, NC: Duke University Press, 2006.

Osella, Filippo, and Caroline Osella. "Migration, Money and Masculinity in Kerala." *Journal of the Royal Anthropological Institute* 6, no. 1 (2003): 117–33.

Pande, Amrita. "Mobile Masculinities: Migrant Bangladeshi Men in South Africa." *Gender and Society* 31, no. 3 (2017): 383–406.

Peeren, Esther. "Compelling Memory: 9/11 and the Work of Mourning in Mike Binder's Reign over Me." *Cultural Critique* 92, (2016): 57–83.

Pegues, Julianna. *Space-Time Colonialism: Alaska's Indigenous and Asian Entanglements*. Chapel Hill: The University of North Carolina Press, 2021.

Pietsch, Tamson. "Many Rhodes: Travelling Scholarships and Imperial Citizenship in the British Academic World, 1880–1940." *History of Education* 40, no. 6 (2012): 723–39.

Pitt-Rivers, Julian. "The Paradox of Friendship." *HAU: Journal of Ethnographic Theory* 6, no. 3 (2016): 443–52.

President's Commission on Higher Education. *Higher Education for American Democracy*. Report. Washington, DC: US Government Printing Office, 1947.

Puar, Jasbir. *Terrorist Assemblages: Homonationalism in Queer Times*. Durham, NC: Duke University Press, 2007.

Puar, Jasbir, and Amit Rai. "Monster, Terrorist, Fag: The War on Terrorism and the Production of Docile Patriots." *Social Text* 20, no. 3 (2002): 117–48.

Radhakrishnan, Smitha. *Appropriately Indian: Gender and Culture in a New Transnational Class*. Durham, NC: Duke University Press, 2011.

Ramnath, Maia. *Haj to Utopia: How the Ghadar Movement Charted Global Radicalism and Attempted to Overthrow the British Empire*. Oakland: University of California Press, 2011.

Rana, Junaid. *Terrifying Muslims: Race and Labor in the South Asian Diaspora*. Durham, NC: Duke University Press, 2011.

Rao, Shakuntala. "The Globalization of Bollywood: An Ethnography of Non-elite Audiences in India." *The Communication Review* 10, no. 1 (2007): 57–76.

Readings, Bill. *The University in Ruins*. Cambridge, MA: Harvard University Press, 1997.

Reinert, Hugo. "Sacrifice." *Environmental Humanities* 7, no. 1 (2016): 255–58.

Richwine, Jason. "Indian Americans: The New Model Minority." *Forbes*, February 24, 2009. https://www.forbes.com/2009/02/24/bobby-jindal-indian-americans -opinions-contributors_immigrants_minority.html.

Roy, Basanta. "Self-Support in American Universities." *Bulletin of the Hindusthan Association of U.S.A.*, no. 1 (August 1913): 9–11. South Asian American Digital Archive. https://www.saada.org/item/20110930-387.

Roy, Tania. "India's 9/11: Accidents of a Moveable Metaphor." *Theory, Culture & Society* 26, no. 7–8 (2009): 314–28.

Sachar Committee. *Social, Economic and Educational Status of the Muslim Community in India: A Report*. New Delhi: Cabinet Secretariat, Government of India, 2006. http://www.zakatindia.org/Files/Sachar%20Report%20(Full).pdf.

Sarkar, Benoy. "Hindu Sociology." *Hindusthanee Student* 2, no. 1 (April–July 1915): 28–32. South Asian American Digital Archive. https://www.saada.org/item/20110830-311.

Saxenian, AnnaLee. "From Brain Drain to Brain Circulation: Transnational Communities and Regional Upgrading in India and China." *Studies in Comparative International Development* 40, no. 2 (2005): 35–61.

Scheffauer, Herman. "The Tide of Turbans." *Forum* 43 (1910): 616–18.

Schiller, Nina G., Linda Basch, and Cristina S. Blanc. "From Immigrant to Transmigrant: Theorizing Transnational Migration." *Anthropological Quarterly* 68, no. 1 (1995): 48–63.

Shastri, K. D. "Inaugural Address." *Hindusthanee Student* 2, no. 1 (September 1915): 2–5. South Asian American Digital Archive. https://www.saada.org/item/20110830-311.

Sibley, David. *Geographies of Exclusion*. London: Routledge, 1995.

Simmel, Georg. "Faithfulness and Gratitude." In *The Sociology of Georg Simmel*, edited by K. H. Wolff, 379–95. Glencoe: Free Press, 1950.

Singh, Saint Nihal. "Opportunity in India and America." *Hindustan Review*, March 1908, 273–79. South Asian American Digital Archive. https://www.saada.org/item/20111018-419.

Slaughter, Sheila, and Larry Leslie, *Academic Capitalism: Politics, Policies, and the Entrepreneurial University*. Baltimore: Johns Hopkins University Press, 1999.

Smith, Dorothy E. *Institutional Ethnography: A Sociology for People*. Lanham: AltaMira Press, 2005.

Sohi, Seema. "Repressing the Hindu Menace: Race, Anarchy and Indian Anticolonialism." In *The Sun Never Sets*, edited by Vivek Bald, 50–74. New York: NYU Press, 2013.

Somerville, Siobhan. "Notes toward a Queer History of Naturalization." *American Quarterly* 57, no. 3 (2005): 659–75.

Sood, Malini. *Expatriate Nationalism and Ethnic Radicalism: The Ghadar Party in North America*. New York: Garland Science, 2001.

South Asia People's Organization. "Report: Diplomatic 'Excesses.'" *India Today*, November 1977, 70–71. South Asian American Digital Archive. https://www .saada.org/item/20131031-3245.

South Asia People's Organization. "Two Years of Janata: Continuity of Class Rule [Statement]." Berkeley, CA: South Asia People's Organization Board, 1978.

South Asian Students Association. "Political Activists Hanged by the Government of India [Pamphlet]." Berkeley, CA: South Asian Students Association Board, 1976.

South Asian Students Association. "A Running Dog Under Sheep's Hide [Statement]." Berkeley, CA: South Asian Students Association Board, 1976.

Standing, Guy. *The Precariat: The New Dangerous Class*. London: Bloomsbury Academic, 2011.

Stein, Sharon, Vanessa Andreotti, and Rene Susa. "'Beyond 2015,' within the Modern/Colonial Global Imaginary? Global Development and Higher Education." *Critical Studies in Education* 60, no. 3 (2016): 281–301.

Subramanian, Ajantha. *The Caste of Merit: Engineering Education in India*. Cambridge, MA: Harvard University Press, 2019.

Taguba, Antonio M. *Article 15-6 Investigation of the 800th Military Police Brigade*. Washington, DC: Department of Defense, 2004. https://irp.fas.org/agency/ dod/taguba.pdf.

Thomas, Susan. "The Precarious Path of Student Migrants: Education, Debt, and Transnational Migration among Indian Youth." *Journal of Ethnic and Migration Studies* 43, no. 11 (2017): 1873–89.

Thomas, Susan. "Student-Migrants and the Diasporic Imagination: Educational Migration, Nationhood, and the Making of Indian Diaspora in the United States." *Interventions: International Journal of Postcolonial Studies* 21, no. 2 (2019): 255–72.

Tsing, Anna. "The Global Situation." *Cultural Anthropology* 15, no. 3 (2000): 327–60.

Tuchman, Gaye. *Wannabe U: Inside the Corporate University*. Chicago: Chicago University Press, 2009.

Tuck, Eve, Marcia McKenzie, and Kate McCoy. "Land Education: Indigenous, Postcolonial, and Decolonizing Perspectives on Place." *Environmental Education Research* 20, no. 1 (2014): 1–23.

Tuck, Eve, and K. Wayne Yang. "Decolonization Is Not a Metaphor." *Decolonization: Indigeneity, Education & Society* 1, no. 1 (2012): 1–40.

Turner, Victor. *The Ritual Process: Structure and Anti-structure*. New York City: Routledge Publishing, 1995 [first published in 1969].

Urciuoli, Bonnie. "The Compromised Pragmatics of Diversity." *Language & Communication*, 51, 2016: 30–39.

Volpp, Leti. "The Citizen and the Terrorist." *UCLA Law Review* 49, (2002): 1575–1600.

Vora, Neha. *Teach for Arabia: American Universities, Liberalism, and Transnational Qatar*. Stanford, CA: Stanford University Press, 2019.

Wang, Chih-Ming. *Transpacific Articulations: Student Migration and the Remaking of Asian America*. Honolulu: The University of Hawai'i Press, 2013.

Warikoo, Natasha. *The Diversity Bargain: And Other Dilemmas of Race, Admissions, and Meritocracy at Elite Universities*. Chicago: University of Chicago Press, 2016.

Whitehead, Stephen. *Men and Masculinities: Key Themes and New Directions*. Cambridge: Polity Press, 2002.

Wilder, Craig. *Ebony and Ivy: Race, Slavery and the Troubled History of America's Universities*. London: Bloomsbury Press, 2013.

Zaloom, Caitlin. *Indebted: How Families Make College Work at Any Cost*. Princeton, NJ: Princeton University Press, 2019.

Index

www.ingramcontent.com/pod-product-compliance
Lightning Source LLC
Chambersburg PA
CBHW032134020426
42334CB00016B/1163